Marxism: The View from America

A VOLUME IN THE SERIES

COMMUNISM IN AMERICAN LIFE

Clinton Rossiter, General Editor

BOOKS PUBLISHED TO DATE:

The Roots of American Communism by Theodore Draper

The Communists and the Schools by Robert W. Iversen

The Decline of American Communism by David A. Shannon

American Communism and Soviet Russia by Theodore Draper

Marxism: The View from America by Clinton Rossiter

Clinton Rossiter

MARXISM: THE VIEW FROM AMERICA

Harcourt, Brace and Company · New York

To
Herbert W. Briggs
and
Mario Einaudi
My senior colleagues
with esteem and affection

PREFACE

"Of making many books there is no end; and much study is a weariness of the flesh." Thus spoke the Preacher more than two thousand years ago, and so would he speak today if he were to labor through the card catalogue of any major library under the headings of "Marxism" and "Democracy—U.S."

With some uneasiness I send to press a book that will mean still another card under both these headings. I send it, nevertheless, because I do not think that there has been another exactly like it.

It might be useful, and I trust not too presumptuous, if I were to say a word or two about how this book came to be written. In 1954 I was invited by the officers of the Fund for the Republic to direct a survey of Communism in American life. I had no illusions why I, or rather someone like me, was chosen for this cheerless task. I was a scholar who had devoted most of his life to studying American thought and institutions, and none of his life to practicing radical politics. My knowledge of Communism, either as practice or as theory, was slight. I had never heard, even in my most hypercritical sophomore days, the seductive call of the Left. Perhaps I am the poorer, both intellectually and spiritually, because I did not; but that, in any case, is the direction in which my own conscience carried me: pretty much down the center of the American road. I had brushed against Marx lightly in a seminar in political theory, but I knew no more about him than I did about

Aristotle or Hobbes, and a good deal less than I knew about Jefferson and John Adams.

This was certainly not true of most of the estimable scholars who consented to share the burden of this assessment of American Communism. Several had been Marxists of one kind or another, and all had given years of patient study to the evolution of Communism from an idea that stirred in the mind of one man to a faith that holds sway over the minds of one-third of a world. I learned soon enough that I was a novice among schoolmen, and I thereupon set out to do what plainly had to be done: to educate myself in the whole range of Marxist studies. I read Marx, Engels, Lenin, Stalin, Mao, Trotsky, Kautsky, Bukharin, Vyshinsky, and Plekhanov, as well as Hegel, Feuerbach, Saint-Simon, Proudhon, and Ricardo. I read Plamenatz, Schumpeter, Wilson, Hunt, Hook, Berlin, and Popper, as well as Calvez, Wetter, Sombart, Aron, and Berdyaev. I read Kelsen, Hazard, Moore, Fainsod, Inkeles, Arendt, and Brzezinski, as well as Cole, Carr, Wolfe, Wittfogel, and Deutscher. And I learned about Marxism from friends who had an understanding of it that even now I cannot hope to match.

This book is a summing up of the conclusions I reached about Marxism in this manner and for this purpose. It may well be judged naive by men who have lived with Marxism all their lives, but that, in my opinion, is the reason for its existence. There are some things about a complicated historical and intellectual phenomenon like Marxism that the Outsider can see (and perhaps even understand) more clearly than the Insider. In any case, I think it high time for us to look at the emperor with eyes unclouded by awe or fear or disgust—or, more to the point, by excessive familiarity.

I am grateful to Theodore Draper, Mario Einaudi, David Spitz, Jan Triska, Steven Muller, Andrew Hacker, George Kahin, Frank Meyer, Richard S. Weckstein, C. Peter Magrath, Gladys Kessler, and Mary Crane Rossiter for their criticisms and suggestions.

CLINTON ROSSITER

Ithaca, New York
May, 1960

CONTENTS

Marxism: The View from America

ONE · MARX AND AMERICA

The reigning intellectual fact of the age is the division of those who do the world's thinking into three major groups: the Marxists, most of whom are Communists; the anti-Marxists, the best of whom are democrats of one breed or another; and the uncommitted, most of whom have not been forced by their own quest for understanding or by the pressure of events to make a choice between the first two ways of life and thought. This is an especially unsettling state of affairs for the Marxists, since they have been promised by the prophets of their faith that they will, in the fullness of time, inherit the whole earth. The mixed state of Marxism—triumph in the U.S.S.R. and China, failure in most of the West, desperate uncertainty in India and Iraq and Indonesia—holds the world in a state of intellectual tension. The repercussions in politics, economics, science, and diplomacy have shaken the world to its basalt foundations.

Of the triumph of Marxism there can be no doubt. The political and intellectual leaders of two great countries and a half-dozen satellites are more Marxist than Marx ever found it comfortable to be. The people of these countries, who like most people pick up their ideas through early indoctrination and late hearsay, are at least as good Marxists as most Americans are democrats. In

3

almost all countries of the world, even in those most militantly anti-Communist in law and spirit, there are dedicated Marxists to take part in, and often to take over, public discussion of the issues of the day. And all men who think, certainly all such men in the West, harbor thoughts that bear the imprint, however faint, of the Marxist dispensation.

Of the failure of Marxism there is, if that were possible, even less doubt. Whatever inroads Marx may have made on the minds of men in countries such as Britain, Canada, Sweden, and Belgium, he is now in retreat in all of them, and their intellectual defenses are the stronger because he forced them to look to these defenses anew. Whatever political successes Marx may have achieved in France, Italy, Spain, and Germany, they were not large or lasting enough to carry Communism to power; and from this time forward he will have to labor in these countries—and in all countries with a free press, an average memory, and a quick conscience—under the burden of Stalin, Kadar, and Serov. Whether this burden will mean defeat for Marx in the uncommitted countries of Asia and Africa remains to be decided by a course of events over which the men of the West can still exercise a great deal of influence.

The most stunning failure of Marxism has been recorded in the United States. Intellectually as well as politically and militarily, America presents an almost solid front against Communism. Quite the contrary to Marx's prediction that the most advanced industrial countries would be the first to make the transit from capitalism to socialism and beyond to communism, this most advanced of all such countries has never been insulated so thickly against the appeals of Marxism nor ever behaved in so thoroughly un-Marxist a fashion. Even among intellectuals, whom Marx expected to be trailblazers of the coming order, he has few disciples and not a great many more admirers. As a thinker he is much quoted by social scientists; as a counselor he is simply ignored.

The failure of Marxism is, of course, only one special aspect of the general failure of radicalism in the United States. The darling of the world's radicals in the early years of its existence, this country has now become their despair. American writers, well aware of the implications and dimensions of the failure of radicalism, agree almost unanimously on its social, political, and personal causes.[1] First among these is what historians of the early Republic called "the history and present state of the United States of America." However full of rough spots the history—depressions, upheavals, insurrections, wars, repeated acts of exploitation of men and nature—we have had less than our share of misery and frustration, more than our share of happiness and fulfillment. However full of soft spots the present state—racism, corruption, vulgarity, obscurantism—we are clearly the most fortunate and well-situated of all the nations of the earth. The appeals of radicalism have gone unheeded in America because the promises of radicalism have been largely fulfilled. Socialism has foundered, as Werner Sombart once noted, "on the shoals of roast beef and apple pie." The vision of the classless society has been fogged by reality; the summons to the proletariat has found few proletarians to listen; the cry of revolution has been smothered in the busy little sounds of evolution. To most Americans radicalism has seemed not so much wrongheaded and dangerous as simply irrelevant.

Friedrich Engels, the good Sherpa of Marx's assault on the summit of capitalism, put his reluctant finger on a related reason for the hard times of radicalism in the United States. In a letter to Friedrich Sorge, a German revolutionary who had settled down in Hoboken to teach music and spread socialism, Engels complained of the staying power of America's "bourgeois prejudices," which he found to be almost as "strongly rooted in the working class" as among businessmen.[2] He saw clearly that the bigness, uniqueness, success, and freshness of the American experiment had created a collective state of mind unusually hostile to comprehensive radicalism. If he were alive today he would see even more clearly that the hostility has grown to frightening proportions—

frightening, that is, to the hopes of Marxist radicalism. Today as in his time the American political mind harbors a stubborn prejudice against the kind of large-scale social experimentation in which Marx invites us to take part.

Our hostility to radicalism has not, to be sure, prevented our borrowing useful ideas piecemeal from radicals in our midst, although we do not engage in this practice quite so casually as did our fathers before us. One of the major causes of the decline of the Socialist party, and of a dozen other radical parties that have orbited crazily around it, has been the cannibalistic tastes of the two major parties. Republicans and Democrats alike have gathered some of their most appealing issues from the Socialist platforms of, say, 1912 and 1932 and have been proclaiming them happily ever since as examples of "100 per cent Americanism"—which, to tell the truth, most of them were from the beginning. Nor should it be forgotten that everything else about American politics—the broad appeal of the two major parties, the costs of political campaigning, the widespread refusal to adopt proportional representation, the statutory difficulties of getting on and staying on the ballot in many states—seems to be loaded against the rise and prosperity of third parties.

Not all the troubles of the American Left have arisen from conditions outside the movement. At least two reasons for the failure of radicalism, and especially of Marxist radicalism, were bred in the bone: first, the intense and self-defeating sectarianism of the Marxists and their fellows in dissent, which led Marx himself to complain to Karl Kautsky that the "Yankee Socialists" were "crotchety and sectarian," and Engels to plead with German-American Socialists to submerge their differences in the quest for votes; [3] and second, the alien stamp, which has been imprinted for at least three generations on the purposes and personalities of the Socialist movement. Neither Daniel De Leon, who wrote orthodox Marxist tracts in "an authentic American idiom," [4] nor Eugene V. Debs, who emerged from Terre Haute to "afflict the comfortable and comfort the afflicted," were typical radicals in the decisive years of the American Left. Too few of our leading radicals have been Americans in birth, interests, inspiration, or even language, and this visible fact has nourished the natural xenophobic prejudices of the American mind. The closer one looks at the history of American Marxism, the more visible and damning the alien stamp becomes. The fact that not more than 10 per cent of the American Communist movement in the founding year of 1919 could speak English was a heavy enough cross for native radicalism to bear.[5] The facts of Lenin, Stalin, the Comintern, the Cominform, and Hungary have buried American Marxism under a pile of debris from which it may never again emerge; and buried with it are the hopes of hundreds of decent American radicals who have even more cause to hate Communism than do their fellow citizens of the Right. The too easy identification of radicalism with socialism, of socialism with communism, of communism with Soviet tyranny, and of all these isms with subversion and ungodliness, has well-nigh shattered the hopes of any brand of political radicalism in the United States. America has never, certainly since 1800, been a consciously importing nation in the area of political and social ideas, and Marxism now stands first on the list of embargoed goods.

There is, I think, one last nail in the coffin of Marxist aspirations in America, one conclusive reason for our failure to bid Marx and his followers a decent welcome. The fact is that Marxism, whether we see it as science, judgment, myth, or plan of action, rushes into head-on collision with almost every principle with which Americans have attempted to explain or justify or purify their way of life. Even if Marxism had encountered none of the other difficulties I have mentioned—the success of our institutions, the prejudices of our political mind, the cannibalism of our parties and two-headedness of our politics, the curse of sectarianism, the stigmata of alienism—it would have held little appeal for the minds of men who had been brought up, however carelessly, in the American tradition. Nothing in that tradition prepares men to share Marx's anger, to accept his advice, or to answer his summons—even, to our present disadvantage, to understand his appeal to the less fortunate peoples of the earth. Everything in it, as we learned in 1932, forbids most Americans to turn to Marx even in their desperate hours.

My purpose is to inquire into this final aspect of the failure of Marxism in America. Why, I propose to ask, has this giant new theory of the nineteenth century—now the giant new religion of the twentieth—been rudely ignored in one of the few countries for which it was supposed to hold the most immediate appeal? Why did we, the people who converted Liberalism from a permissive faith into a national monument, shy away skittishly from what Raymond Aron describes as the "synthesis of all the principal schemes of progressive thought"? [6] Why, even now, do we find it difficult to go to Marx for instruction in those fields in which he was a provocative if not always trustworthy teacher? And I propose to answer that it is not enough to lay out the historical reasons for the failure of Marxism as a basis for political action, nor even enough to prove that our minds are insulated by "bourgeois prejudice" against its collectivist, irreligious, anti-bourgeois temptations. What we come down to in the end is a fundamental conflict between two bodies of principle, two faiths, two ideologies (if I may use that word in a Pickwickian rather than Marxist sense), a conflict so severe that peace between them has always been and remains today impossible to achieve. My intention is to draw the main outlines of this conflict. In doing this, as my readers will soon discover, I plan to probe the mysteries of Marxism with three different if not dissimilar techniques: 1) exposition; 2) confrontation; and 3) criticism. Most of this book is given over to expounding the principles of Marxism from a "characteristically American" point of view, but from time to time, when it appears to suit my purpose, I expect to move beyond exposition to describe and assess the confrontation of principle between Marxism and the American tradition, and beyond confrontation to criticize those Marxist teachings that seem especially disquieting or unpalatable. When I have finished, I hope that others will agree that it is exaggerating only a little to say that Marxism never had a chance in America.

If this inquiry is not to raise more questions than it answers, there must be no doubt what is meant by *Marxism* and *the American tradition*. By *Marxism* I mean generally what most men mean by it: that protean body of principles, assumptions, warnings, hopes, slogans, dogmas, and prophecies that emerged first from the astonishing brain of Karl Marx, and from the hardly less astonishing brain of Friedrich Engels, and then spread its magic over the minds and hearts of most of the intellectual and political radicals of the world. It is, as all the world knows, a total view of life with an answer to every question in every field. It is a way, straight and narrow, for those who will follow it, to the understanding and mastery of history, politics, philosophy, psychology, social relations, economics, and esthetics; of men, nature, science, and technology; of the bees in their hives, the seeds in their pods, and the stars in their courses. If it is science, sociology, and philosophy of history, it is also myth, dogma, and religion—and it has always been a call to revolution and promise of salvation.

There are many Marxisms, as men so different in mood and purpose as Lenin, Stalin, Khrushchev, Mao, Trotsky, Eduard Bernstein, Daniel De Leon, Earl Browder, William Z. Foster, Karl Kautsky, G. D. H. Cole, Harold Laski, Leon Blum, Georg Lukacs, J. B. S. Haldane, Paul Sweezy, and Sidney Hook have proved. Indeed, it often appears to the man outside the magic circle that every self-proclaimed Marxist is his own Marxist. Yet one version, surely, is still more Marxist than the rest: the Marxism of Marx and Engels themselves, to whose teachings even the weirdest brands of twentieth-century Marxism can be traced back directly and without affront to common sense, and it is on their writings that

I will concentrate attention throughout most of this book. At the same time, I will have something to say about the "hard" Marxism of Lenin, who did several things to Marx that might have affronted the master but could hardly have surprised him, and about the Marxism of Lenin's heirs, who have carried his "hard" principles all the way to their tragic conclusion and perhaps beyond. It would make my task a great deal easier if I could ignore the development of Marxism since 1917, but the Soviet Union is a reality—to an important extent a *Marxist* reality—and no one, I fear, can write on this subject without dealing with modern Communism openly. I hope to make especially clear those points at which Lenin and Stalin remained faithful to Marx or went visibly astray. Finally in Chapter VIII, I plan to elaborate on an assumption I will simply proclaim at this early stage: that the Communists are not only devoted Marxists but the best Marxists, the chief heirs of Marx and Engels themselves. My respect for those left-wing democrats whom I would call, not at all pejoratively, the "soft" Marxists is civil,[7] but they are (and know they are) men whom the history of Marxism has left behind. In any case, I think it should be understood clearly that the present political and intellectual leaders of the U.S.S.R., China, and the satellites, as well as those men in the West who proclaim themselves Communists, are at least as close to Marx in principle and purpose as most Jeffersonians are to Jefferson, most Freudians to Freud, and—I do not mean this facetiously or irreverently—most Christians to Christ. Marxism, as John Plamenatz has written, may often be incoherent and self-contradictory, but "that does not mean that [it] is a mere collection of doctrines to which new doctrines can be continually added without regard to what they are." It has "its own vocabulary, and its dominant themes." [8] One chants these themes or one is not a full-blooded Marxist. Just what they are and why they all blend together in a chorus that prophesies our doom will be one of my major points of inquiry.

Let me review briefly the cast of Marxist characters who will be seen and heard in the course of this book. The writings of these men are what most historians of modern thought (excepting always the "soft," or revisionist Marxists) would include in the canon of Marxism.[9] In addition to Marx himself,[10] the giant among all radical thinkers, these are the great contributors to the orthodox Marxism that holds sway in our times:

Friedrich Engels (1820-1895), the friend, supporter, collaborator, and editor of Marx, whose own judgment of his role in their common labors was certainly too modest,* and whose *Anti-Dühring, Socialism: Utopian and Scientific, Ludwig Feuerbach and the Outcome of Classical German Philosophy, Dialectics of Nature,* and *The Origin of the Family, Private Property and the State* are sacred texts in the canon: The philosophers of the Soviet Union still salute Engels as the "co-founder with Marx of scientific socialism," [12] and well they might salute the man who coined the phrases "dialectical materialism" and "historical materialism." Like Marxists everywhere they consider his statements exactly as authoritative as those of Marx himself, and that should be a conclusive enough opinion for the rest of mankind. The number of times Engels will be quoted in these pages is an accurate measure of his standing in the annals of Marxism.

V. I. Lenin (1870-1924), the chief Marxist of this century, whose additions to the canon in the area of political strategy and tactics carried Marxism beyond the point of no return into the harsh realm of Bolshevism: The question of how good a Marxist Lenin really was will continue to be argued so long as there are

---

* "I cannot deny that both before and during my forty years' collaboration with Marx I had a certain independent share in laying the foundations, and more particularly in elaborating the theory. But the greater part of its leading basic principles, particularly in the realm of economics and history, and, above all, its final, clear formulation, belong to Marx. What I contributed—at any rate with the exception of a few special studies—Marx could very well have done without me. What Marx accomplished I would not have achieved. Marx stood higher, saw further, and took a wider and quicker view than all the rest of us. Marx was a genius; we others were at best talented. Without him the theory would not be what it is today. It therefore rightly bears his name." [11]

Mensheviks to cry havoc, but to men who are not Marxists themselves he has the awesome look of a very good, sincere, and faithful Marxist indeed. Few will deny, certainly with much conviction at this late date, that *What is to be Done?, Materialism and Empirio-Criticism, The Teachings of Karl Marx,* and *State and Revolution* are substantial additions to the Marxist legacy. Lenin's intellectual kinship and spiritual affinity with Marx are obvious to all who have studied both men with fresh eyes, and I would be willing to concur for once in a statement of Stalin, "Leninism is Marxism in the epoch of imperialism and of the proletarian revolution" [13] —provided, of course, that I could define those words in a non-Marxist way.

Joseph Stalin (1879-1953), whose entire intellectual baggage, however dumpy, was the Marxism of Lenin, and who added his own little bit in such writings as *Foundations of Leninism* and *Marxism and Linguistics:* I would think that he had the poorest claim of all the major characters of Marxism to be included in this list, but we must recognize the claim for reasons I will mention in Chapter VI. Moreover, it is quite possible that he will be known in the future as the last Russian leader to have made any significant contribution to the development of Marxism. The age of the statesman-as-theoretician may well have passed in the Soviet Union.

Leon Trotsky (1879-1940),[14] the most heretical of Marxist heretics, whose heresy, however, was political rather than intellectual in character: Although it may seem monstrous to most exponents and critics of Marxism to place Trotsky on the list, a work like *Dictatorship versus Democracy* is Marxist to the core. The student of the subject cannot safely or sensibly pass it by. No amount of defamation can erase Trotsky's substantial contributions to the Marxist theory of revolution.

Mao Tse-tung (b. 1893),[15] who has recently emerged, unchallenged by any theoretician in the Soviet Union, as the most interesting contemporary exponent of Marxism: It remains to be seen whether Mao's musings on contradictions in socialist societies and his theory of the prime role of the peasantry will be permanent growths on the Marxist trunk, but there are signs that the third, or Asian phase of Marxism may have already begun. Mao will not be seen or heard much in this book, but his presence in the wings will be felt from time to time.

Three groups of minor characters might also be announced:

Karl Kautsky, Georgy Plekhanov,[16] Nikolai Bukharin, Antonio Labriola, and Andrei Y. Vyshinsky, who are very minor indeed compared with the six men I have already singled out, yet who did have walk-on parts of some little significance: Studies such as Kautsky's *Economic Doctrines of Karl Marx,* Labriola's *Essays on the Materialistic Conception of History,* and Plekhanov's *The Role of the Individual in History* are, if I may mix the metaphor, attractive embroideries on the Marxist tapestry.

Daniel De Leon, Algie M. Simons, Louis B. Boudin, Morris Hillquit, John Spargo, Max Shachtman, Earl Browder, Lewis Corey, V. J. Jerome, William English Walling, Paul M. Sweezy, Howard Selsam, Vernon Venable, and Harry K. Wells,[17] who are, except perhaps for the first two, even more minor, but who form the panel of Marxist theoreticians from whom Americans would learn their lessons if the kindest dreams of William Z. Foster should ever come true: [18] I am assuming, to be sure, in a flush of calculated naiveté, that American Communism would be compelled to "let a thousand flowers bloom," something no one really has a right to assume at all. The writings of all these men, which I shall draw upon for occasional thoughts and suggestions, would in that case seem to be acceptable hybrids of the original flower. No one of them has had a major idea of genuine originality or interest to add to Marxism, but many of their observations on American themes—for example, the strictures of hard Marxists like Selsam on morality and Wells on pragmatism—are revealing glimpses into the Marxist mind.

Finally, in the very back of the stage, a crowd of "lords, heralds, officers, soldiers, grooms, gardeners, and other attendants," some of whom are named Wilhelm Liebknecht, Rosa Luxemburg, H. M. Hyndman, Jules Guesde, Paul LaFargue, Rudolf Hilferding, Franz Mehring, Georg Lukacs, Harold Laski, G. D. H. Cole, J. Middleton Murry, John Macmurray, Emile Burns, Maurice Dobb, Maurice Cornforth, Christopher Caudwell, R. Palme Dutt, J. B. S. Haldane, J. D. Bernal, Roger Garaudy, John Lewis, and Auguste Cornu, may be noted milling about and shouting the war cries of Marxism. I hope they will understand, those of them who are still living and still Marxists, that the line had to be drawn somewhere between the dozen or so most important and relevant Marxists and the many thousands of intellectual radicals who have offered their mites to this vast storehouse of ideas.

By *the American tradition* I mean, again, what most men mean by it: that less extensive but no less influential body of principles and aspirations which have guided the conduct of our political and social affairs since the founding of the Republic.[19] No American has made, as many Marxists have made for Marxism, an authoritative statement of its essentials. The American tradition has no Marx, no teacher identified and revered as the First Source; its essence is pluralism, which means that each of its children is encouraged to make his own interpretation of its principles; and it is, after all, the product of centuries of unplanned accretion rather than of a few years of imperious dogmatizing. The implacable hostility of the American tradition to intellectual and spiritual authority must always frustrate even the most well-meaning, self-effacing efforts to describe it in terms that most Americans will accept as conclusive.

Even if I could construct what no man has yet constructed, this would certainly not be the setting in which to do it. This book is primarily a study of Marxism, and whatever descriptions I make of certain principles of the American tradition are intended solely to help us get a sharper focus on related principles in the Marxist system. I certainly do not wish our view of the object of scrutiny to be blurred by lavishing too much attention on the microscope. More than that, I know from experience that a detailed exposition of the American tradition raises more questions than it answers, not least because some of its principles have always been fuzzy or unfinished and others need to be reshaped in the face of growing obsolescence. But that is a subject for another book, and for this book it should be enough to state briefly, wherever it seems useful to establish a confrontation, the American consensus (as best I can interpret it) about such institutions and values as liberty, property, constitutionalism, and individualism. In doing all this, I will draw principally upon the explicit principles of men like Benjamin Franklin, John Adams, Thomas Jefferson, James Madison, and Abraham Lincoln, and upon such latter-day academic interpreters of the tradition they established as Carl Becker, Ralph H. Gabriel, and Ralph Barton Perry. I will draw, too, on the implicit principles of the American tradition—the principles, that is to say, implicit in the structure and functioning of our institutions rather than explicit in the writings and speeches of our leading men. There is a growing school of intellectual historians who insist that the American tradition is something "given" and "acted upon" rather than "asserted" and "thought upon," [20] and I intend to honor if not join up with this school.

In either case, whether we make use of explicit words or implicit understandings to describe the American tradition, we are dealing with a body of principles that has a unity of its own. No more than Marxism is the American tradition "a mere collection of doctrines to which new doctrines can be continually added without regard to what they are." It has no high priests to keep it undefiled, no sanctions with which to punish those who bend it into grotesque shapes, but it does have ways of protecting its integrity as a body of ideas. The American tradition is the latest and most colorful flower of the Liberal tradition. It is the prudently democratic outlook of a race of men for whom many of the ideals of Liberalism have been made reality, and as such it is remarkably resistant to the ravages of the authoritarian creeds of Left and Right. If we honor it more often in the breach than in the observance, that is because it asks a great deal more in the way of reasoned decency than we have ever been willing to give. Perhaps a close look at the most powerful of alternate faiths can inspire us to redouble our efforts to obey the commands of the American tradition.

Let me now announce certain ground rules that I hope to follow in this study of Marxist principles. First, I must declare out-of-bounds many questions that agitate students of Marxism. I have been instructed most agreeably by Herbert Marcuse's fresh appraisal of Marx's debt to Hegel,[21] by Vernon Venable's profound discourse on Marxist epistemology,[22] by Sidney Hook's razor-edged analysis of the seven meanings of "dialectic" in Engels,[23] by at least a dozen discussions of the difference between "permanent" and "uninterrupted" revolution,[24] and by the memorable debate between Eugen von Böhm-Bawerk and Rudolf Hilferding on the Marxist theory of value.[25] I have sat in on several fascinating discussions of "the real reason for Marx," in which Germany, the Rhine, the rabbinic tradition, Jewishness, the flight from Jewishness, the bourgeois background, Romanticism, anti-Romanticism, alienation, exile, isolation, straitened circumstances, and carbuncles were all given a hearing. But these and many other points of interest in the vast range of Marxist studies are really quite irrelevant to my purpose. The charge of irrelevancy may be leveled with particular force against most of the theory (if not the message) of Marx's writings in political economy. I cannot define what Marx would not define, nor solve what he could not solve; and it would be unseemly in a book about Marx and America to get trapped in the bog of his theory of value. Most important, I refuse to beat dead horses, with which the plains of Marxism are littered, although I will call attention to some of the deadest when they cannot sensibly be ignored.

Second, I will try conscientiously to present Marx and Marxism in a fair light, although there will be times when this will not be easy to do. A study of this sort could, I suppose, equate the illegitimate Liberalism of Marx with the Byzantine cruelty of Stalin and close itself out abruptly. But this would be fair neither to Marx, who was a noble figure compared with Stalin, nor to Marxism, which was not transformed into Bolshevism until years after his death. The only useful way to make this study, it seems to me, is to give Marx at least an even break—to recall constantly his profound humanitarian impulse, to present the most kindly interpretation possible of his strictures on the family and private property and parliamentary democracy, to refuse to blame him for all the tortuous vulgarities of the latter-day Marxists, to be very clear about where Lenin went beyond Marx, and Stalin beyond Lenin, and finally to agree with Veblen that Marx was "neither ignorant, imbecile, nor disingenuous" and ought to be interpreted as if he might make sense.[26] I will do my best to honor J. S. Mill's wise counsel that one should grapple with the most reasonable rather than with the most absurd version of a wrong opinion. One way of doing this will be to quote—at reasonable length and, I trust, in context—the portentous words of the great men of Marxism. They deserve to be heard, and we should make an extra effort to hear them without benefit of paraphrase.

Third and most important, I intend to look at Marx steadily from the American point of vantage, which means, for example, that I will resolve many of his ideas into categories with which we are familiar, pay close attention to some of his minor ideas and only passing attention to some of his major ones, and present these ideas in words as defined in our dictionary rather than in his. This, I think, is what justifies this study: It seeks to tell American readers in American words what Marx had to say about the political and social issues to which the shapers of the American tradition directed their best thoughts. All great creeds, of which Marxism is surely one, can be carried across the boundaries of faith and tradition and made intelligible to men who could never subscribe to them, and this is exactly what I hope to do.

Let me give a preliminary example of what I mean by dealing with Marx on our terms rather than on his. In several parts of the book, especially in the chapters on government and society, I will make use of a rough conceptual scheme that divides Marx's thought along chronological lines into four categories. As I survey Marxism from this angle of vision, it appears to deal with any particular phenomenon in four successive stages. Here, for example, is this four-ply scheme applied to the class structure:

Description, an account of how things are in the Western world, and also of how they developed: Society is divided into irreconcilably antagonistic classes.

Prediction, a promise that things are going from bad to worse and must soon reach a state of unbearable tension: All classes are being swallowed up into two major groups, the exploiting bourgeoisie and the exploited proletariat, and the institutions through which the former have hitherto operated are on the verge of collapse.

Prescription, a call to arms, directed primarily to those who grasp this situation and thus can steer it toward desired ends: The exploited, led by their farseeing friends, must rise up against the exploiters, seize the power that has been so long abused, and begin the noble work of rebuilding society.

Prophecy, a vision of how things will be when the rebuilding is completed: The society will be classless; the exploitation of men by men will be only a vague memory.

There are a hundred other equally valid schemes for analyzing Marx's political and social theory, and I do not propose to become a prisoner of this particular pattern. It is, nevertheless, a most useful tool, and it will be put to work at several points in the discussion.

•

Yet even this technique can do little more than throw a flickering beam of light onto a shadowy area of human knowledge and experience. There are discouraging obstacles in the path of anyone who intends to survey Marxism from the point of view of liberal democracy. The vocabularies, the judgments, the purposes, the tempers, the habits of thought, even the "facts" are sharply at odds. What we hold in respect Marxists hold in contempt; what they call science we call nonsense; where we go deep they go shallow; where they stop to think long thoughts we rush ahead impatiently. For us, perhaps the most discouraging obstacle of all is Marx himself, who of all great social thinkers is the most difficult to understand, however easy he may be to quote. It may seem impolite, after what I have just said about being fair to Marx, to go through the catalogue of his trespasses against intelligibility. But they are, after all, still another reason for his failure to attract many Americans to his cause, and I feel constrained to list these charges against him:

1) That he was unclear to the point of incoherence about some of the cardinal elements in his theory: Marx had no gift whatever for expounding fundamentals, and it will always be a wonder that he gets so many people to read him. Long before he died he was complaining of the way even his followers misunderstood his teachings, but it is hard to put the blame anywhere but on Marx himself. As Pareto said, one looks at a passage in *Capital* and sees a bird, then looks again and sees a bat.[27] His failure, for example, to make up his mind whether science and technology were to be placed among the "modes of production" or in the "superstructure" of civilization leaves the student of Marx in a swamp of uncertainty. More than that, his lack of clarity makes certain that any exposition of large parts of his thought will give it an intelligibility it never possessed.[28]

2) That he failed to define many of the key words in his famous vocabulary: It is discouraging enough to discover that he has no precise and consistent meaning for words like "conscious-

ness" and "matter" or a phrase like "relations of production," but almost frightening to learn that he never stated exactly what he meant by a "class." Marx could have spared mankind the making of hundreds of books if he had spent one of his good years on a short philosophical dictionary.

3) That he failed repeatedly to bring the available facts, or often any facts at all, to the support of his important generalizations: [29] What are we to think of an economist who used reports and statistics which, as he could have learned from even a short trip about the country, were hopelessly out-of-date? What are we to say of a "scientific historian" who forged an iron law of history out of practically no evidence whatever? Benedetto Croce exposed the softest spot in *Capital* when he wrote that it was concerned with "an ideal and formal society, deduced from certain hypotheses, which could indeed never have occurred as actual facts in the course of history." [30]

4) That he almost deliberately refused to anticipate questions that he must have known would occur to his serious readers: A classic instance was his failure to make clear, as he could have in a few sentences, whether and how the dialectic of history, hitherto powered by the class struggle, would continue to operate in the classless society. If I may again call on Croce, Marx "despised and neglected all such preliminary and exact explanations as might have made his task plain." [31]

5) That he casually brushed off several major questions about the behavior of all mankind: An example was his cavalier treatment of the religious impulse, which he dismissed with a shrug as a figment of men's frustrated imaginations—and thereby proved himself a child of his own times. "One might have thought," F. J. Sheed writes,

that in a matter so vital to his whole system as the non-existence of God, he would not have glided lightly on without the most careful consideration. Even if the generality of men from the beginning of history have been in error, the mere persistence of the error should have warned him that he was in the presence of a human tendency which might survive to wreck his system. And even short of concern about a denial essential to his system, there are certain questions which the theist answers with God but even the atheist ought to recognise as questions.[32]

6) That he was woefully silent about his prescriptions for building the new society: Marx may be excused for framing his prophecies of the golden future in the vaguest kind of language, but not for his failure to give at least broad marching directions to the men who would hold power in the transitional stages. When a man comes to destroy a society, especially a man who poses as a scientist, we have a right to hear a few proposals about the stage of reconstruction. How is production to be planned, or the dictatorship to be exercised, or law to be enforced, or the new generation to be educated? His answers might not have pleased us, but at least we and the Marxists would have been instructed.

7) That, worst of all, he inhabited a simple world where there were no shades, only blacks and whites: He ascribed all the dying corruption of capitalist society to the owners, all the rising goodness to the workers; he insisted on a one-to-one correspondence between the mode of production and the form of the state; he reduced all the fabulous struggles among the world's philosophers to the collision of materialism and idealism, and all the tortured struggles among the world's peoples to the conflict of exploiters and exploited. Marxist theory, which is more Germanic than we often recall, is a mass of false antitheses. Marx and Engels are convincing witnesses to the fact that simply to reverse a one-sided view of man or society or history is not in the least to arrive at the truth.

There are many other charges that could be leveled against Marx on strictly intellectual grounds: his penchant for pressing useful insights beyond their proper limits; his confusion of the real with the ideal, indeed, his habitation of a world that is a "wholly abstract, artificial and unreal construction"; [33] his insistence that he was a scientist even when he was most obviously a moralist or mystic; his use as philosopher of the most baffling Hegelian terms and his use as economist of obsolete apparatus; his amazing capacity for getting many facts about society just plain wrong; and his poor showing, since his death, as guide to the present or prophet of the future.[34] But I think I have said enough to show that we are dealing with a man who is perversely anxious to rebuff those who go to him in any but the most determined mood for enlightenment about the human predicament. Those who go to him for slogans with which to dream or slash their way out of it are sent away much better satisfied.

Many of these criticisms, to be sure, can be made of all the great thinkers who took humanity as their province. Yet Marx is especially vulnerable for two reasons: first, because of the sweep of his influence over the minds of men, an influence that may some day be judged to have matched that of Aristotle or St. Paul; and second, because of his own insistence on the scientific certainty of his descriptions, predictions, and even his prescriptions and prophecies. When a great thinker supposes and suggests, he may be forgiven the average burden of intellectual faults. But when he claims to speak the truth and lay down the law, he should be judged by more rigorous standards, which is exactly what I have tried to do. The most charitable judgment we can make of Marx in this matter is that he failed magnificently to meet these standards. Yet he was, for all his failures, a very great thinker, and we, like all men, must make our reckoning with him. If he demands that we come to him in the determined mood of which I spoke, then let us by all means put ourselves in such a mood. Like Darwin and Freud he changed the minds of men, even of men who hate him, and like Darwin and Freud he must therefore be treated with respect and keen attention. Even if his system were not the secular creed of one-third of the world, it would be a living force of huge proportions in the shaping of all our minds. I shall try to say something in the concluding chapter about the lasting appeals and contributions of Marxism, but I would make clear at this early stage that they are both enormous.

If all this backing and filling has led some of my readers to conclude that my posture toward Marx is one of pronounced ambivalence, I hasten to confess that such is the case, at the same time begging leave to remind them that ambivalence is the natural posture of anyone who looks at Marx with open eyes from the direction of the American tradition. He was an irritating, perplexing, angry man who passed a sentence of death on the American system, and for that we can hardly be expected to admire him. He was also a brilliant, far-ranging, eloquent man who told us things about capitalism and democracy that we needed to be told in the worst way. He is one of those few great men of whom it may truly be said: We should be both glad and sad that they lived and wrought.

Let me close this chapter with a few comments on Marx's relations with men and events in the United States and on his knowledge and understanding of American conditions. Although Marx never spent a day, and Engels only one month, in this country, both were free with public and private comments on many aspects of American life.[35] Marx had many reasons to look westward to the United States. It gave him an audience in Charles Dana's *New York Tribune* and paid him money for his remarks (even when they were written by Engels); harbored exiled comrades like Sorge and Joseph Weydemeyer; offered a place of burial for the First International; found him publishers for his books; provided him with the fascinating spectacle of the Civil War (topped off with a message straight from Lincoln, "the single-minded son of the working class");[36] and raised a native son on the banks of Lake Cayuga, Lewis Henry Morgan,[37] who led both Marx and Engels astray in their study of primitive societies. Yet he never looked westward long or carefully enough to add anything to our own or Europe's grasp of the uniqueness of the American experiment,

and there is not much point in speculating about what he might
have learned from, say, a six months' journey along de Tocque-
ville's route. If he could live in England for more than thirty years
and never meet or know "any honest-to-God workers," [38] whom
would he have met to tell him the truth about the United States?
One is tempted to think that after a fussy month with Sorge in
Hoboken, he would have been on his way to London.

Engels was a keener observer of what he and Marx, like Winston
Churchill a half-century later, called "the Great Republic." He
was aware of the strength of the "bourgeois prejudices" and "prac-
ticality" that governed "America . . . the idol of all bourgeois";
he understood why "Brother Jonathan" (we call him Uncle Sam)
was "the greatest organizer in existence of religion as a trade"; he
predicted in 1881 the removal of "the center of the world's industry . . . to the United States"; [39] and he repeatedly expressed the
opinion, so popular today among historians, that America was different because it had no feudal tradition, "no medieval ruins (to)
bar the way" to the onrush of history.[40] Indeed, if he had ever
freed himself for a spell from the chains of Marxist dogma, he
might have been persuaded by the sight of America that the laws
of capitalist development did not work out the same in every country. He might even have been persuaded to consider the possibility
that the absence of a feudal tradition would prove a boon to political democracy as well as to capitalism, permitting the former
to harness the latter to popular ends. But neither Engels nor Marx
was ever persuaded by external evidence to alter their common
conclusions, which they came to early and stayed with to the end.
The United States was only one of the phenomena which they
never really understood.

Whether we, in our turn, have understood them is a question
worth arguing, but there is no argument about the fact that we
have rejected them harshly. The number of conscious Marxists
who have raised their voices influentially in American intellectual
or political debate is amazingly small, and the contribution of these

men to Marxist thought has been almost negligible. I would except only Daniel De Leon from this harsh judgment.[41] Their contribution to American thought has not been much greater. The attempts of men like Algie M. Simons, Morris Hillquit, and John Spargo to freshen the ideals of American democracy with Marxist techniques of social analysis were, to say the best we can of them, crowned with small success. The attempts of William English Walling and, some years later, Sidney Hook to mix the turbid oil of Marxism and the clear water of pragmatism were even less successful.[42] America occupies a minor place in the intellectual history of Marxism—whether of the hard, soft, orthodox, revisionist, evolutionary, vulgar, or democratic variety.

Some of our non-Marxist intellectuals appear to have learned a few lessons from Marx, but what they learned was already so much a part of the common stock of critical ideas that we can never hope to be precise in measuring the direct influence of Marx. Charles A. Beard is one prominent American thinker who is thought by some to have drunk deep at the Marxist spring, but Beard himself insisted to the end that he and Marx, to the extent that they agreed on the primacy of economic forces in history, had drunk together at a much older spring with Aristotle, Machiavelli, Harrington, Madison, and others.[43] Reinhold Niebuhr made serious use of Marx's teachings—especially his historical diagnosis of the decay of capitalism—in *Moral Man and Immoral Society* (1932), but he has long since moved on to a position of criticism of "the Marxist illusion." [44] Even disenchanted intellectuals like Henry Adams, who thought he should have been a Marxist "by rights," [45] and his brother Brooks, who had many affinities with Marx,[46] have been unable to make themselves converts, or if converted, to stay converted. Marx is just not a master to whom men of an American cast of mind have been able to go for lessons in radical criticism.

I do not mean to say that the American mind has been untouched by Marx. A pervasive Marxist influence has spread all through the American intellectual community in the twentieth century, and many men who would deny flatly any debt to Marx have thought in Marxist categories and employed Marxist language. Yet in this instance I use *Marxist* (as do most historians of the American mind) as a word to describe a general pattern of radical, naturalistic thought rather than a particular source of inspiration. My own judgment is that Marxism has had less success in this country than in any other in the world. I hope this book will explain one of the reasons why.

TWO · THE MARXIST IDEA

Marxism makes much of the power of ideas to shape the behavior of men and the course of history. To some students of Marx this statement may appear ridiculous, for was it not he who proclaimed (if not first, certainly with the loudest voice) that ideas have no life of their own, that they are responses to the play of material forces, that they are always and everywhere rationalizations of positions taken or interests vested or hopes raised? And was it not he who predicted that philosophy, the ancient workshop and playground of ideas, is destined to decay and finally to disappear in the happier years ahead?

It was Marx, no doubt of that; and his broadside against the "ideology" of the bourgeoisie was a key operation in the grand assault on capitalism and parliamentary democracy. But the guns with which he fired the broadside, and indeed the position from which he launched the whole assault, were themselves an ideology in every sense of that stormy word.[1] Almost from the time he first advertised his ideas widely in the *Manifesto,* they have been a mighty force in the unfolding of human events—as he surely intended them to be. However rigidly his followers may ascribe these ideas to the shaping hand of "the mode of production," however cleverly they may demonstrate the conformity of these ideas to the realities of history, we know, and they know, too, that the teachings of Marx have had a life of their own, and that they have conformed to the inner necessities of men as often as to the outer realities of events. Their influence has been visited powerfully on the activities of men all over the world, not least upon those activities through which men produce and distribute the essentials of human existence. "Marxism," H. J. Muller writes, "is the clearest illustration of how history is made by man's beliefs about what has happened, what is happening, and what should happen." [2]

Any doubts about the central position that Marxism accords to ideology have long since been dispelled by the career of Marxism itself. Everything about Communism today, from the amount of money spent on propaganda to the revival of "consciousness" as a factor in psychology, supports Stalin's observation that ideas are "significant and important." Marxists in and out of the Soviet Union may harp on the "unity of theory and practice," [3] they may take a rigidly instrumentalist approach to ideas, they may shout the slogans of the *Manifesto* no more intelligently than many Christians mumble the verities of Matthew, chapters 5-7, but the truth is that no men in history have known better than they that "ideas are weapons" or that "ideas have consequences," and no men, certainly since the Scholastics, have indulged more enthusiastically in juggling the sacred texts in which their ideas were first proclaimed. Again in the words of Stalin, who in this passage has the ring of a faithful Marxist:

> The strength and vitality of Marxism-Leninism are derived from the fact that it relies upon an advanced theory which correctly reflects the needs of development of the material life of society, that it elevates theory to a proper level, and that it deems it its duty to utilize every ounce of the mobilizing, organizing and transforming power of this theory. [4]

What is "this theory," this total view of life, this Marxist chain of all natural and social phenomena in which man is the link between things and thoughts? What are the key elements of the Marxist philosophy?

Lenin once described Marxism as a "solid block of steel" in which the principal elements were the *dialectic* and *materialism*. "Dialectical materialism," his disciple Stalin wrote with even less fear of contradiction than usual,

is the world outlook of the Marxist-Leninist party. It is called dialectical materialism because its approach to the phenomena of nature, its method of studying and apprehending them, is *dialectical*, while its interpretation of the phenomena of nature, its conception of these phenomena, its theory, is *materialistic*.[5]

Let me separate these two inseparables, to the horror of many Marxists, and see what each of them means to American minds.

The primary meaning of *dialectic*, a legacy from Socrates and Plato, is "the art or practice of logical discussion as employed in investigating the truth of a theory or opinion." It is, in essence, a method of searching for truth in which two persons of contradictory opinion take part. The first makes a statement (*thesis*) which becomes the subject of discussion. The second produces objections to the thesis and develops a position (*antithesis*) which contradicts it. The two expositors then move on and up in a spirit of give-and-take to seek a position that combines the unassailable truths of both positions, and thus transforms them into a new and higher truth (*synthesis*). This position then becomes the opening step in a new dialectic—and so on endlessly through thesis, antithesis, and synthesis in search of knowledge.[6]

Hegel, as is well known, applied the dialectical pattern to history, which he interpreted as a vast process that moves from stage to higher stage through a series of contradictions and resolutions in the realm of ideas. He summed up the operation of the dialectic, which he preferred to call "development," in three great laws:

1) The Law of the Unity of Opposites, which affirms that opposites or contradictions do not exclude but imply one another.

2) The Law of the Negation of the Negation, which affirms that the conflict of two contradictions (thesis and antithesis) must result in a higher synthesis.

3) The Law of Transformation of Quantity into Quality, which affirms that this synthesis comes about through a sudden transformation, the way for which is prepared by a series of quantitative mutations. Thus does water rise degree by degree to 212° F. and suddenly take a "dialectical leap" to steam; thus does the child form in the womb and suddenly, through "an act of revolution," leap into life; thus, above all, does the class struggle move inexorably toward violent resolution.[7] These examples, I hasten to add, are Marxist and not Hegelian. For Hegel the dialectic unrolled (or rather spiraled upward) in the direction of the Absolute Idea.

Marx, the pupil of Hegel,[8] carried the dialectic out of the realm of ideas and into the realm of social and economic institutions. "My dialectic method," he wrote in his preface to *Capital,*

is not only different from the Hegelian, but is its direct opposite. To Hegel, the life-process of the human brain . . . is the demiurgos of the real world, and the real world is only the external, phenomenal form of "the Idea." With me, on the contrary, the ideal is nothing else than the material world reflected by the human mind, and translated into forms of thought. . . . The mystification which dialectic suffers in Hegel's hands, by no means prevents him from being the first to present its general form of working in a comprehensive and conscious manner. With him it is standing on its head. It must be turned right side up again, if you would discover the rational kernel within the mystical shell.[9]

Engels, the friend of Marx, carried the dialectic beyond society and applied it to everything in nature from the growth of barley to higher mathematics. Whether it was used to analyze the behavior of chemicals or of classes, it was man's "best working tool" and "sharpest weapon" and "highest form of reasoning." [10] Lenin, the pupil of Marx and Engels, who saluted the dialectic as "that gem in the rubbish of Absolute Idealism," went even further to find all nature conforming to the dialectical scheme.[11] And the Communists, the self-proclaimed children of Marx and Lenin, have tried ever since to apply the dialectic to any problem with which they may be faced, even when the result is to hide the solution completely. What was and still is an interesting scheme for analyzing some situations has become for Marxists a rigid technique for analyzing and manipulating all situations. In the words of a British Marxist:

> The *dialectical* logic of Hegel provides for the first time a logical instrument for the description and analysis of processes of development. . . . By means of this dialectical instrument all organic processes of development can be analyzed and grasped—and by no other means. The Hegelian dialectic is, therefore, the only available instrument which is adequate to provide the scientific understanding of organic processes and consequently to secure the control of such processes, based upon understanding.[12]

I do not wish to engage in either an exposition or a demolition of the Marxist dialectic. To expound it any further would be irrelevant to my purposes; to demolish it would be to repeat the labors of many better men.[13] But I do think it important to recall the central implications of this mode of thinking, for these explain why it continues to grip the imagination of all true Marxists. And the implications, each in a word, are:

Change, "the view," as Engels wrote, "that the whole of nature, from the smallest element to the greatest, from grains of sand to suns, from protista to men, has its existence in eternal coming into being and passing away, in ceaseless flux, in unresting motion." [14]

Conflict, the view that every phenomenon in nature and society is opposed by internal forces that contradict its very being, that even the most impressive unity is a sum of polar opposites.

Interdependence, the correlative view that phenomena are not isolated or disconnected, but are necessarily dependent upon other phenomena.

Progress, the view that the dialectic is, as it were, pointed upward, that every new synthesis is of a higher order than the old thesis.

Revolution, the view that significant changes in nature and society come as "leaps" or "jumps," that slow and steady progress has no other purpose than to prepare the way for sudden transformation.

While all these implications of the dialectic are dear to Marxists (as we shall learn repeatedly in the pages to come), the last point explains particularly why this technique has such a strong appeal, and why it may be argued, persuasively if not conclusively, that without it Marxism would have been a quite different system of insight and advice. Marx and Engels had need of a theory of history that would make revolutions a necessary part of progress and not simply accidents that happen along the way, and in the dialectic they found exactly what they needed. Marxism makes room for accidents in the development of natural and social phenomena, but not at the decisive point where the important advances take place. In Stalin's thoroughly Marxist explanation:

> Contrary to metaphysics, dialectics does not regard the process of development as a simple process of growth, where quantitative changes do not lead to qualitative changes, but as a development which passes from insignificant and imperceptible quantitative changes to open, fundamental changes, to qualitative changes; a development in which the qualitative changes occur not gradually, but rapidly and abruptly, taking the form of a leap from one state to another; they occur not accidentally but as the natural result of an accumulation of imperceptible and gradual quantitative changes.[15]

If there are doubts about the role of the dialectic in Marxism, there are none about the role of *materialism.* It is, by all odds, the most powerful and revolutionary of Marx's teachings, the stoutest rebuff he ever issued to the world that had produced him. I will try in this book to avoid overlong quotations from Marx and Engels, and I will repeatedly cut them short in the midst of flights of eloquence. But when Marx himself took special pains to sum up the central proposition of his system, as he did in his *Contribution to the Critique of Political Economy* (1859), he deserves to be quoted in full:

My investigations led to the conclusion that legal relations as well as forms of State could not be understood from themselves, nor from the so-called general development of the human mind, but, on the contrary, are rooted in the material conditions of life. . . . The general conclusion I arrived at—and once reached, it served as the guiding thread in my studies—can be briefly formulated as follows:

In the social production of their means of existence men enter into definite, necessary relations which are independent of their will, productive relationships which correspond to a definite state of development of their material productive forces. The aggregate of these productive relationships constitutes the economic structure of society, the real basis on which a juridical and political superstructure arises, and to which definite forms of social consciousness correspond.

The mode of production of the material means of existence conditions the whole process of social, political and intellectual life. It is not the consciousness of men that determines their existence, but, on the contrary, it is their social existence that determines their consciousness.

At a certain stage of their development the material productive forces of society come into contradiction with the existing productive relationships, or, what is but a legal expression for these, with the property relationships within which they had moved before. From forms of development of the productive forces these relationships are transformed into their fetters. Then an epoch of social revolution opens. With the change in the economic foundation the whole vast superstructure is more or less rapidly transformed.

In considering such revolutions it is necessary always to distinguish between the material revolution in the economic conditions of production, which can be determined with scientific accuracy, and the juridical, political, religious, esthetic or philosophic—in a word, ideological forms wherein men become conscious of this conflict and fight it out. Just as we cannot judge an individual on the basis of his own opinion of himself, so such a revolutionary epoch cannot be judged from its own consciousness; but on the contrary this consciousness must be explained from the contradictions of material life, from the

existing conflict between social productive forces and productive relationships.

A social system never perishes before all the productive forces have
developed for which it is wide enough; and new, higher productive
relationships never come into being before the material conditions for
their existence have been brought to maturity within the womb of
the old society itself. Therefore, mankind always sets itself only such
problems as it can solve; for when we look closer we will always find
that the problem itself only arises when the material conditions for
its solution are already present or at least in process of coming into
being.[16]

This passage, one of the three or four most celebrated in the
Marxist canon, deserves to be read in a Baconian spirit: not simply
tasted and swallowed but "chewed and digested." It states the
basic doctrine of materialism, applies this doctrine specifically to
the realm of ideas, infuses it with the dialectic, and then projects
the fusion—dialectical materialism—into history. I shall return in
a few pages to the problem of history. Let me comment here on
the three other principles or applications of Marxism incorporated
in this momentous statement.

The one point upon which Marxists and anti-Marxists can be
said to agree most enthusiastically is that materialism is the essence
of all those attitudes and exhortations which men identify as Marxism. Beyond this point, however, agreement usually comes to an
abrupt end, not least because many anti-Marxists insist on imputing to Marxism all the worst sins and most naive theories that can
be read into this word. This is unfair to Marx and Engels, who,
when they did not use *materialism* as a synonym for *science* or
realism or *naturalism* or *atheism,* had something more complicated
and less vulgar in mind than the notion that men are incapable of
acting contrary to their economic interests, or than the notion that,
as Engels put it ironically, the real joy of man is to engage in
"gluttony, drunkenness, lust of the eye, lust of the flesh, arrogance,
cupidity, avarice, miserliness, profit-hunting, and stock-exchange
swindling." [17] To them, especially to Engels (who was a more con-

vinced materialist than Marx), this word stood for a view of man, ideas, society, history, and the universe that was diametrically opposed to what they despised as *idealism*. Indeed, it is impossible to grasp the nature of materialism in Marxism unless we take note of this obsessive contempt for idealism, which to a Marxist means either the extreme philosophical position that admits no other reality than mind, or the eclectic position that admits some other reality than matter. In the most authoritative recent exposition of materialism, that of Stalin (and friends) in *Dialectical and Historical Materialism,** this necessary, one might say dialectical, connection stands forth sharply:

The principal features of Marxist philosophical *materialism* are as follows:

a) Contrary to idealism, which regards the world as the embodiment of an "absolute idea," a "universal spirit," "consciousness," Marx's philosophical materialism holds that the world is by its very nature *material*, that the multifold phenomena of the world constitute different forms of matter in motion, that interconnection and interdependence of phenomena, as established by the dialectical method, are a law of the development of moving matter, and that the world develops in accordance with the laws of movement of matter and stands in no need of a "universal spirit." . . .

b) Contrary to idealism, which asserts that only our mind really exists, and that the material world, being, nature, exists only in our mind, in our sensations, ideas and perceptions, the Marxist materialist philosophy holds that matter, nature, being, is an objective reality existing outside and independent of our mind; that matter is primary, since it is the source of sensations, ideas, mind, and that mind is secondary, derivative, since it is a reflection of matter, a reflection of being. . . .

* This small book is a chapter from the celebrated (and now defunct) *History of the Communist Party of the Soviet Union (Bolsheviks)* (1938), generally known as the *Short Course*. Stalin upgraded his own part in preparing it, and Khrushchev downgraded it in his speech to the Twentieth Congress. I think we may continue to treat the ideas and mode of expression of *Dialectical and Historical Materialism* as if they were Stalin's, and Stalin's ideas as if they were Khrushchev's. Nothing in the new texts of the past five years, especially the new party history of 1959, deviates one inch from Stalin's orthodox pronouncement on dialectical materialism.[18]

c) Contrary to idealism, which denies the possibility of knowing the world and its laws, which does not believe in the authenticity of our knowledge, does not recognize objective truth, and holds that the world is full of "things-in-themselves" that can never be known to science, Marxist philosophical materialism holds that the world and its laws are fully knowable, that our knowledge of the laws of nature, tested by experiment and practice, is authentic knowledge having the validity of objective truth, and that there are no things in the world which are unknowable, but only things which are still not known, but which will be disclosed and made known by the efforts of science and practice. . . .

Such, in brief, are the characteristic features of the Marxist philosophical materialism.[19]

There are other interesting tidbits floating around in this Marxist stew on which we will chew in course. My chief reason for quoting these words is to present in simplest fashion—from a tract written for the Soviet millions—the essentials of materialism. These are so plainly stated that I hardly need comment on them, except to rephrase the Marxist affirmation that the only reality is material: All life is reducible to matter; all events are simply material processes. If there is a realm of the mind and spirit, the things that inhabit it—ideas, beliefs, traditions, desires, aspirations, "innate characteristics"—are themselves either matter or "products, functions of matter." [20]

This, of course, is the most controversial application of philosophical materialism: to the ideas men hold about themselves and their place in the universe. Marx and Engels knew how frontally they were challenging the most sacred assumptions, not merely of the German philosophers with whom they jousted even in their sleep, but of the men who ruled and were ruled throughout the world. The challenge, therefore, was harsh as well as frontal. Said the *Communist Manifesto:*

Does it require deep intuition to comprehend that man's ideas, views, and conceptions, in one word, man's consciousness, changes

with every change in the conditions of his material existence, in his
social relations and in his social life?

What else does the history of ideas prove, than that intellectual
production changes its character in proportion as material production
is changed? *The ruling ideas of each age have ever been the ideas of
its ruling class.*[21]

And *The German Ideology* echoed:

We do not set out from what men say, imagine, conceive . . . in
order to arrive at men in the flesh. We set out from real, active men,
and on the basis of their real life-process we demonstrate the development of the ideological reflexes and echoes of this life-process. . . .
Men, developing their material production and their material inter-
course, alter, along with this their real existence, their thinking and
the products of their thinking. *Life is not determined by consciousness,
but consciousness by life.*[22]

"Or," Stalin wrote, "to put it more crudely," which is the way
he liked to put things, "whatever is man's manner of life, such is
his manner of thought." [23]

We will never know what Marx and Engels meant by that key
word "determined" (*bedingt*), and thus never be able to trace any
more carefully than they (which is to say not at all) the causal
links between the mode of production of a given society and the
ideas of its ruling class. Yet for all the intricacies, deficiencies, and
sheer mysticism of the Marxist concept of materialism, I do not see
how we can mistake its chief message: that the things men prize
most in this world—such institutions as the family and the law, such
values as self-sacrifice and integrity, such faiths as God and country
—are shaped primarily, and in the long run exclusively, by the
manner in which they organize themselves for economic production.

As the mode of production changes, so sooner or later will all
these other things change, too; and at some point the process will
take the form of a sharp break with the past. This is the further
message of dialectical materialism, which is, the Marxists insist,
the only correct kind of materialism.[24] It was Marx's and Engels'

magnificent achievement, they add, to put the best of Germany and the best of England and France together, to blend in our consciousness (as nature had already blended in reality) the dialectic of Hegel and the materialism of Hobbes and of Holbach.[25] The fact that outsiders can detect no logical connection between the two, no reason why one must be a believer in both or neither, does not mean there was no such connection in the understanding of the founders.[26] To them, and to all Marxists who have followed them faithfully, the two were fused together forever in that "solid block of steel" of which Lenin boasted. Marx and Engels wanted to make the proletarian revolution doubly certain, and this was their truly ingenious way of doing it. We have listened already to the revolutionary promise of the dialectic; in a moment we shall hear the same promise from materialism.

The American tradition dictates no particular way of thinking about man, nature, and the universe. Rather, it invites all Americans, so long as they try to obey the rules of common sense and intellectual honesty, to think as they please. Those who have tried to grapple with essential truth are spread all along the spectrum of thought: empiricists, rationalists, idealists, fundamentalists of a dozen varieties, positivists of a dozen more, skeptics, agnostics, Calvinists, deists, Thomists, pragmatists, instrumentalists, and even a few materialists.[27] If one were to fix on any way of thought as "characteristically American," it would include, I suspect, two parts empiricism and one part Christian rationalism, with a dash of idealism and a twist of pragmatism. But one would quickly add that many other blends were no less entitled to the bonded label of "100 per cent Americanism."

What, then, does the American tradition say to the doctrine of dialectical materialism, to this "most powerful instrument of human thought and understanding," [28] this "philosophy which illuminates all events whatever, from the falling of a stone to a poet's imaginings"? [29] To the first half of the doctrine it says nothing more than "how interesting." An American who wished to make use of the dialectic in his thinking would not thereby become any less American. If he tried to apply it rigidly and exclusively to the pattern of American history, he might be considered a crank; if he tried to apply it to all the phenomena of nature from river valleys to skidding cars, he might be called a fool.[30] He might even be judged by some to have dishonored the American tradition, but the essence of the charge against him would be that he had been an extremist, not a dialectician. There are those who, like the Marxists, think of the dialectic as an entering wedge for the proletarian revolution and, unlike them, are horrified by the thought of using it at all. But they seem to have forgotten that Hegel used it as a stout defense of the Prussian state, a fact that leads me to observe that every man is his own dialectician.[31] To the extent that Engels used the dialectic to explain all life, he is simply out of order on the counts of mysticism and irrelevancy. To the extent that Marx used it to dramatize the dynamic quality of much in society that seems stable on the surface, he is due a cautious vote of thanks. I would conclude these few remarks with the thought that although the dialectic is not a key to nature or history, it is an open window into Marx's mind and style.[32] The window is still open, and we would do well to keep looking through it as we survey Marxism "from China to Peru." *

We cannot be so forbearing about the second half of the formula. When the Marxists insist that we are hopeless idealists, they are not too far from the truth. The American tradition puts great value on the human spirit as an independent force. It believes that ideas shape society just as surely as society shapes ideas, and it makes

* If one did not know that Mao Tse-tung was a devoted child of Marx, a man whose mind dwells in a misty vale of dialectical contradictions, how could one make sense of his concept of war?

A revolutionary war is an offensive yet has also its defensive phase and retreat. To defend in order to attack, to retreat in order to advance, to take a flanking action in order to take a frontal action, and *to be devious in order to go direct—* these are inevitable occurrences in the process of development of many things, and military events cannot be otherwise.[33]

room for the existence, above and outside the known or knowable, of a realm of eternal mystery. To be specific, it makes room for God, and that is the sum of the reasons why we find materialism unacceptable as an explanation of life and society.

At a lower level, too, we cannot agree to the rigid, all-controlling primacy of economic forces. We have learned a lot in the last few generations, most of all from Marx himself, about the role of economics in shaping faith, morals, behavior, and institutions. But that man's essence is economic, that the root of all his miseries is economic, that his redemption will be economic, that the explanation of all history is economic—these are a few of the hard implications of Marxist materialism that we cannot possibly accept. Engels went out of his way, late in life, to call a halt to the absurd lengths to which certain Marxists had driven the doctrine of economic determinism; [34] and Marx, as Berdyaev wrote, behaved like an extreme idealist in calling upon the proletariat to lead the world to redemption.[35] But this hardly excuses them, and excuses Lenin not at all, for having neglected the countless forces that have made man and history in constructing their pattern of ideas.

In the end, it is not so much the doctrine itself but the role assigned to it that makes dialectical materialism unacceptable to American minds. The truth is that the Marxists, who ridicule our notion of a higher law as the sum of "idealistic nonsense," [36] have converted dialectical materialism into a far more rigid, all-embracing, all-controlling law than any we have ever imagined—and thus, in fact, have beat a retreat to idealism.[37] Engels tried to laugh his adversary Dühring out of court with these words:

As is well known, we Germans are of a terribly ponderous *Gründlichkeit*, radical profundity or profound radicality, whatever you may like to call it. Whenever anyone of us expounds what he considers a new doctrine, he has first to elaborate it into an all-comprising system. He has to prove that both the first principles of logic and the fundamental laws of the universe had existed from all eternity for no other purpose than to ultimately lead to this newly-discovered, crowning theory. And Dr. Dühring, in this respect, was quite up to the national mark.[38]

Dr. Marx and Mr. Engels, however, had already set a new national mark, one that is not likely ever to be topped in Germany or anywhere else. Hegelians to the core, they thought they had found in dialectical materialism the one fundamental law of the universe, and on this law they hung their own "newly-discovered, crowning theory." The twentieth-century Marxists, led by Lenin, have carried this faith in one mighty law of nature to the very pole of monism.[39] Any suspicion that there may be some pattern of events or phenomenon of nature to which dialectical materialism does not apply has been discarded out-of-hand, and with it the notion that there is a place in every system for a leaven of empiricism. Dialectical materialism is a science, a "truly scientific world outlook," [40] whose laws are so manifest and certain that no one who uses them to survey the world need ever admit he may be mistaken—until, of course, he is shown to be mistaken by someone entitled to point out his mistakes. In that event he will hold himself responsible for having stupidly misread the plain commands of dialectical materialism. It takes considerable ingenuity for Soviet intellectuals to reconcile much of their work with this most sacred of Marxist symbols, for they must live always with the revealed truth that dialectical materialism "enables the Party to find the right orientation to any situation, to understand the inner connection of current events, to foresee their course and to perceive not only how and in what direction they are developing in the present, but how and in what direction they are bound to develop in the future." [41]

The American tradition is permissively pluralistic, Marxism severely monistic about the ways man can think deep thoughts about himself and all the wonders around him, and this is where the final philosophical break occurs. The Marxists have taken special pains to brand our idealism, pragmatism, empiricism, and rationalism as "reactionary tendencies in contemporary bourgeois philosophy." We are thoroughly uncomfortable in the presence of a system that relates all thoughts and all wonders to a single determining principle. This, we think, is the supreme ideology of all time, in the worst, or Marxist sense of the word.

Let us turn now to two great questions that men have pondered since the beginning of recorded time—the meaning of history and the existence of God—and let us hear and appraise the answers of Marxism. The breach between Marxism and the American tradition in both of these matters of universal concern is so open as to defy the healing power of even the most imaginative attempt at a "higher synthesis."

The Marxist interpretation of history is known as *historical materialism*.[42] This phrase is a shorthand way of saying that the laws of dialectical materialism apply in all their force to the development of human society. Whether there is in fact any logical connection between dialectical and historical materialism is fortunately not necessary for me to decide. It may be proved to the satisfaction of all reasonable men that historical materialism could be true even if dialectical materialism were false,[43] and that the connection between them is therefore merely formal; [44] but if Marxism insists that the two are one, then in this context we should by all means treat them as one.

Marx placed history at the center of his system, and his followers have always kept it there. A devout belief in history—in its laws, lessons, and promises—is the beginning of Marxist wisdom. It is not, of course, any history whatsoever that is the object of reverence, but Marxist history: history as interpreted by Marx and Engels, history as made by the Commune and Lenin. We must take constant notice of this essential dualism in Marxism: history as science, an object of contemplation, and history as purpose, an area of action.

The essence of the Marxist philosophy of history is caught in two passages from Engels, in the first of which he defined historical materialism as

that view of the course of history, which seeks the ultimate cause and the great moving power of all important historic events in the economic development of society, in the changes in the modes of production and exchange, in the consequent division of society into distinct classes, and in the struggles of these classes against one another.[45]

In the second, he put the case for materialism even more boldly:

The materialist conception of history starts from the proposition that the production of the means to support human life and, next to production, the exchange of things produced, is the basis of all social structure; that in every society that has appeared in history, the manner in which wealth is distributed and society divided into classes or orders is dependent upon what is produced, how it is produced, and how the products are exchanged. From this point of view the final causes of all social changes and political revolutions are to be sought, not in men's brains, not in man's better insight into eternal truth and justice, but in changes in the modes of production and exchange. They are to be sought, not in the *philosophy,* but in the *economics* of each particular epoch.[46]

Here, in a small room, are laid out the elements of historical materialism. The first of these is the dialectic, which Marx applied remorselessly to all history. It was not enough for his purposes to portray human society in "fluid movement" since the beginning of recorded time. He needed to believe himself and to prove to his followers that this restless transformation of even the most apparently stable patterns of life resulted from the emergence and resolution of sharp antagonisms. His allegiance to the dialectic, which discourages three-cornered fights and free-for-alls, made it possible for him to resolve the antagonisms of his own time into two clear-cut forces: the exploiters and the exploited, thesis and antithesis, each hating yet needing the other to fulfill its destiny. Further, it encouraged him to impose on history a grand scheme— the notion of a series of stages progressing inexorably from ancient

communal society through the slave and feudal societies to the
capitalist society of his time—that answered his gnawing Hegelian
need for the One Big Explanation. The dialectic enabled him to
rise above the view of history as "a wild whirl of senseless deeds
of violence." [47] More than that, it seemed to point beyond his own
time to a socialist and then a communist future. The dialectic, as
I have mentioned, embodied the notion of rational progress, of
an eternal pattern of motion upward and onward. It pleased Marx
to think of history as a vast dialectical parade moving grandly
from the primitive golden age of the communal past to the fabulous
golden age of the communist future.[48] He was pre-eminently a
historian of Progress, an heir of Condorcet who not only imagined
bravely but predicted scientifically the establishment of a terrestrial
paradise.[49] He believed confidently throughout his life in the "revolutionary reconstitution of society at large." It was Marx who
cried out with Dimitrov from the prisoner's dock at Leipzig in
1933, "The wheel of history moves on towards the ultimate, inevitable, irrepressible goal of Communism." [50]

The second element is materialism, which Marx also applied so
remorselessly that we may consider him one of the great teachers,
perhaps the greatest, of the economic interpretation of history. In
his *Poverty of Philosophy,* which appeared in 1847, he made his
first clear statement of this idea:

Social relations are closely bound up with productive forces. In
acquiring new productive forces men change their mode of production; and in changing their mode of production they change their
way of earning their living—they change all their social relations.
The hand-mill gives you society with the feudal lord; the steam-mill,
society with the industrial capitalist.

The same men who establish their social relations in conformity
with their material productivity, produce also principles, ideas and
categories, in conformity with their social relations.[51]

Several lovely forests in Sweden and Canada have been denuded
to feed the endless paper-war over the question: How far did Marx

and Engels really mean to go with their economic determinism? Engels, in particular, has been quoted again and again as expressing horror over the extreme applications the younger Marxists had made of his and Marx's teachings, and as reminding his friends of the influence of law, politics, ideology, and religion on the course of history.[52] But there is not much doubt, certainly from the point of view of men who sit outside the magic circle of Marxism, about the finality of their commitment to economics as the giant force in history, one on which all other forces and events must in the end be causally dependent. As Samuel Beer points out, Marx cannot wander far from the strict version of economic determinism, because only such a version is consistent with the other parts of his system.[53] Engels himself, in the same breath in which he chastised the younger Marxists, affirmed that "amid all the endless *host* of accidents . . . the economic movement finally asserts itself as necessary." Both Engels and Marx used the words "inevitable" and "necessary" so often in describing the influence of the mode of production on the course of history that they ought to be treated as men who meant what they said. Their descendants have tried their best to agree with Bukharin that, in the long view, "there can be no such thing as accident in history." [54]

And now to lay all doubts at rest, let us stand at Marx's grave on March 17, 1883, and hear what Engels claimed for his senior partner:

Just as Darwin discovered the law of evolution in organic nature, so Marx discovered the law of evolution in human history; he discovered the simple fact, hitherto concealed by an overgrowth of ideology, that mankind must first of all eat and drink, have shelter and clothing, before it can pursue politics, science, religion, art, etc.; and that therefore the production of the immediate material means of subsistence and consequently the degree of economic development attained by a given people or during a given epoch, form the foundation upon which the state institutions, the legal conceptions, the art and even the religious ideas of the people concerned have been evolved, and in the light of which these things must therefore be explained, instead of vice versa as had hitherto been the case.[55]

The third major element in the Marxist philosophy of history is the class struggle, the mighty lever through which the mode of production applies its exclusive power to direct the dialectical course of events. "The history of all hitherto existing societies," the *Manifesto* proclaims, "is the history of class struggles."

Freeman and slave, patrician and plebeian, lord and serf, guild-master and journeyman, in a word, oppressor and oppressed stood in constant opposition to one another, carried on an uninterrupted, now hidden, now open fight, a fight that each time ended, either in a revolutionary reconstitution of society at large, or in the common ruin of the contending classes. . . .

The modern bourgeois society that has sprouted from the ruins of feudal society has not done away with class antagonisms. It has but established new classes, new conditions of oppression, new forms of struggle in place of the old ones.

Our epoch, the epoch of the bourgeoisie, possesses, however, this distinctive feature: It has simplified the class antagonisms. Society as a whole is more and more splitting up into two great hostile camps, into two great classes directly facing each other—bourgeoisie and proletariat.[56]

The class struggle thus emerges as the supreme expression of dialectical materialism. The mode of capitalist production has created the bourgeoisie and proletariat, and these two classes must contend with one another in the most dramatic of all contradictions until they are resolved into the higher synthesis of the classless society. Before this happens, however, the proletarians will show themselves to be "the creators of history and the motive force of progress." [57] There is no doubt where Marx's preference lies in this particular contradiction. It is only because he can promise the bloody negation of the bourgeoisie that he proclaims the class struggle as bravely as he does. Marx hated and welcomed this struggle at the same time—hated it because of the misery it had caused, welcomed it because it promised an end to all misery. It was, indeed, the only means through which man could finally bring his destiny under his own control.

The last element, to which all the others lead, is revolution. The dialectic, it will be remembered, is a theory of development in which progress is achieved by "leaps" or "jumps," by the "transformation of quantity into quality." The leap in the dialectic of history can be nothing else than revolution; and Marx, although he wavered occasionally, was almost certain that any decisive transition from one stage to another in history would be marked by a violent revolution. Since Lenin wrought and wrote, there has been no wavering of any kind. Without class antagonisms that build up slowly to an unbearable crisis, and without the resolution of this crisis through a violent leap into the future, there can be no genuine progress: [58] this is the firm opinion of all orthodox Marxists. The bourgeoisie will bleed before it will surrender its power; the proletariat must bleed before it will be purged of the poisons of capitalism. Societies, like men, are born in pain and die in agony. To conclude with Marx and not with the Bolsheviks:

> Would it, moreover, be matter for astonishment if a society, based upon the *antagonism* of classes, should lead ultimately to a brutal *conflict,* to a hand-to-hand struggle as its final *denouement?* . . .
>
> It is only in an order of things in which there will be no longer classes or class antagonism that *social evolutions* will cease to be political revolutions. Until then, on the eve of each general reconstruction of society, the last word of social science will ever be:
>
> "Combat or death; bloody struggle or extinction.
> It is thus that the question is irresistibly put." [59]

Marx the historian was a dialectician, a materialist, a class-conscious revolutionary, and a prophet of glory. Was he also, as is generally asserted, a determinist? Was he a man who believed that the face of the future was already drawn, that events like the proletarian revolution and the dictatorship of the proletariat were fixed "on the agenda of history," that men were powerless to turn these events aside by their own heroics?

The answer is both Yes and No, with the balance of the evidence leaning toward Yes. On one hand, he can be quoted, especially when he is talking theoretically about stages of history or forces of production, as a complete determinist who finds that all men, both great and small,[60] are chips on the surface of vast social and economic tides that move in obedience to "inner, general laws." [61] Many of his followers, no longer orthodox to be sure, still draw comfort from those passages in which men appear as "necessary agents of a necessary system." [62] This, one might say, is the Menshevik answer to the dilemma of determinism versus free will in history: passivity, acquiescence, a disposition to wait confidently for the inevitable.[63] On the other hand, Marx can be quoted, especially when he is talking about specific persons and agents, as a historian who leaves a wide range of choice and influence to men and nations. His other followers, to whom Moscow is Rome, draw inspiration from such passages as "men make their history themselves." [64] This, one might say, is the Bolshevik answer: activity, decision, a disposition to force the hand of the inevitable.

Marx thus appears as a dualist who preaches both the historically necessary and the humanly possible—with no apparent concern for the dilemma such dualism raises.[65] He likes to have it both ways, and so do his orthodox heirs, who handle the dualism in their own way by preaching activity to themselves and passivity to us. Thus, perhaps unwittingly, they resolve the dilemma, which turns out to have been no dilemma at all. The course of history *is* determined: it will move, whether men like it or not, from capitalism through revolution to socialism and beyond to communism. But men can influence it markedly if—and this "if" is the key—if they are Communists, men who understand the great laws of social development. As is so often the case, the text is from Engels:

> Active social forces work exactly like natural forces; blindly, forcibly, destructively, so long as we do not understand and reckon

with them. But when once we understand them, when once we grasp their action, their direction, their effects, it depends only upon ourselves to subject them more and more to our own will, and by means of them to reach our own ends.[66]

The situation of history is transformed for those who are prepared to work with it. Since Communists understand and accept the laws of history, they are free to do great things: to speed up revolutions, to bypass supposedly inevitable stages, to make their own history. For those who are not prepared to work with it the situation is just what it has always been; for capitalists and bourgeois democrats there is no way out. History is a bandwagon, rolling dialectically to glory.[67] Those who get on board can make it go faster and even steer it a bit; those who prefer to walk will be run over and left behind. Did not Bukharin say, before he fell from grace, that "when Marxists organize the Communist Party and lead it into battle, this action is also an expression of historical necessity which finds its form precisely through the will and actions of men"? [68] If Marx had been a novelist his double attitude toward men in history might have been a source of great insight,[69] but a novelist was the last thing he would have chosen to be. He wanted it both ways in the real world, and who is to say that he did not get what he wanted?

In the American tradition there is room for many ways of explaining the march of human events.[70] We, too, profess great respect for history and historiography, for the former because we think it has been especially kind to America, for the latter because we think it is one of the most reliable of all teachers. Indeed, if history is defined as what has happened up to now, our respect is large and that of the Marxists small. We look upon history as a wonderful tapestry of successes and failures, with the successes becoming more numerous as it approaches our own time. They seem to look upon it as a series of failures leading painfully if necessarily to the immediate future (which is said to have arrived in Russia) when it will score its first genuine success. In the preface to his *Contribution to the Critique of Political Economy,* Marx speaks of the bourgeois present as "the closing chapter of the prehistoric stage of human society," [71] thus apparently withholding the designation of "history" from everything that has happened thus far in the world.

Let me again attempt a description of the American tradition and a critique of Marxism in one operation. First, our pluralistic tradition is opposed to a historical determinism that places the causes of history not only entirely in this world, but in that part of the world where men labor to produce the essentials of existence.[72] We have had our determinists, followers of Calvin as well as of Marx, but we have paid small attention to them. Most Americans think of history as something that moves toward an "open future" not foreordained by the past, that is propelled by many forces including social co-operation and creative thinking and unscheduled accidents, and that calls on men to bend it to their will. Even those historians who have detected the hand of God in the American experiment have thought of it as little more than a cosmic pat on the back. They have assumed that we were just as free to rise or fall by our own efforts as if there were no God. We are not determinists, and we are even less materialists. Engels called economics a "red thread" running through history. Most of us would now agree with him, but we also think there are other threads that have run right with it, two of which—religion and politics—historians ignore at their peril.

The American historical tradition is full of faith in progress,[73] although not quite so full as it was a generation ago. We still have little use for theories, cyclical or otherwise, that predict the decline of the American Republic. On the other hand, we have so many reservations about the progress described by Marx that it is quite useless to seek a meaningful identity between his promises and our hopes. The progress of which we speak is a matter of wishful faith rather than of scientific proof; it has been achieved through a process much more complicated than the dialectic; and it has made its greatest strides through co-operation and evolution rather than through antagonism and revolution. Just where history is leading us we find hard to say, but surely not toward the "perfections" of Communism.

The breach between Marxism and the American tradition in the field of history goes deeper than this. Once again, it is not so much what Marx and Engels said that puts us off as it is the narrow certainty with which they said it. We have little use for the deterministic, materialistic, revolutionary explanation of history, even less for men who insist that there is, in the long run, no other explanation. History was not that easily made, and it is not that easily written. Marxism is no less monistic in the writing of history than it is in philosophy or psychology or political theory, and Marx, for all his brilliance, is no less misleading than the other historians who have offered us single-factor theories of the march of events, including the man who came up with the "syphilitic interpretation of history." They have all, Marx included, given us not an explanation but a description, "and a highly selective one at that." [74] In the words of John Dewey, an American progressive whose pluralism and pragmatism forbade him to be tempted by Marxism:

> The thesis that all societies must exhibit a uniform, even if uneven, social development from primitive communism to slavery, from slavery to feudalism, from feudalism to capitalism, and from capitalism to socialism, and that the transition from capitalism to socialism must be achieved by the same way in all countries, can be accepted only by those who are either ignorant of history or who are so steeped in dogma that they cannot look at a fact without changing it to suit their special purposes.[75]

The fact is, of course, that Marx the historian passes out of the laboratory of imitation science and into the kingdom of genuine mysticism; and although we are not necessarily hostile to mysticism as such, we cannot follow him into a realm where the reigning mysticism is mystical exactly because it denies all mystery. Marx and the Marxists claim to have discovered the causation and goal of the historical process, which is to say that they claim to know things we believe to be unknowable. The very words Marx uses to reveal the mysteries of history—proletariat, bourgeoisie, super-structure, substructure, condition, determine, class struggle, mode of production—are incantations mumbled to an unknown god, who is not much better known today than he was in Marx's time.

I feel bound to make two final criticisms of Marx and Engels: First, they were, as anyone who has read them knows to his disappointment, poor historians from the purely technical point of view.[76] They came to their conclusions early along the paths of pure speculation, refused to let events or documents ever shake these conclusions, and made commanding generalizations about whole periods of history of which they knew nothing. Indeed, when one sits down to assess the flimsy evidence they gathered [77] (or swallowed whole, as they did the fancies of Morgan's *Ancient Society*), when one notes to his amazement what a tiny portion of their writings is devoted to history, when one considers the cardinal questions (will the dialectic operate in communist so-ciety?) that they left unasked as well as unanswered,* one is tempted to wonder how they ever got to be thought of as historians at all. Those who presume to construct general laws of history should do at least as much digging for foundation materials as did Spengler or Toynbee. If Marx and Engels had done any real digging, we may ask, would they still have been historical ma-terialists?

Second, they have failed the one test on which they were willing to stake their claim to be the world's first "scientific historians": the test of history itself.[79] The class structure has not polarized

---

* The Communists have attempted, without much success, to answer this question by asserting that "a new aspect of movement, a new type of de-velopment, a new dialectical law" has already begun to operate in the Soviet Union. Progress is powered by "the rational method of criticism and self-criticism" rather than by "violent social conflicts and upheavals." [78]

and hardened; the bourgeoisie has not fed upon itself; the working class has not sunk ever deeper into misery. Most telling blow of all, more than a century has passed and the proletarian revolution in the West has not come. It could be argued, I suppose, that events in Russia and Asia have borne out some of their grand prophecies in a perverse and unexpected way, but this is only to say that as prophets they were at their best when they spoke to the future in Delphic language. Prophecy is a thankless business, and we would not blame them for being so poor at it if they had not insisted that we were fools to question their "science" and its power to foretell the future. They were, as Karl Popper has shown, the supreme historicists of all time, a historicist being one who believes "that history is controlled by specific historical or evolutionary laws whose discovery would enable us to prophesy the destiny of man." [80] As they were supreme, so, too, were they the most misleading among those who proclaim that the future is closed. Any doubts on this score should long since have been settled by a cataloguing of their false prophecies about Europe and the United States. In the words of a scholar who has spent his life with Marx:

> With a zeal, a fanfare and an explicitness that no fortuneteller would risk, Marx was forever climbing out on a limb of prophecy, and forever falling from the dead branch. No other serious thinker of the nineteenth century was so frequently, egregiously, and totally wrong in his predictions.[81]

Again, perhaps, I have been too hard on Marx and Engels. The tactical situation in their time forced those who challenged the reigning theories of history to do so with force and passion, and in issuing their own challenge they naturally went too far toward the opposite extreme of the heroic and idealistic and dynastic schools. If they failed to convince men of common sense that there is a meaningful pattern to history, still they turned the attentions of many writers of history back to the basic activities of the race. Out of the wreckage of historical materialism, there has come, to

those not afraid of the ghost of Marx that haunts it, a new understanding of a key factor in shaping the course of events, a new
lead in our eternal quest to learn more about the "unknown god"
of history. For this great insight, which we have elected to use
with un-Marxist moderation, we may give them thanks. For the
rest of their philosophy of history we dare not, if we are democrats, have any use.

In the light of what we have learned already about the Marxist
commitment to materialism, we need pause only briefly to survey
the field of religion. To Marx and Engels religious conviction, in
whatever form it appeared, was the extremity of idealism. "All
religion," Engels wrote, "is nothing but the fantastic reflection in
men's minds of those external forces which control their daily
life." "The religious world," Marx added, "is but the reflex of the
real world." [82] It was idealism, moreover, forced upon man by his
alienated condition, about which we shall learn in the next chapter.
"Religion," Marx wrote, "is the fantastic realization of man's
essence because man's essence is not realized in fact." [83]

Marx and Engels were more than just another pair of secular-
ists and anticlericalists among the social critics of their day. They
were men determined on principle to see the end of all religion.
They stated their case so positively that no dedicated Marxist has
ever been left in doubt about the line he must take. As a young
man, Marx proclaimed his Promethean hatred for "all the gods,"
not just for the god who blessed bourgeois capitalism; and neither
he nor Engels gave much special consideration to Christianity.
Theirs is a theory of religion, or rather of no-religion, that finds
every idea of God equally culpable before the bar of materialism.
"All religious ideas," Lenin wrote to Gorky in a Marxist vein,
"all ideas about any little god, even of flirting with a little god are
an unspeakable abomination." [84]

This, then, is the first and, for our present purposes, most significant count that Marxism levels against religion: that in a uni-

verse in which there is nothing but matter or phenomena relating to matter, the whole notion of God, of any power or presence the least bit supernatural, is a monstrous fantasy in the minds of frustrated men. Marx took over from Feuerbach the proposition that man created God in the act of imagining that God had created him. Religion first arose, according to Marxism, from "the helplessness of primitive man before the menacing phenomena of nature, the content of which he did not understand," [85] and it has persisted because men remain in ignorance of the real nature of the world. Religion, in two words, is the "direct opposite" of science, and as such it has no place in the minds of enlightened men.

Religion is more than an affront to the scientific truths of dialectical materialism. It is the most reactionary of social forces: the product of an imperfect social order, the symptom of a deep-seated social disease. It is, moreover, the most effective way ever devised for men to forget their troubles, in Marx's memorable metaphor the "opiate of the people" (*das Opium des Volks*).[86] (Lenin called it "sivushka," a Russian drink about the same in price and effect as the gin of old London or the moonshine of old Kentucky.) Unable or unwilling to rise above the level of suffering and degradation at which most of them live, they are sustained by the promise of heavenly salvation. By dosing themselves constantly with this opiate, the men of the working class are drugged into accepting the fact of exploitation passively, the men of the bourgeoisie into thinking of themselves as goodhearted philanthropists. For the former religion is, as Marx put it, the ideology of despair, "the sigh of the harassed creature, the heart of a heartless world, the soul of soulless circumstances." [87] For the latter it provides, as Lenin put it, "cheap justification for their whole exploiting existence" and tickets to heavenly bliss "at a reasonable price." [88] The proletarian takes the opiate to forget his own troubles, the bourgeois to forget the troubles he inflicts on others. One way or the other, Lenin wrote, "The roots of modern religion are deeply embedded in the social oppression of the working masses, and in their apparently complete helplessness before the blind forces of capitalism." [89] As for the man who preaches it:

> All oppressing classes of every description need two social functions to safeguard their domination; the function of a hangman, and the function of a priest. The hangman is to quell the protest and the rebellion of the oppressed, the priest is to paint before them a perspective of mitigated sufferings and sacrifices under the same class rule. . . . Thereby he reconciles them to class domination, weans them away from revolutionary actions, undermines their revolutionary spirit, destroys their revolutionary determination.[90]

Religion, then, is wrong, the wrongest thing that man ever imagined or practised, for two major reasons: In the realm of ideas, it is unscientific and lacks even a trace of truth; in the realm of reality, it is oppressive and lacks even a trace of decency. All religions are equally guilty on the first count; the Christian religion, because of its pious hypocrisy, is especially guilty on the second. In 1847, Marx wrote in a revolutionary newspaper in Brussels:

> The social principles of Christianity justified ancient slavery and glorified medieval serfdom, and if necessary they are prepared to defend the oppression of the proletariat even if with a somewhat crestfallen appearance.
> The social principles of Christianity preach the necessity of a ruling and an oppressed class, and all they have to offer to the latter is the pious wish that the former may be charitable.
> The social principles of Christianity transfer the reparation of all infamies to heaven and thus justify the perpetuation of these infamies on earth.
> The social principles of Christianity declare that all the villainies of the oppressors against the oppressed are either just punishment for original or other sin, or tribulations which God in his inscrutable wisdom causes the elect to suffer.
> The social principles of Christianity preach cowardice, self-abasement, resignation, submission and humility, in short all the characteristics of the *canaille*.[91]

Marx prophesied the passing away of religion as even a wisp of memory in the minds of men. The advance of science would reduce and finally eliminate the area of mystery in which religion has flowered corruptly; the end of social and economic oppression would put a stop to all craving for ideological opiates. Communist man, no longer alienated from a world he never made, would feel no urge to seek refuge in illusion. For religion, as Marx wrote, "is only the illusory sun which moves around man as long as man does not move around himself." [92] His whole system rested on the assumption that soon, for the first time in history, man would begin to "move around himself." With the abolition of the last capitalist institution there would come, as inevitably as there comes the death of all men, the death of all religion. Engels wrote in *Anti-Dühring:*

When this act has been accomplished, when society, by taking possession of all means of production and using them on a planned basis, has freed itself and all its members from the bondage in which they are now held by these means of production which they themselves have produced but which confront them as an irresistible alien force; when therefore man no longer merely proposes, but also disposes—only then will the last alien force which is still reflected in religion vanish, and with it will also vanish the religious reflection itself for the simple reason that then there will be nothing left to reflect. [93]

Neither Marx nor Engels, nor Lenin after them, paid much attention to the question whether Communists should assault religion frontally. They were confident that it would die with the death of capitalism, and they therefore counseled their followers to concentrate their fire on the capitalists rather than on the priests. Lenin in particular resented "the religious question" being "pushed into the foreground where it does not belong."

We must not allow the forces waging a genuinely revolutionary economic and political struggle to be broken up for the sake of opinions and dreams that are of third-rate importance, which are rapidly losing all political significance, and which are being steadily relegated to the rubbish heap by the normal course of economic development.[94]

It should be pointed out, by way of summary, that Marx's hatred of religion had its taproot in his resentment of social injustice. He hated it for its "falsehood," but he hated it even more for its "hypocrisy." It was as revolutionary rather than materialist that he first swung his mace against Christianity. In condemning religion he condemned a world in which religion was personally necessary and socially possible, a world in which "the law of God invariably proves to be the law of the possessing classes." [95] Thus, as he wrote, the "criticism of heaven is transformed into the criticism of the earth, the criticism of religion into the criticism of the law, the criticism of theology into the criticism of politics." [96]

The American tradition has always been friendly to religion. Its own taproot goes so deep into the teachings of Judaeo-Christianity, spiritual as well as social and ethical, that it could not reasonably be imagined as indifferent, much less hostile to religion. It is, to be sure, easy-going and permissive to those who have no religion. One does not have to believe in God in order to share in the American dream. Yet it cannot be denied that those who do believe in God, especially in the God of Paul or the God of Abraham, are a little nearer to the center of the tradition than those who do not. This may seem unfair to a man whose god is love or money or all mankind or himself or no-god, but a feeling of resentment is the only price he must pay for his unorthodoxy —unless, of course, he runs for public office and insists on being honest at the same time. In any case, the American tradition makes room gladly for beliefs that Marxism despises heartily: that there is in fact a God who watches over men; that the religious spirit is itself real and not a mere "reflex of the real world;" that the basic truths of religion, especially those of Christianity, have nothing to do with classes or stages of history or modes of production;

that religious institutions are a bulwark of decency and liberty; and that religion is the chief support of that condition of public and private morality in which free government becomes possible. Marxism despises all these beliefs; it is merely indifferent to that part of the American tradition which proclaims freedom of conscience and separation of church and state. The whole structure of law and custom we have erected stone by stone over the centuries is a screen behind which the bourgeoisie can feel free to exploit the proletariat.

It would be fruitless to elaborate upon each detail and dimension of the wall between the Marxist and American views of religion.[97] The wall is so high, the exact ground to be occupied on our side of it so much a matter for personal decision, that I think it best for each American to make his own survey of the situation. I will say only three things: First, since Marx's case against religion rests on the case for a science destined to conquer the unknown, it must be judged to have failed badly. The one thing we have come to learn about science, and also to respect about it, is that as it expands the boundaries of knowledge it also expands those of ignorance. The unknown and unknowable are far more imposing today than at any time in the history of human consciousness, and what Soviet scientists scorn as the "hypothesis 'God' " has never seemed to enjoy so favorable an intellectual situation. Science and religion can, after all, dwell happily together.* Second, it is in the light of religion that Marx's low opinion of man, of which more presently, emerges in sharpest detail. We, too, think that social justice is highly important, but it is only one aspect of the good life we aspire to for every man. We cannot imagine that man is exclusively a secular animal, that the outpourings of his spirit are mere reflections of his role in the mode of production,

---

* If the "hypothesis 'God' " is not necessary to Soviet science, it certainly is to Soviet rhetoric aimed against the West. Khrushchev's speeches during his tour of America in 1959 were punctuated repeatedly with appeals to the Almighty.

that he needs an opiate (let us call it a refuge) only because the mode is out of joint. Even those Americans who deny God do not deny the reality of the human spirit and its persistent longing for the eternal, which may be one reason why the Christian ethic retains its appeal to many Americans who cannot believe in Christ. And third, it is in this area that the clash of Marxist monism and American pluralism, to which I shall devote a few thoughts in Chapter VIII, is most violent and, for all our pluralism, uncompromising. That Marx should hammer all explanations of the world's religions into a narrow strip of social and economic factors is presumptuous; that he should squeeze all the varieties of religious experience into one formula is unforgivable. We have seen enough of the cruelties of monism in religion over the past centuries to want no part of his.

It would not seem right to end this discussion of Marxism and religion without offering an answer to the popular question: Can a man be both a Marxist and a Christian? I should think that this entire chapter gave a flat enough answer to that question, and how could the answer be anything but No? One may admire Khrushchev, vote Communist, despise capitalism, call for proletarian revolution, prophesy a classless society, and regard the history of Christianity as a cruel fraud, and still be a Christian, that is, a believer in the God to whom Jesus bore witness. But one cannot be a Christian, one cannot be a Buddhist or Mohammedan or Taoist or Druid or pantheist or "friend of elves and little folk" and still be a genuine Marxist. For to be that kind of Marxist one must be a genuine materialist, and to be that kind of materialist one must deny categorically the possibility of any reality beyond that of matter, deny with Lenin the possibility of even "flirting with a little god." In a word, a Marxist must be an atheist. Agnosticism is not enough. Science, not religion, is the sanctuary of Marxist man.

The philosophy of Marxism-Leninism—the theoretical foundation of the Communist Party—is incompatible with religion. . . . The world outlook of the party is based on scientific data, while religion contradicts science. As the party bases its activity on a scientific foundation, it is bound to oppose religion.[98]

And religion, it seems certain, is bound to oppose it.

Let me conclude this chapter with two short statements that reveal the authentic flavor of the Marxist idea. I do this not to open the gap even wider between Marxism and the American tradition, but to catch the spirit that infuses everything that Marxists think and do in this broad arena we have surveyed, to leave no doubt in anyone's mind about either the role or influence of the Marxist ideology. The first quotation is from an American Marxist, Howard Selsam, who says of the "partisanship" that distinguishes Marxism "from all other positions":

It is not above the battle of humankind for a better life, but holds, on the contrary, that the one great task of philosophy should be to contribute to the winning of that battle. It is partisan to socialism as against capitalism; it is partisan to the working class as against the capitalist class; it is partisan to materialism as a world view as against all forms of idealism, spiritualism, and mysticism.[99]

The second is from Marx himself; it is the last and most momentous of the eleven *Theses on Feuerbach* in which, in Engels' words, Marx first "deposited the brilliant germ of the new world outlook":

The philosophers have *interpreted* the world in various ways; the point however is to *change* it.[100]

THREE · MARXIST MAN

Deep in the core of every political and social theory lies a psychology. In some theories it is stated in stark detail; in others it is buried under a thick layer of comforting clichés. In most it consists of a loose array of facts and assumptions about man's behavior and capacities, ranging from the freshest evidence of the clinical laboratory to the stalest prejudices of the human heart. Whatever it says about man and however frankly it says it, this psychology is the surest key to an understanding of the theory of which it is a part. There is a remarkable correlation—not always exactly one-to-one but almost always direct and logical—between what a theory teaches about the nature of man and what it expects of him in politics, prescribes for him in education, and leaves him free to do in the realm of being and to think in the realm of conscience. The contrasting political prescriptions of Hobbes and Locke or of Calhoun and Jefferson are familiar evidence of this correlation.

My first concern in this chapter is the view of man held by those who call themselves Marxists. My second concern, which I will dwell upon briefly for purposes of contrast, is the view held by those who honor the American tradition. Out of these views have arisen two major systems of thought; upon them stand two mighty ways of life. We and the Communists have different instruments of law and politics, different techniques of social and economic control, and different understandings of the role of education and art because at bottom we hold different opinions about man—about his urges and needs, his capacity for growth, his relations with other men, and the rights he may properly claim. For this reason we turn next in our study of Marxism to the study of Marxist man.

Marxism is at its most frustrating when it deals with human nature.[1] Neither Marx nor Engels was much interested in psychology—because the field was shrouded in the fog of "bourgeois nonsense," because the few solid lessons it could teach them denied most of the hopes they cherished, because they were so much more happily concerned with social phenomena than with personal problems.[2] They had very little to say about the behavior and capacities of man, and what they did say was tossed off casually and obscurely. They talked of classes rather than of individuals, of systems rather than of persons, of abstracted types rather than of genuine people, of what should and could be rather than of what was and ever had been. They were sociologists, not psychologists; and their followers have picked up where they left off. It is not surprising, considering the inadequacies of Marxist psychology in particular and the pitfalls of all psychology in general, that this remains the most rigidly controlled and narrowly unproductive field in the whole range of the social sciences in the Soviet Union.

Having dug long and hard in the writings of Marx and Engels for evidence of a reasonably consistent psychology, I can say with some confidence that such a psychology exists, and that it is made up of four key assumptions about human nature. These assumptions have always served the Marxist purposes with uncommon effectiveness.

First, the nature of man, like all things in the universe, is constantly changing. The fundamental assumption of Marxism in the vital area of psychology is the fluidity of all those elements— urges, aspirations, fears, needs, instincts, motives, habits, and traits—which conspire to shape the behavior of men. Men are not at all today what they were yesterday; and tomorrow, if all goes well, they will be something new and different. Human nature is not an entity but a process of dialectical development. "The whole of nature," Engels wrote in words I have already quoted, "from protista to men, has its existence in eternal coming into being and passing away, in ceaseless flux, in unresting motion and change." [3] And Marx echoed, "The whole of history is nothing but a continual transformation of human nature." [4] So relentless has been this change since time out of mind that it may almost be said of man that he has no original nature.

Almost, but not quite—for Marx and Engels never push their allegiance to the assumption of changeability so far as to deny the possibility of innate characteristics. In this matter, as in so many other matters of importance, the clarity of their message does not match its gravity. Sometimes they ascribe such varied qualities as dignity, sociability, inertia, acquisitiveness, and self-interest to all men everywhere; at other times they seem to think that the behavior of men is entirely determined by the world about them.* Sometimes they assert that the changing of the world, which is their chief aim, will bring out the best and suppress the worst of certain qualities that have inhered in man since first he rose above all other animals; at other times they sound as if a wholly new man with wholly new traits will be created by communism. Despite their ambivalence, Marx and Engels linger long enough in the first of these veins to appear finally as willing to attribute two qualities to all men in all societies.

The first is the need and desire to labor. In Marx's deepest and

---

* In an exploiting society, according to Marx and Engels, the "vicious tendencies" of men are always symptoms rather than causes of the human condition. In a nonexploiting society, according to their heirs, such tendencies are "birthmarks of capitalism."

most imposing thoughts, labor is the essence of life. It is more than the primary force impelling the world on its way; it is the only means through which man can express his inmost nature. Through labor alone is man distinguished, historically as well as logically, from all other animals. The urge to labor, and to labor consciously, is engrained in his nature. In his early and highly Hegelian phase,[5] Marx liked to express his conviction about the importance of labor in such statements as "the whole history of the world is nothing else than the creation of man through man's labor," and "Hegel . . . grasps the essence of labor and conceives objective man, true, real man as the result of his own labor."[6] From this conviction he never strayed, even when he expressed his loathing for the kind of labor in which most men are forced to engage in bourgeois society.

And the second quality is reason, the force that directs man's labor into the channels of self-realization. Marx is no friend of Cartesian reason, of the notion that abstract speculation is the surest guide to personal conduct and social reconstruction. But he does have profound faith in man's capacity to take off from the firm ground of knowledge and experience and to fly far and wide in search of truth. Even in his most determinist mood Marx grants huge importance to man's conscious power of rational self-direction.[7] The urge to labor and the capacity to reason are subject, to be sure, to the great law of constant change, but they may nonetheless be considered as innate characteristics of the human race.

Third, the nature of man, again like all things in the universe, is changing for the better. Marx's psychology, like his view of history, is permeated with optimism. Whenever he has occasion to express the notion of innate characteristics, he finds most of these to be the characteristics of the good natural man of Rousseau, not of the bad natural man of Calvin. The concept of man as immutably weak, wicked, and irrational has no place in Marxism. Men are placed on the road of ceaseless change with their faces pointed in the right direction and their backs relieved of the burden of original sin, and the dialectic of history is carrying them inexorably along. The men of tomorrow are bound to be finer, abler, truer, and kinder than the men of today. Indeed, there are no visible limits to man's capacity for change and growth. Marx is more than an optimist; he is a perfectibilist, insisting dramatically that all men will someday rise to and even above the level of virtue and wisdom that only a few giants have hitherto occupied. Trotsky caught the spirit of the Marxist view of man perfectly when he wrote in 1924:

> Man will become immeasurably stronger, wiser and subtler; his body will become more harmonized, his movements more rhythmic, his voice more musical. The forms of life will become dynamically dramatic. The average human type will rise to the heights of an Aristotle, a Goethe, or a Marx. And above this ridge new peaks will rise.[8]

The final assumption of Marxist psychology has the most profound implications for political theory: the chief influence in the changing of man's nature is the environment in which he lives and works. Marx feels no urge to exempt men from the operation of the iron laws of materialism. The behavior of men, like the working of their institutions and the substance of their ideas, is shaped by the manner in which they are organized to produce the essentials of life. As the manner changes, so, too, does their behavior. Marx and Engels joined to observe in *The German Ideology:*

> The way in which men produce their means of subsistence . . . must not be considered simply as being the reproduction of the physical existence of the individuals. Rather it is a definite form of activity of these individuals, a definite form of expressing their life, a definite *mode of life* on their part. As individuals express their life, so they are. What they are, therefore, coincides with their production, both with *what* they produce and with *how* they produce. *The nature of individuals thus depends on the material conditions determining their production.*[9]

Engels often speaks of either "class" or "labor" as the force determining man's political and social behavior, but these are just two more dramatic ways of proclaiming the decisive influence of the system of production. The way men make their living determines the kind of men they are. They cannot *be* anything more or other than what they *do* in the system of production and *are* by virtue of their class's role in it. To the extent that men can change their environment, they can, of course, change themselves; and Marx is fond of saying that men really make their own nature. If "men are products of circumstances and upbringing," and "changed men are products of other circumstances and changed upbringing," [10] then the fact that "circumstances are changed precisely by men" is the hope of man in the future as it has been his pride in the past. By laboring unceasingly since time began, man has made himself a giant in knowledge and skill. Yet, Marx adds, the giant is a pygmy in contrast to what he will make of himself through labor in the future, a pygmy, moreover, who lies in chains of his own forging. The present condition of man is low and miserable; his spirit is suffering along with his mind and body. But if he will be up and doing in obedience to the iron laws of history, he will move triumphantly into a golden future.

If I may sum up the Marxist psychology in one phrase, it is: the perfectibilist assumption of the infinite plasticity of human nature in response to purposeful manipulation of the social environment.

Let me turn now from the generalities of Marx's view of human nature to the specific things he had to say about man in his time —about man in bourgeois society. The sum of his explosive thoughts about the human condition is expressed in the famous word *alienation* (*Entfremdung*), which he borrowed from Hegel and Feuerbach, converted from a metaphysical concept to a critical tool in some of his earliest writings,[11] and carried in his mind as both tool and goad until the day he died. The concept of alienation is extremely slippery, and some of the most learned friends and critics of both Hegel and Marx have attempted to subdue it without entire success. I do not propose to attempt what German philosophy has found so difficult,[12] but I do think it important for us to understand at least the practical implications of this concept.

What Marx meant by *alienation* in his early writings (and what he assumed in *Capital* [13]) was that the conditions of life and work in bourgeois society have estranged man from his fellows and thus from himself—economically, politically, socially, spiritually, and psychologically. They have cut him off so abruptly from control of his own plight and sympathy for the plight of others that he is not really a man at all. He is, rather, a mutilated and depersonalized fragment of a man. Marx has a dozen ways of expressing what he means by alienation, but they all come down to the idea that man's most precious possession, his labor, has been stunted by drastic specialization, and placed on the market to be made off with by the quickest bidder—whose bid is always too low for the worker. Worse than that, the fruits of his labor have been snatched away from him by other men. The life of the ordinary man is an exercise in unremitting frustration, for if he wants to live at all, he must "perform tiresome labor on objects that he will not himself use or own." [14] Marx has a dozen ways of accounting for alienation, but they all point to one villain: private property in the means of production—or, to be short about it, capitalism. As Henri Bartoli points out, the economic alienation of Marxist man is at the root of all his other troubles.[15] There is a touch of Rousseau in the Marxist concept of alienation, for it seems to premise a natural man in a golden age who lived in perfect harmony with nature, with his fellow men, and with himself, and who was driven from paradise—and into a perpetual state of war with society—by the coming of property and its train of evils. The system of private ownership of productive property has revived "fetishism" by enslaving man to the commodities he makes, turned his own labor into a commodity, impeded his intellectual and even physical growth by forcing him to spend his days performing one task, set up the state to coerce him, robbed him of his dignity, and wreaked such havoc on his spirit as to send him howling after something called God.

Marx appears especially disturbed by the careless, heartless way in which capitalism has reduced the job of every man, even of the directing capitalist himself, to a specialized routine.[16] The division of labor in any advanced society entails "some crippling of body and mind," Marx wrote in *Capital*,[17] but capitalist society has made the worker "a crippled monstrosity" by forcing him to acquire one particular skill "at the expense of a world of productive capabilities and instincts; just as in the States of La Plata, they butcher a whole beast for the sake of his hide or his tallow." [18] Men no longer think creatively but react stupidly; they no longer produce purposefully but work brutishly at "ossified particularizations." They have been, in fact, "dismembered." [19]

Nor is it only the worker who is alienated from himself, from his fellows, from nature, and from history. The exploiting bourgeois, although he may be materially secure, feels spiritually and psychologically estranged. He, too, finds the world "basically unreasonable," [20] a force that controls him when he should be able to control it. He, too, is confronted by "alien and coercive powers" in the form of "unintended consequences of human actions." [21] He, too, is a victim of "fetishism," and thus mistakes the relationships between men for relationships between things. He, too, is at war with society. All men, in short, are alienated men, mere fragments of their natural and potential selves. They are, in a word, "dehumanized," for their talents are so organized and directed that the one thing they have in common, their sense of humanity, is smashed into jealous pieces. The fact of private property in the means of production condemns all men, whether they own much or little or none at all, to suppress their better natures and struggle viciously with one another. Their lot is to

exist in a "life situation which brazenly and decisively contradicts
. . . human nature," especially the nature of the man who labors
with his own hands. In a memorable passage in *Capital,* Marx
described the alienated worker:

> Within the capitalist system all methods for raising the social pro-
> ductiveness of labour are brought about at the cost of the individual
> labourer; all means for the development of production transform them-
> selves into means of domination over, and exploitation of, the pro-
> ducers; they mutilate the labourer into a fragment of a man, degrade
> him to the level of an appendage of a machine, destroy every remnant
> of charm in his work and turn it into a hated toil; they estrange from
> him the intellectual potentialities of the labour-process in the same
> proportion as science is incorporated in it as an independent power;
> they distort the conditions under which he works, subject him during
> the labour-process to a despotism the more hateful for its meanness;
> they transform his life-time into working-time, and drag his wife and
> child beneath the wheels of the Juggernaut of capital.[22]

Alienated man is really no man at all—physically, intellectually,
or psychologically. And even if his material lot were improved,
even if he lived like the sleekest bourgeois, his psychological estrangement would go on without relief. Only the building of a new
society will bring man peace of mind; [23] only socialism will put
a halt to the absurdities of specialization and fetishism; only communism will redeem man and make him whole.

The last and cheeriest element in the Marxist psychology is a
radiant vision of communist man. Marx was, as I have noted, an
unabashed perfectibilist, and he looked confidently beyond the
human nature of the present to the human destiny of the future.
Released from the chains of capitalist society, man will emerge at
last as what he was always intended to be: a whole person. In
Marx's words, obscure yet portentous as ever, the future lies in
"the positive abolition of private property, as human self-alienation," and "the real appropriation of the attributes of humanity by
and for humanity," and thus leads to a "completely conscious
return, on the basis of the whole wealth of previous development

of the human being as a social, that is to say, as a real human being." [24] No longer will man be degraded by owning or coveting large amounts of property; no longer will his thoughts and desires be shaped by his membership in a class; no longer will he be forced to channel his diverse potentialities into one narrow occupation. His labor will offer him an "opportunity to develop and exercise all his faculties, physical and mental in all directions," and it will also fulfill a genuine social need.

The vision of the average communist man as a sort of Aristotle or Leonardo da Vinci never lost its appeal to Marx and Engels. In their younger years they wrote in *The German Ideology:*

> In communist society, where nobody has one exclusive sphere of activity but each can become accomplished in any branch he wishes, society regulates the general production and thus makes it possible for me to do one thing to-day and another to-morrow, to hunt in the morning, fish in the afternoon, rear cattle in the evening, criticize after dinner, just as I have a mind, without ever becoming hunter, fisherman, shepherd or critic. [25]

And years later in his *Anti-Dühring,* Engels promised confidently:

> In time to come there will no longer be any professional porters or architects. . . . The man who for half an hour gives instructions as an architect will also act as a porter for a period, until his activity as an architect is once again required. A fine sort of socialism that would be—perpetuating professional porters! [26]

If Marx and Engels were ever conscious of the element of fancy in such promises, they did not betray it publicly. Their writings still exude an intense belief that the future of man will be marked by a complete reversal of his relations to the institutions he has created. Man will take command of the things he has made and force them to serve him instead of tyrannize over him. His stunted capacity for purposeful reasoning will flower into mighty plans for mastering his environment and for turning it from a hostile into a benevolent force. With the passing of private property in the means of production there will be an end to crime; with the coming of communism there will be an end to suffering. This will not be a return to the golden age of primitive communism, for then freedom from alienation was a happy chance bestowed by nature and now it will be a higher reality achieved and maintained by conscious striving. The new man will be like ancient man only in his inner sense of perfect harmony with the world about him. His intellect, spirit, and skills will make him truly a giant; and the nice thing, according to Marx, is that every one else will be a giant too—"ten feet tall," as Fourier promised.

This, then, is the Marxist message on the future of human nature: men may and will improve indefinitely in mind, body, and spirit by merging their labor and reason with the progressive laws of history. In promising soberly the rise of a new race of men, Marx carried the old radical dream of perfection to the end of the line.

The Marxists of the Soviet Union continue to believe, at least in public, in the validity of this message. Soviet psychology has gone well beyond Marx himself in stressing conscious self-direction and education as determining factors in human behavior,[27] while salutes to the influence of environment have been somewhat muffled. Yet the appearance in Soviet men of "vicious tendencies" is still ascribed officially to the fact that they "came from the bowels of capitalist society," that the "birthmarks of capitalist consciousness have remained with many of them." [28] The assumptions of orthodox Leninism, even of neo-orthodox Stalinism, are no less perfectibilist than those of Marx himself. Maxim Gorky once spoke of Lenin's "burning faith that suffering was not an essential and unavoidable part of life, but an abomination that people ought to and could sweep away." [29] The burning faith has cooled to a hard dogma that excuses some of the worst suffering men have yet endured, but even today the Marxist promise is one of perfection on earth. The neo-Lamarckianism of the Russian botanists Michurin and Lysenko is, in one sense, simply a disingenuous attempt to take Marx's message seriously.[30] If plants can acquire new characteristics and then pass them on through the channels of heredity, why cannot men? Why not, indeed? As Bukharin said many years ago, "If we were to take the point of view that racial and national characteristics were so great that it would take thousands of years to change them, then, naturally, all our work would be absurd." [31] No one has yet arisen publicly in the Soviet Union to say that the notion of rebuilding man is quite absurd.

When I wrote in Chapter I of the essential pluralism of the American tradition, I had our view of the behavior and capacities of man uppermost in mind. To say the very best we can about it, this view is pleasantly clouded. Few American political thinkers have moved more than a step or two into the trackless field of psychology, and among these men there have always been serious disagreements. Thanks to the stern Calvinists among us, we have never been able to laugh off entirely the Augustinian warning that all men are miserable sinners; thanks to our happy Liberals, we are still tempted by the Pelagian (if not Marxist) dream that all men can be made perfect. We are distinctly more sanguine about the nature of man in the explicit words with which we exhort one another than in the implicit assumptions that account for our laws and institutions.

Yet having taken note of both the inadequacies and the contradictions in the view of man professed in the American tradition, I am prepared to draw at least the broad outlines of a consensus. We seem to have operated through most of our history in response to a mixed view of man's nature and capacities; yet, except for a deep suspicion we entertain of man in power, the mixture is still made up largely of the ingredients of hope. If the American tradition is not perfectibilist, it is certainly meliorist. It makes more of man's benevolence than of his wickedness, more of his educability than of his perversity, more of his urge to be free than of his need to submit, more of his sense of justice than of his capacity for injustice; and it plainly lacks any secular counterpart to the doctrine of Original Sin. It assumes that the forces of good, if nurtured carefully by education and supported by a favorable environment, can generally hold the upper hand; at the same time, it insists that the forces of evil may be checked but never completely driven from the field, neither from the conduct of any one man nor from the behavior-patterns of the race. If we have been entertained but not impressed by the old line of revivalists, we have been excited but not convinced by the new breed of psychologists. The man of the American tradition is a rational man, one who, when given half a chance, will make political decisions calmly and thoughtfully with the aid of Aristotelian reason—reason tempered by experience. What we mean by "half a chance" is a decent environment and a system of constitutional restraints that can hold his ineradicable love of power in fairly close check. No matter, then, how we look at man, we see him as a jumble of cross-cutting tensions between good and evil; and no matter how far we look ahead, we see no final resolution of any of the tensions, especially of the tension between his sense of justice and capacity for injustice. The nature of man is changeable only slowly and within limits ordained by God and nature.

To men who stand on this ground the Marxist psychology presents a mixed picture of appealing insight and distressing prescription. We may be happy to find support for our own long-standing confidence in the power of human reason, but we are obviously not as prepared as Marx—certainly not in our political and social calculations—to give it first place among the forces that direct men's minds. We may rouse to his proclamation of human perfectibility, but in this instance, too, the sober side of our tradition forbids us to act too impetuously on such an assumption. The new man of Marxism, we are bound to say, is a dream in which a line of tough-minded thinkers from John Adams to Reinhold Niebuhr has forbidden us steadily to indulge at all purposefully.

Where we begin to part company decidedly is with Marx's view of man as "the *ensemble* of the social relations," [32] as the exclusive creation of labor, class, and the system of production; for this, we think, is to see man as a collectivized and abstracted image of his unique and robust self. We give much credit to social and economic environment, but certainly not half so much as does Marx. We are far more skeptical than he in our evaluation of its role in the development of the species in history and its influence on the behavior of each individual in his own time. As to history, the American tradition teaches that forces deeply implanted in human nature had a great deal to do with the making of modern man; as to the individual, it assumes that he can rise above or fall below his alleged destiny, and that his class and occupation may often have little to do with his behavior. Our tradition asks us to believe that there is such a thing as a good man, and not just a good member of an economic class. The notion of proletarian man and bourgeois man as two different species is one that we cannot accept on proof or principle. The American tradition insists that there are some things common to all men, at all times, and in all classes, and that men can transcend society, as they have transcended nature, by virtue of their spirit, self-reliance, and desire for freedom. Many things have made each man what he is, and one of these has been the man himself.

We are not totally deaf to the argument for the plasticity of human nature, yet we are bound to say that Marx carries it much too far for our tastes with his call for "the alteration of men on a mass scale." [33] Man's nature is malleable, yes, but even continuously favorable circumstances existing over a long period of time can do little to erase or even recast those traits in his make-up which have set him eternally far below the angels. What Marx calls "vicious tendencies" are not wholly a product of present environment or a relic of past environment; rather they are a burden that man is destined to carry with him on his pilgrimage as far as the eye of sober imagination can see. The doctrine of plasticity, to tell the truth, is doubly unacceptable from the American point of view, for it appears politically dangerous as well as psychologically unsound. If we were to concede the point that a new race of men can be created by conscious manipulation of the social environment, what power could we then properly withhold from those in whose hands have been placed the levers of political control? The assumption of the infinite plasticity of human nature is a major intellectual support of the total state, and for this reason, if for no other, we cannot admit its validity.

The concept of alienation touches upon matters about which we have begun to think seriously only recently, and Marx deserves much credit for having made us think about them. Americans, I trust, cry out as loudly as do the Marxists at the sight of fragmented, depersonalized, dehumanized men, but we deny that such men exist in very large numbers, and deny further that capitalism or any other merely economic arrangement is the sole cause of their estrangement. We are not ignorant of the particular dangers to a healthy mind and spirit that flow from overspecialization and "fetishism," but we consider these the price of industrialism rather than of capitalism (a price, incidentally, which the whole world seems willing to pay). To the extent that men in Western society are alienated, the fault lies with them as much as it does with their surroundings. Life without anxiety, which appears to be the essence of the Marxist promise, is a will-o'-the-wisp, a Utopian dream that can never be made reality. Life without anxiety, I am tempted to add, would not be life at all, and it might well be argued that the elimination of all the tensions and frustrations that we label collectively as "alienation" would be undesirable as well as unattainable. The perfectly integrated mass-society would very likely be a sink of boredom and mediocrity in which creativity would be lost without a trace. Man, in any case, will always be alienated, troubled within and estranged without, simply because he is trapped in the paradox of human existence that we see fuzzily and the Marxists simply ignore: that he is always one alone and yet one among many.[34] The American tradition assumes that man has his best chance of self-fulfillment in a system that cuts him loose from the state and puts a large part of the responsibility for his conduct on his own will and capacities. If there is perhaps a little too much naiveté in this assumption, surely we can correct that without going outside the bounds of the tradition. This is one of those points at which we can learn from Marx's insights without embracing his prescriptions.

In the final reckoning, we reject the Marxist psychology because of two curiously related misjudgments it makes of the realities and potentialities of human nature. On one hand, Marx gives too much to man, which also means that he asks too much of him. His doctrine of perfection is more than just a pleasant hypothesis that beguiles men in their present condition. It is a tough reality—in which he believes deeply—that calls them to revolutionary action. Marx's vision of communist man I have already called a dream, and now I would move closer to the point by labeling the dream dangerous. For by promising that all men in time will be perfect in wisdom and reason, and by insisting that a few men, the "most advanced and resolute" communists, are already exempt from "vicious tendencies," Marx takes the easy way out of the massive dilemma with which political theorists and statesmen have wrestled for thousands of years: how to organize the instruments of power so that those who wield them are held accountable to those who do not, so that they can be persuaded, even against their will, to "do justly and love mercy." I will return in Chapter VI to the blunt question of political power; it should be enough at this stage to point out that Marx's perfectibilism removes him almost completely from the area of political reality, and that anyone who chooses to follow him must abandon belief in the necessity of checks on political power. This, of course, is a denial of our whole tradition, which is why the tradition has always forbidden us to take political advice from those who assume that any man or class or group is either perfect or perfectible.

On the other hand, Marx gives too little to man, so little indeed that it is hard to think of him, as do many non-Marxists, as a passionate humanitarian. This is one of those points at which we must be particularly fair to Marx. We must refrain from rehearsing the Soviet treatment of man and from quoting the Bolsheviks, for instance Trotsky, on the petty bourgeoisie as "human dust" or on "the Kantian-priestly and vegetarian-Quaker prattle about the 'sacredness of human life.' " [35] It is Marx—Marx in the most favorable light—in whom I am interested; and this Marx, I insist, seems to have a deep-seated contempt for humanity that we cannot excuse and cannot accept. By insisting on the prime, indeed exclusive influence of "social relations" in the shaping of human behavior, Marx leaves man no personal responsibility for his conduct and no private way out of his situation, whatever it may be. He forbids him, in effect, to move outside the narrow line of behavior and development laid down by his place in the scheme of production. By dealing with man solely as a member of a class, he deprives him of personality. It has been truly said that Marx never sees persons, only members of a class; his men, even his new men, are little better than abstract automatons. By denying even the remote possibility of man's divine origin or nature, he robs him of dignity. He insists that man, like any other natural phenomenon, can be known and explained entirely in terms of the material world, and thus he puts an abrupt end to the saving grace of mystery. And by basing his political prescriptions on the assumption of plasticity, he ignores man's claim to security against power. The Soviet presumption to total control over man has at least one live root in the Marxist insistence on the infinite malleability of human nature.

This is severe treatment, I realize, especially since it seems to ignore the fact that Marx had to do battle with some very ignorant and obscurantist people who used the dogma of wicked, unchanging human nature to justify the most sordid laws and practices, and the further fact that the society he observed (nineteenth-century England) was full of men who had been exploited mercilessly.

I do not mean to ignore these facts at all, but I do not see how they can make a great thinker who claimed the mantle of "science" any less responsible for his teachings. When a man asserts dogmatically that men have behaved a certain way in history because of this or that system of production, and will behave entirely differently in the future because another system will come to replace the last one, then he should be taken at his word, or words. The words, as we seem to hear them, are *alienation, plasticity,* and *perfectibility,* and the American tradition, I am certain, has only a limited place for them in its understanding of the human condition and in its prescriptions for improving it.

In later chapters, I will touch upon such aspects of the Marxist view of man as education and individualism. Let me round off this chapter by inquiring into Marx's thoughts on two conditions or qualities of human existence to which Americans have always paid special attention: liberty and equality. Marx promised men that he would carry them out of a dying world of bondage and illicit privilege and into a new world of freedom and equal justice. What did he mean by *liberty* and *equality?* What did he think of the meaning we give these words? What in truth was the substance of his promise?

Marx never dipped so exclusively into inky blacks and dazzling whites as he did in his portraits of liberty under capitalism and communism, and by capitalism, be it remembered, he meant any of the Western systems that had not yet passed through the proletarian revolution and into socialism. In this system, whether it was the France or England or United States or Switzerland of his own time, he found nothing that he was willing to acknowledge as human liberty. There was "bourgeois liberty," to be sure, but this was simply a façade behind which a few men could exploit the lives and energies of all other men. The many were no closer to genuine freedom than had been the slaves of Rome, and the few were not a great deal better off themselves. For in seeking more freedom at the expense of the proletariat, they were committing themselves to a struggle from which there was no way out.

The liberty of any man, Marx insisted, was determined by his membership in a class, just as were his nature, conduct, and morality. Each man was free to the extent that his class was free, and no man, therefore, was free at all. Even the vaunted liberty of the English and Americans was a weak, stunted, imperfect abstraction. Marx surveyed with arrogance what he liked to call "the narrow horizon of bourgeois right." [36] He had withering contempt both for the philosophical foundation on which Western man has grounded his claims to personal liberty, the concept of natural and inalienable rights, and for the practical machinery through which he has exercised his claims, the "pompous catalogue" of laws and customs that guarantee the freedoms of speech, press, worship, suffrage, assembly, petition, association, and fair trial.[37] The foundation of Western liberty was the rankest sort of idealism, the machinery was a legal cloak for the exploitation of the working class. As for constitutions and bills of rights, Engels had this to say of the most famous one:

> It is significant of the specifically bourgeois character of these human rights that the American constitution, the first to recognize the rights of man, in the same breath confirms the slavery of the colored races existing in America: class privileges are proscribed, race privileges sanctioned.[38]

In this context Marx made his famous distinction between "formal" and "effective" freedom.[39] Formal freedom is the kind that exists under capitalism and bourgeois democracy. In theory, it is the freedom to pursue one's ends in the absence of legal restraints; in fact, it is the harsh mixture of privilege and bondage that is guaranteed—privilege to the few, bondage to the many—by the complicated legal structure of "bourgeois right." Effective freedom is the kind that Marx promised in the future. In theory, it is the power to realize the ends one has chosen to pursue; in fact, it will be the happy condition of life for the proletariat under socialism and for all men under communism. Formal freedom, Marx warned, will never become effective until private property in the means of production is rooted out and destroyed. The unequal distribution of control of property leaves most men in a state of subjection— as commodities to be bought and sold—and no amount of "prattle" about freedom of speech or the right to vote can mask this cruel fact from the honest eye. Marx was never more certain of the truth of his analysis of contemporary society than when he looked upon its painfully wrought structure of political rights and judicial safe-guards, and pronounced it an extravagant fraud from top to bottom. And the most fraudulent part of the whole formal structure, in his opinion, was the boasted "freedom of contract." No one who studied the history of this "right" so precious to the bourgeoisie could fail to grasp the essential connection between freedom and exploitation in even the most "democratic" bourgeois societies. The "free" labor market, he wrote with savage irony in *Capital,* "is in fact a very Eden of the innate rights of man." [40]

Several refinements of Marx's theory of liberty should be noted briefly. The first was his refusal to admit the validity of the ancient distinction between public and private man, a distinction that re-serves to every individual an area of conscience and activity that is all his own. Marx called for the end of "man the egoist, man the member of bourgeois society—that is, an individual withdrawn into his private interests and private willfulness, separated from the community." [41] He demanded that man rise above the division that bourgeois society tries to make of him—"an egoistic, inde-pendent individual on the one hand, and . . . a citizen on the other hand."

Only when the real, individual man reintegrates into himself the abstract citizen and becomes, as individual man in his empirical every-day life, in his individual work, in his individual relations, a common existence; only when man has recognized and organized his *forces propres* as social forces, and therefore no longer separates these social forces from himself in the guise of political forces, only then is his human emancipation accomplished. [42]

I am no more confident than any other student of Marx that I understand the full meaning of such a passage, but I am certain that he meant to declare war on the assumption that a man has any need or right to hold some part of himself aloof from the community, certainly from the community that will rise from the rubble of bourgeois democracy. One wonders what he would think of the massive invasion of privacy in Communist countries today, and of the continuing resentment among the mass of men against this invasion.[43]

The second refinement was his Hegelian affirmation, which still echoes through the Soviet Union, that freedom is action taken in obedience to necessity, that knowledge of social and historical necessity is the open door to freedom, and that freedom and knowledge are therefore identical. "Freedom," Engels wrote in *Anti-Dühring,*

does not consist in the dream of independence from natural laws, but in the knowledge of these laws, and in the possibility this gives of systematically making them work towards definite ends. . . . The *freer* a man's judgment is in relation to a definite question, the greater is the *necessity* with which the content of this judgment will be determined. . . . Freedom therefore consists in the control over ourselves and over external nature, a control founded on knowledge of natural necessity; it is therefore necessarily a product of historical development.[44]

The individual is free, in short, when he understands the laws of human and social development and identifies himself with the necessity they incorporate. "Real knowledge of the subject" becomes, as Vernon Venable points out, the "mark and sanction" of man's free will.[45] Since "real knowledge" of history and society is knowledge of what Marx and Engels have found to be true, the only truly free men in their society would seem to be the vanguard of the proletariat.

Third, Marx called attention loudly, for which he deserves great credit, to the notorious fact that the normal working day of his time was twelve hours or more. This fact alone, in his angry opinion, made a mockery of the promise of formal freedom, as indeed it did for the mass of men. Whether Marx meant to assert that a man engaged in productive labor could never be entirely free, even under the pleasant and varied conditions of communist society, is not quite clear, although this view would hardly seem consistent with the vital place he gave to labor in the development of both man and society. In any case, there can be no doubt what he considered the first step to freedom in bourgeois society and the second step in any better society. In the third volume of *Capital* he wrote:

> The realm of freedom does not commence until the point is passed where labor under the compulsion of necessity and of external utility is required. In the very nature of things it lies beyond the sphere of material production in the strict meaning of the term. Just as the savage must wrestle with nature, in order to satisfy his wants, in order to maintain his life and reproduce it, so civilized man has to do it, and he must do it in all forms of society and under all possible modes of production. . . . It always remains a realm of necessity. Beyond it begins that development of human power, which is its own end, the true realm of freedom, which, however, can flourish only upon that realm of necessity as its basis. The shortening of the working day is its fundamental premise.[46]

Even more fundamental is the Marxist premise that genuine liberty cannot exist for anyone under capitalism and bourgeois democracy, and that only with the destruction of this outworn system and its replacement by communism will man find the true freedom that has been promised him by history. The whole condition of man will be so different that it is hard to imagine the kind of freedom he will enjoy—certainly if we try to do it with our present categories of thought. The most we can say is that "on the job," where he will spend very little of his time, he will be free because he will no longer be exploited, and that "off the job," where he will spend most of it, he will be free because he will have the power and opportunity to do whatever he pleases.

The bourgeois "rights" will fade from memory, and effective freedom will fill the vacuum of formal freedom. Communist man will not need religious freedom because there will be no religion; he will not bother about the rights of property because he will own no property to speak of; and he will wonder how there could have been so much fuss over freedom of contract because he will not be forced to bargain away his labor. Most important, he will be as free in the collective as in the individual sphere; indeed, the false line drawn between these spheres by the imperatives of bourgeois morality will be wiped out without a trace. Then at last will that wondrous event take place: "the ascent of man from the kingdom of necessity to the kingdom of freedom." [47]

It hardly seems necessary to make an elaborate statement of the meaning of liberty in the American tradition. There are a dozen ways of making such a statement, and no one who reads these pages will fail to have his own version of American liberty in mind. It will be enough, I think, to move directly into a critique of the Marxist theory of liberty, in the course of which the essentials of the American tradition should emerge into sufficiently clear view. In making this critique I will refrain from beating Marx over the head with the fact of the Soviet Union. Let us once again concentrate on Marx himself.

The first thing to be noted is that any meaningful debate with Marx and the Marxists on liberty is quite impossible to conduct.[48] This is not so much because our approach to liberty, which concerns itself largely with the relation of man to authority and is therefore concrete, contrasts so sharply with that of Marx, which concerns itself largely with the relation of man to history and is therefore metaphysical—although this difference in approaches does raise at least one insoluble problem. It is, rather, because our definitions and assumptions are so radically at odds with those of all the Marxists who have ever lived. We and they seem truly to live in two different worlds. What they call freedom, we call either

airy fancy or real bondage; what they scorn as "formal," we cherish as real. They, too, as we know to our despair, define our freedom as bondage, and they do it so confidently that we cannot deny
their sincerity.⁴⁹ Yet even if we were to accept their definitions,
how could we then take the next step, which is to agree that the
minimum price of genuine freedom is the root-and-branch destruction of our entire social, economic, and political system? And
even if we were to agree to that—for the sake of the argument,
I hasten to add—what concrete things can they tell us about freedom in the communist society of the future, a society about which
Marx and Engels were never more vague than when they spun
their fine words about the "kingdom of freedom"? At no point
is the gulf between Marxism and the American tradition so impossible to bridge, even for the sake of a verbal duel.

There are a few adverse comments, however, that we can make
about Marx's view of liberty in language that Marxists can understand. No matter how his words are twisted and turned, he cannot
escape these criticisms:

1) that he never came to grips with the paradox of freedom,
the pattern of unceasing tension between liberty and authority,
which he may have thought he had resolved by prophesying the
"withering away of the state," but which, as the Soviets have
proved,⁵⁰ he had not resolved at all;

2) that, as a result, he had nothing to say about political power,
at once a mighty threat to, and stout guardian of, personal liberty;

3) that he failed to understand the importance of the instruments of "mere formal freedom," of laws and charters and elections, in protecting men against the abuses of public authority and
the exploitations of private power; *

4) that in grounding the case for human rights exclusively on
the fact of human needs, he did a serious disservice to the concept

---

* This is why, as an English Marxist points out, a "higher synthesis" of
the "earlier inherent individual rights" and communist "social and economic
rights" is an impossible dream.⁵¹

—so necessary to liberty as either fact or aspiration—of human dignity;

5) that in denouncing the distinction between public and private man he passed a sentence of death upon privacy, one of the most cherished of our legacies from the past and one of the saving refuges of our present;

6) that in this, as in all matters of importance to mankind, he put too much stress on economics, and thus refused to tell us how men might move beyond the negative if essential freedom from exploitation to the positive and creative practice of liberty;

7) that in this, as in all matters, he put too much stress on class, and thus failed to place the chief responsibility for the day-to-day practice of liberty, now or in the future, where it surely belongs: on man himself;

8) that in concentrating his attention on the element of effective power in personal freedom, he ignored the central question of who was to hold control of this power—the individual or some authority outside him? Few Americans will now deny a place to power in the formula of liberty, but not at the expense of independence and privacy.

Marx and Engels were most remiss, I think, in making so absolute a connection between liberty and necessity, and in making it—how else can we put it?—in so offhand a manner. Since the time of the Flood we have told ourselves, and have been told, that liberty is obedience to necessity, that (to state this principle in the Scholastic version) it is the freedom to do that which is right and good. Now most of us have no quarrel with the argument, in either its metaphysical or practical form, that the freedom to do wrong is less sacred than the freedom to do right, and that those who do wrong will suffer sooner or later for having ignored the dictates of necessity. But the question we go on to ask is: Who is to say in fact, in the real world of laws and penalties, what is right and what is wrong? Who is to judge what is necessary and therefore proper? John Winthrop's answer was the Word of God, to be spoken by the Puritan elect; Rousseau's was the General Will, to be interpreted by the people massed in the public square; Hegel's was the Absolute Idea, to be brought to earth by the rulers of Prussia; and Marx's was the Laws of History, to be proclaimed by those who understand them best, by "the most advanced and resolute" of the communists. With none of these solutions, all of which put final authority in the hands of supposedly infallible men, can we have anything to do. Law, popular will, tradition, and custom must all have a hand in deciding what is right and what is wrong, and a way out must be left to men who cannot agree with the definitions operative at any particular time.

I said that I would not beat Marx over the head with the fact of the Soviet Union, and the truth is that I do not need to. For it was Marx, not the Bolsheviks, who first came up with the notion that a few men could and must tell the rest what the necessity of history required of them. It was Marx, not Lenin, who insisted on the unity of truth among the vanguard of the proletariat, Marx who placed the authority to speak this truth in the keeping of the dictatorship of the proletariat. We cannot escape the final judgment that his affirmation of the link between freedom and necessity, as he forged the link, is a deadly blow to liberty as most of the world understands it. We do not ask exemption from the laws of history or the commands of society. We ask only that the meaning of the laws be left open to discussion, in the course of which we must be free to decide that there are no such laws, and that the commands be worked out slowly through the agencies of "mere formal freedom." To place either the laws or the commands in the hands of any man or class or party appears to us a total denial of individual liberty. We will continue, I trust, to aspire to a higher plane of freedom than the freedom always to embrace and never to reject the truth Marx thought he had found, "truth" that now rests in the keeping of his most ruthless heirs. Whatever his hopes for liberty, and in a sense they were as high as any we have ever held, his prescriptions were thoroughly authoritarian. By these prescriptions we are bound to judge him.

The appeal of Communism to millions of unfortunate people all over the world lies chiefly in its promise of an end to unjust privilege and degrading discrimination. It is therefore essential for us to learn what Marx and his followers have had to say about equality. The first and most surprising thing to learn is that they have had very little to say, that no leading Marxist, from Marx himself to Mao, has given himself over to long or searching thoughts about the matter.[52] For a man who is celebrated for having made equality the essence of justice, Marx was amazingly reticent in dealing with its philosophical supports or practical applications. This, in any case, is the sum of his ideas about equality; if the sum be trifling, let the blame fall on Marx himself:

To begin with, as we have learned to expect of Marx, he branded all other affirmations of equality, even those of the radicals who had gone before him, as nothing more than "obsolete rubbishy phrases." [53] The "equality" for which men had struggled in the French and American Revolutions was, in Engels' words, simply a "bourgeois demand for the abolition of class privileges." [54] The political and judicial "equality" guaranteed in the laws of the bourgeois democracies was, like the "liberty" they also proclaimed, "mere formal" equality that masked the most shocking of all inequalities: the division of men into exploiters and exploited.

Marx and Engels refused to be lured into any rhetoric about the brotherhood of man. They recognized that men are not created equal and cannot be made equal; they even went so far in the *Manifesto* as to charge the Utopian socialists with preaching "universal asceticism and social leveling in its crudest form." [55] The Marxists of the Soviet Union, who gave up on equality long ago in the face of human nature and in the interests of an advanced technology,[56] have even less patience with those who insist on being naive about social and economic equality. "It is time it was understood," Stalin told the Seventeenth Party Congress in 1934, "that Marxism is opposed to leveling." [57] It is opposed, moreover, during the long period of socialist transition to anything resembling equality of income—to what Vyshinsky castigated as "petty bourgeois wage-leveling." [58] Marx himself made the great and careful distinction in his *Critique of the Gotha Programme* between the lot of men under socialism, who would continue to be rewarded on the basis of their contributions to society, and of men under communism, who would be satisfied, like the members of a family, on the basis of their needs.[59] Thus the Communists are able to rest their present case against the "left-egalitarian" call for equality of income—"a petty bourgeois deviation"—directly on scripture.[60]

What, then, we may ask, is equality in Marxism? And the answer comes in two parts: first, in words of Engels that are held sacred by the orthodox:

> The demand for equality in the mouth of the proletariat has . . . a double meaning. It is either . . . the spontaneous reaction against the crying social inequalities, against the contrast between rich and poor, the feudal lords and their serfs, the surfeiters and the starving; as such it is simply an expression of the revolutionary instinct, and finds its justification in that, and in that only. Or, on the other hand, this demand has arisen as a reaction against the bourgeois demand for equality, . . . and in this case it stands or falls with bourgeois equality itself. In both cases the real content of the proletarian demand for equality is the demand for the *abolition of classes*. Any demand for equality which goes beyond that, of necessity passes into absurdity.[61]

And second, in words of Marx that are even more sacred:

> In a higher phase of communist society, after the enslaving subordination of individuals under division of labour. and therewith also the antithesis between mental and physical labour, has vanished, after labour has become not merely a means to live but has become itself the primary necessity of life, after the productive forces have also increased with the all-round development of the individual, and all the springs of co-operative wealth flow more abundantly—only then

can the narrow horizon of bourgeois right be fully left behind and society inscribe on its banners: *from each according to his ability, to each according to his needs.*[62]

Abolition of classes in the socialist future, equal satisfaction of human needs in the communist future beyond: this is the Marxist promise of equality. This promise has obviously been of little value in preventing the resurgence in the Soviet Union of the sharpest disparities in rank, privilege, and income. Yet in fairness to Marx it should be said that his own impatience with easy egalitarianism never blinded him, as it has blinded the Communists, to this great hope and truth: that while society must take the differences among men into honest account, it must not exploit these differences to the illicit advantage of the naturally superior and unseemly degradation of the naturally inferior. Most important of all, it must be careful always not to confuse artificial with natural inequalities.

The American tradition of equality is also, in essence, a protest against the existence of unjust, unnecessary, unnatural privileges. But it looks beyond the limited horizon of class determinism to account for the origin and persistence of such privileges. As a result, it prescribes quite different methods for achieving meaningful equality among the American people. Instead of concentrating passionately on one kind of equality, it proclaims the excellence and necessity of many: moral equality, the right of each man to be treated as end and not means; judicial equality, the right of each man to justice on the same terms as other men; political equality, the right of each man to a vote that counts no more and no less than any other man's vote; legal equality, the right to be exempt from class legislation; and, at the heart of the tradition, equality of opportunity, the right of each man to exploit his own talents to their natural limits. No American with a conscience can deny the existence of a grim wall between the ideal and the reality of equality in our way of life. Every American with a conscience is anxious for the wall to be torn down stone by stone, especially to demolish the crazy-quilt structure of privilege and exploitation that sits upon the treacherous foundation of racial discrimination. But we are determined, thanks to our tradition, that the struggle for equality be carried on through constitutional and customary processes, that it be directed exclusively toward the reduction of illicit privilege, and that it not sacrifice genuine liberty to spurious equality.

I think it useful to close on this very last point, for it represents one of the most serious breaks between Marxism and the American tradition. There can be no doubt that in a showdown between liberty and equality, which must often take place in both theory and practice, the Marxist chooses for equality and the American for liberty. There are many reasons for the choice that each of them makes, but the most important, I think, is the two different views they have of man. Marxism, by its own admission, is interested primarily in the "toiling masses" and therefore treats any one man as an abstraction of millions of men. Whenever it may be necessary for revolutionary purposes, Marxists have not the slightest trouble voicing the slogans of equality. The American tradition is more concerned with "self-reliant individuals." It therefore treats any one man as just that—one man—and even when we talk of equality, as we do with feeling, we tend to emphasize equality of rights rather than of goods or position.

It may be, as wise men have argued, that we can never hope to match the Marxists in our appeal to underdeveloped countries so long as we talk of liberty more than we do of equality. That, however, is a price worth paying for a tradition that takes man largely as he is and grants him the responsibility for his own freedom. Marxists may talk of man as "the ensemble of social relations" and go on to promise him unearthly virtue, talent, and happiness. We would do well to continue with our view, which gives far more dignity to man because it makes no false promises. The nature and destiny of man, we think, both lie in his being a man.

FOUR · MARXIST SOCIETY: THE CLASSES

Lrom any point of view that is not dogmatically Marxist, dialectical materialism appears to be a mixture of overworked truisms and mystical humbug. Why, then, do so many men, even obdurate anti-Communists, still turn to Marx for instruction and stimulation? The answer, of course, is that Marx was far more than a third-rate philosopher. He was a first-rate sociologist, a man who shook the science of society to its foundations, and he stands even today not far from the top— some would say at the very top—of the social thinkers of the industrial age. Men must read him carefully, at least as carefully as they read Comte or Weber or Mannheim or Veblen, before they take off on their own over the darkling plains of sociology. Those plains, I might add, are far better known today than they were a hundred years ago because of the spectacular if irregular explorations he undertook.

Marx's constant purpose was to inspire men not so much to change their way of thinking as to change their way of living. He called upon them to demolish one mighty structure of social existence and to erect upon its rubble a far mightier and more splendid structure. His intellectual energies were therefore directed largely to proving that the society of his own time was wicked, oppressive, and decayed. In making his case against capitalist society, which he did to the satisfaction of several hundred million persons, he used techniques and spun hypotheses and drew generalizations that mark him indelibly as a sociologist. Even his economic theory was, in the strictest sense, a social philosophy stated in economic terms. He may have arrived at conclusions for which the evidence hardly existed, he may have fogged his vision by trying to examine his data through the lens of the dialectic, he may have confounded completely the roles of social analyst and revolutionary prophet, yet he issued a series of challenges to Western society that its defenders must still take altogether seriously.

Let us, too, take him seriously, much more seriously than we have taken him so far, and let us set up a confrontation of principle and purpose between the Marxist and American views of society. In this chapter, I plan to deal with his ideas about certain general aspects of society, especially the cardinal question of social classes; in the next, with capitalism and with those institutions and arrangements like property, family, and education which give every society its characteristic flavor. And as this view of Marxist sociology unfolds, I suggest that one fact be remembered constantly: Marx was talking about our society. In all his writings there are not more than a dozen pages that describe the new society he would like to see rise out of the ruins of the old. It is the old society, the society dominated by the bourgeoisie, on which Marx centered his attention. He was a sociologist of capitalism, not of socialism, and that is perhaps the most pressing reason of all for us to learn what he had to say.*

Working with what we know already of Marx's philosophy and psychology, we should not find it difficult to reconstruct the main outlines of his theory of society. In the first place, he was an even more convinced materialist in the dull republic of institutions than

* In the light of Marx's stature as a sociologist, it is interesting to note that there is no distinct discipline of sociology in the U.S.S.R. today.

he was in the heavenly city of ideas. In Marx's sociology, the entire range of social phenomena, from the oldest way of raising children to the newest way of cooking and serving, is determined primarily by the manner in which the community is organized to produce and distribute the means of material existence. Church and school and family, the laws of inheritance and the pattern of charity, the virtues men admire and the vices they practice, the sacred cow of monogamy and the black lamb of prostitution, even the ways most men sing and dance and write poetry and paint pictures—all are what they are, and could be nothing very different, because the society in which they flourish is at a certain stage on the inevitable road from feudalism through capitalism to socialism, and because its class structure corresponds, with only a small lag, to the economic conditions of that stage. The decisive force in shaping society is the class struggle. The decisive force in shaping the classes that do the struggling is the mode of production.[1] Indeed, the classes of every society that has existed since the first golden age have been largely instrumentalities of property; the struggle of the classes has been carried on between owners and nonowners. So thought Marx, and thus we may say that as a sociologist he was a thoroughgoing economic determinist.

He was likewise a thoroughgoing dialectician, which means that he viewed society essentially as a process, as a plastic mosaic of institutions, laws, customs, and arrangements that was never the same from one moment to the next. All things in society, like all things in nature, are in constant flux, and the flux moves onward and upward in fits and starts. Marx, who admired Darwin as much as he could admire any man, was a kind of premature Social Darwinist.[2] In the rise and resolution of conflict, especially conflict among classes, he found the mainspring of human progress. Engels wrote:

Since civilization is founded on the exploitation of one class by another class, its whole development proceeds in a constant contradiction. Every step forward in production is at the same time a step backwards in the position of the oppressed class, that is, of the great majority. Whatever benefits some necessarily injures the others; every fresh emancipation of one class is necessarily a new oppression for another class.[3]

Marx broke away from Darwin exactly because he was a dialectician, because he insisted that decisive social progress could be achieved only by "leaps" and "jumps" and "catastrophes," that is, by revolutions. When Marx looked at society he searched for real change amid apparent stability, for clusters of social tensions that would grow steadily larger until they would burst asunder and be transformed into some entirely new pattern. Not stability but progress, not harmony but conflict, not evolution but revolution—these were the working assumptions of his dialectical sociology. He was the same breed of sociologist as he was of philosopher: one for whom "the point" was not to "accept" but to "change" the world, and to change it radically.

Marx's bloodless view of man as an "ensemble of social relations" and his contempt for the bourgeois tradition of personal liberty combined to make him a student of society for whom society itself was the exclusive object of attention. He was, that is to say, an uncompromising collectivist, a sociologist for whom the organic group, especially the ruling class of the present and the ruling class of the future, was something more than a collection of individuals, something with a life and destiny of its own. I will return to the question of individualism and collectivism toward the end of this chapter, but I think that it should be understood at the outset that Marx the sociologist and social technician had no real feeling or concern for individual men. Whether he was describing the inanities of the society in which he lived or calling for the inevitable leap to the society for which he longed, he saw only masses or classes or types. He despised the state, as we shall learn in Chapter VI, but he was fascinated with society.

With these characteristics of Marx's sociology in mind—that it was materialist, dialectical, and collectivist, and that in this as

in all fields he claimed to be a scientist and was in fact a revolutionary—we may move on to learn what he said about bourgeois
society. And the first thing we learn is a lesson we already know
by heart: Marx never took the trouble to define the basic words
in his vocabulary. The basic word of Marxist sociology is *class,*
and it never ceases to astonish—unless we remember that Marx
is one of those few great thinkers for whom the rules are suspended
—that so much careful thought should have been lavished upon
so careless a man, one who could spend most of his life writing
about the class struggle and never say clearly what he meant by
"class." Perhaps a passage from Lenin will help to make explicit
what Marx left distressingly implicit:

> Classes are large groups of people which differ from each other by
> the place they occupy in a historically determined system of social
> production, by their relation (in most cases fixed and formulated in
> law) to the means of production, by their role in the social organiza-
> tion of labor, and, consequently, by the dimensions and mode of ac-
> quiring the share of social wealth of which they dispose. Classes are
> groups of people one of which can appropriate the labor of another
> owing to the different places they occupy in a definite system of social
> economy.[4]

This seems clear enough, and I am confident that Marx would
have applauded Lenin's definition. His own writings on the social
structure of his time assumed consistently that a class is an aggregate of persons who perform the same broad function in the
pattern of production, that birth and education and taste and even
wealth are symbols rather than determinants of class position, and
that relationships between classes are, in the very nature of the
capitalist mode of production, exploitative relationships. If he
had ever found it necessary to put the definition of a class in his
own words, it is likely that he would have gone beyond Lenin to
make at least one qualification and two additions.

The qualification would take the form of heavy emphasis on
the last sentence. For Lenin's "can" Marx would have substituted

"must," to "places they occupy" he would have added "and kinds of power they exert"—thinking in particular of the power of the bourgeoisie to manipulate the techniques of production in such a way as to extract maximum profits from the working class. In every pre-communist society there must be a dominant class, a class that rules in order to exploit, and exploits in order to rule, and in Marx's age this was the bourgeoisie. In every such society there must also be an oppressed class, a class that is both ruled and exploited, and in Marx's age this was the proletariat. What divides one class most sharply from the other is the necessary fact of exploitation. Their natural relationship is therefore one of hostility, which is all the more bitter because each needs the other to fulfill its historic destiny. This basic incompatibility of interest with any other aggregate of persons is, as Vernon Venable has pointed out, an essential part of the Marxist definition of class.[5]

The additions Marx would make to Lenin's definition of a class are implied in a passage from his *Eighteenth Brumaire of Louis Bonaparte,* in which he said of the French peasants:

> In so far as millions of families live under economic conditions of existence that divide their mode of life, their interests and their culture from those of the other classes, and put them in hostile contrast to the latter, they form a class. In so far as there is merely a local interconnection among these small peasants, and the identity of their interests begets no unity, no national union and no political organisation, they do not form a class.[6]

Class consciousness would seem to be a further Marxist requirement for full membership in a class, which is to say that a class does not exist in the fullest sense unless sizable numbers of its members are subjectively alert to their objective condition. Just why some men are more aware of an identity of interests with their fellows than are others—why, for example, the workingmen of France in 1851 should have been a class and the peasants "a sackful of potatoes" [7]—Marx never told us, but it does appear that he meant to include the awareness of common interests with other men in his definition of a social class. One cannot become a bourgeois or proletarian or peasant simply by adopting the appropriate state of mind, but the appropriate state of mind piled on top of the necessary objective relationship to the mode of production will cement any man in his proper class. And, Marx thought, there is nothing so essential to creating the awareness of common interests as the presence of a common enemy.

The last step to full classhood is stimulated by the feeling of identity: it is association for the pursuit of common ends. As Marx wrote in *The Poverty of Philosophy,* the unorganized mass of workers is "a class, as opposed to capital, but not yet for itself." In the ongoing struggle it unites in a political association based on social and economic identity, and then at last "it is constituted as a class for itself." [8] It was Marx's fond belief that his efforts at political organization had done as much as any force or event in the nineteenth century to make the proletariat of Europe a true class. He may have been right.

These, then, appear to be the Marxist criteria for the full existence of a social class. These are what an "aggregate of persons" must have in common: 1) an objective relationship to the means of production, which is determined largely by the ownership or nonownership of productive property; 2) a corresponding position in the camp of the exploiters or exploited; 3) a subjective awareness of their identity of economic interest; and 4) a willingness to translate this awareness into association for common action. If these be the Marxist criteria, what are the Marxist classes?

This is another question that cannot be answered straight off. One looks in *The Eighteenth Brumaire,* or Engels' preface to the second edition of *The Peasant War in Germany,* or the third volume of *Capital* and finds as many as six or seven distinct classes; [9] one looks in the *Manifesto* and learns that there are really only two. Marx the student of society and observer of events was, as Raymond Aron has demonstrated, subtly aware of the varied categories of men in the modern community.[10] Marx the critic of society and prophet of revolution, persuaded and prodded by Marx the dialectician, saw all these categories resolving into two giant, contradictory classes: bourgeoisie and proletariat, owners and nonowners, exploiters and exploited. When he was in this revolutionary mood, he had no trouble projecting the two-class view back through history to find "freeman and slave, patrician and plebeian, lord and serf, guildmaster and journeyman, in a word, oppressor and oppressed" [11]—with all other men of a particular stage in history grouping themselves like sheep around the one class or goats around the other.

The first great aggregate in modern society is the bourgeoisie, the industrial capitalists who own and manipulate the means of production. Toward this class Marx has a somewhat ambivalent attitude. On one hand, it is the ruling class—the men who exploit the workers ruthlessly in pursuit of their profits and destiny—and he hates it because it rules. On the other, it is the producing class—the men whose daring and genius broke the bonds of feudalism and carried the West into the industrial revolution—and he admires it because it produces.

The bourgeoisie, during its rule of scarce one hundred years, has created more massive and more colossal productive forces than have all preceding generations together. Subjection of nature's forces to man, machinery, application of chemistry to industry and agriculture, steam navigation, railways, electric telegraphs, clearing of whole continents for cultivation, canalisation of rivers, whole populations conjured out of the ground—what earlier century had even a presentiment that such productive forces slumbered in the lap of social labour? [12]

Some day the bourgeoisie will be forced to give over control of production to a new class far better equipped to exercise it, but even then historians will record that it filled a necessary role in the dialectical progress of mankind toward the golden age of communism.

I have, of course, overstated Marx's ambivalence, for his natural mood is one of gnawing hatred for the bourgeoisie. To put the matter simply, it has been much too successful a class, and its success may be measured in the misery of the men it has exploited. In the words of the *Communist Manifesto:*

> The bourgeoisie . . . has pitilessly torn asunder the motley feudal ties that bound man to his "natural superiors," and has left no other nexus between man and man than naked self-interest, than callous "cash payment." It has drowned the most heavenly ecstasies of religious fervour, of chivalrous enthusiasm, of philistine sentimentalism, in the icy water of egotistical calculation. It has resolved personal worth into exchange value, and in place of the numberless indefeasible chartered freedoms, has set up that single, unconscionable freedom— Free Trade. In one word, for exploitation, veiled by religious and political illusions, it has substituted naked, shameless, direct, brutal exploitation.[13]

The second aggregate is the proletariat. Toward this class Marx bears nothing but admiration, affection, and high anticipation. The proletariat consists primarily of those men who, owning nothing but their labor, sell it to the bourgeoisie, and man the machines of production. Not every exploited nonowner in society is a member of the proletariat. Here, in particular, class consciousness and the urge to associate are requirements for full membership, and Marx has no words angry enough to voice his contempt for those who are disinherited, exploited, and oppressed, and yet do not think and act as proletarians. Not only these men (the worst of whom are assigned to the *Lumpenproletariat*), but the peasants, too, are excluded from "the class of modern wage labourers who, having no means of production of their own, are reduced to selling their labour power in order to live." [14] To this day it is difficult to get two Marxists to agree exactly on the full membership of the proletariat. Its charter members are the class-conscious urban industrial workers, and that definition of the proletariat will have to suffice. We should note, however, that Marx and Engels make room for themselves:

In times when the class struggle nears the decisive hour, the process of dissolution going on within the ruling class, in fact within the whole range of old society, assumes such a violent, glaring character, that a small section of the ruling class cuts itself adrift, and joins the revolutionary class, the class that holds the future in its hands. Just as, therefore, at an earlier period, a section of the nobility went over to the bourgeoisie, so now a portion of the bourgeoisie goes over to the proletariat, and in particular, a portion of the bourgeois ideologists, who have raised themselves to the level of comprehending theoretically the historical movement as a whole.[15]

Having identified the proletariat, to his satisfaction if not to ours, Marx heaps virtue and duty in lavish amounts on its back. Supporting its claims to virtue, real or potential, are these facts: the proletariat alone can identify itself with all humanity, since its interests are as universal as those of all other classes are particular; it alone is morally and intellectually fit to practice brotherhood, since both its collective character and collective reason are untainted by the ownership of property; it alone is truly progressive, since it has no stake in past or present; and it alone has the developed quality of class consciousness which permits it to grasp the full significance of its duty to history.

The duty to which Marx calls the proletariat, the mission he is certain that history has been saving for it, is to supplant the dying bourgeoisie as "the creators of history and the motive force of social progress" [16] and to carry all mankind through the next revolution to the golden age beyond. The proletariat is the last and greatest of all revolutionary classes. To embody reason and to broadcast truth in the dying bourgeois society, to resolve the fierce contradictions of capitalism by striking at the right moment, to seize power in the form of the dictatorship and thus to hasten the socialist transition, to end the curse of alienation, and then at last in the dawn of communism to dissolve into the mists of history: this is the noble, fateful, self-immolating mission of the proletariat. Since it has such a mission, it cannot be treated as just one class among many. Its unique claim to reason and truth and its decisive role in history make compromise with other classes unthinkable. As the class of the future, the proletariat cannot concede that other classes have any claims upon it. If other men insist on serving the proletariat, it must be on the proletariat's terms, for out of its emancipation will come the "creation of a new society." [17]

We are dealing here, needless to say, with an astounding concoction of reality and myth. The reality is the Marxist assault on bourgeois society. The myth is the notion that history demands this assault and guarantees its success, that it has singled out this despised group of persons to provide the motive power for the last go-round of the dialectic of history.[18] Marx did everything in his power to create the myth, for the language in which he described the workingmen of his day was some of his most mystical and downright confusing. In discussing, in one of his early pieces, the possibility of a genuine revolution, he asked where this possibility lay, and then answered:

> In the formation of a class with radical chains, a class of bourgeois society which is not a class of bourgeois society, an estate which is the dissolution of all estates, a sphere which has a universal character as a result of universal suffering and demands no particular right because no particular wrong has been done to it, but wrong pure and simple, . . . and finally a sphere which cannot emancipate itself without at the same time emancipating itself from all other spheres of society and thus emancipating all other spheres of society also, a class which, in a word, represents the complete loss of humanity and can therefore win itself only through the complete rewinning of humanity. This dissolution of society is the proletariat.[19]

This proletariat is in fact the purest kind of abstraction, and it remains to be seen how Marx and the Marxists clothe it with flesh and blood by assigning the mission and even the substance of this last and greatest class to the Communist party.

In his earthbound moments Marx speaks of at least four other aggregates of persons that he seems willing to look upon as classes for the sake of understanding society if not of making history: the landholders, a tenacious remnant of the ruling class of feudalism; the petty bourgeoisie—owners but not exploiters—the independent farmers, craftsmen, and small merchants who occupy the middle level between bourgeoisie and proletariat; the peasantry, of and yet not of the petty bourgeoisie, men with whom neither Marx nor the Marxists (except for Lenin on one level and Mao Tse-tung on another) have ever known quite what to do in theory or practice; [20] and the *Lumpenproletariat,* which Engels salutes as "the scum of the decaying elements of all classes which establishes headquarters in all the big cities, . . . an absolutely venal, an absolutely brazen crew." [21] In addition, in his *Theories of Surplus Value* (which was meant to be the fourth volume of *Capital*) Marx speaks of "third persons" who function in various roles outside the productive pattern. He includes many representatives of the petty bourgeoisie in this shadow-class, as well as ministers, artists, entertainers, teachers, soldiers, physicians, functionaries, and a host of other persons who simply frustrate his urge to put men into categories and thus to understand all about them.[22]

Marx is not much interested in these groupings of men, for unlike the bourgeoisie and proletariat they have no real meaning for history. Their role in either capitalist production or proletarian revolution is negligible; they are doomed soon enough to be swallowed up in one of the two great classes. The landlords are being transformed into capitalists. The petty bourgeoisie, the core of "the middle class," is sinking "gradually into the proletariat." The peasantry—well, something will happen to the peasantry to make it an arm of the proletariat, if not in the destructive shock of revolution then in the creative purgatory of socialism. In all stages of society the multiplicity of classes tends to polarize as the productive system moves into high gear. Even if this were not entirely true of, say, slave society or feudalism, it is completely true of capitalism. Marx writes in the *Manifesto,* in words I have quoted already:

Our epoch, the epoch of the bourgeoisie, possesses, however, this distinctive feature: It has simplified the class antagonisms. Society as a whole is more and more splitting up into two great hostile camps, into two great classes directly facing each other—bourgeoisie and proletariat.

This, then, is the heart of Marx's sociological message to America and all countries like it: The conditions of industrial capitalism must inevitably drive all grades and interests in society into two giant camps—one a giant in power; the other, in numbers and destiny—and these camps must war implacably upon one another until the iron law of history gives victory to the exploited. And with this message comes a prediction of the end of the middle class, which cannot keep itself afloat in the storms of this struggle, but must sink at last, except for a few of its more clever or corrupt members, into the ranks of the proletariat. There are times when Marx appears to recognize the emergence and staying-power of what we call "the new middle class," [23] but the main direction of his thought points to the eventual disappearance of all groups in the middle. The middle class, however one defines and delimits it, cannot be integrated with the dialectic of history. The advance of capitalism promises the absorption of most of its members into the proletariat.

The sharpening struggle between bourgeoisie and proletariat will go inexorably forward to resolution by revolution. The class struggle, we have learned already, has always been the lever of historical transformation, and it is now to be applied for the last and most decisive time. It cannot be too often emphasized that Marx finds the natural relationship of social classes to be one of hostility, contempt, suspicion, and irreconcilability, and that he cannot imagine the proletariat making any useful sort of compromise with the bourgeoisie. As Bukharin's *ABC of Communism* put it in words still read and believed in many parts of the world:

Peace between the classes is as impossible as peace between wolves and sheep. Wolves want to eat sheep, so sheep must defend themselves against wolves. But if this be so . . . then we have to ask whether it is possible for wolves and sheep to have a common will. Every intelligent person knows that it is absurd to talk of anything of the kind. There simply cannot be a will common to sheep and wolves. . . . It is as clear as daylight that the same thing applies to the two main classes of human society. In contemporary society, class is arrayed against class, the bourgeoisie against the proletariat, the proletariat against the bourgeoisie. Between them there is war to the knife.[24]

In capitalist society, men have no choice but to exploit or be exploited. The men of property are the thesis, the proletariat the antithesis; out of their conflict must emerge not a mechanical compromise of interests but a dialectical synthesis that produces an entirely new set of interests for society. The workingmen can never compromise with those who own the means of production. They must move forward "irrevocably and obviously" to destroy the ruling class and all who serve it. Struggle, contradiction, and conflict until "this person," the bourgeois owner of property, is "swept out of the way, and made impossible" [25]—such is the fate of capitalist society.

While some Marxists have denied the fact or necessity of the class struggle, Marx and Engels had the answer for them when they wrote in 1879:

As for ourselves, in view of our whole past there is only one path open to us. For almost forty years we have stressed the class struggle as the immediate driving force of history, and in particular the class struggle between the bourgeoisie and the proletariat as the great lever of the modern social revolution; it is therefore impossible for us to co-operate with people who wish to expunge this class struggle from the movement.[26]

What kind of society will emerge from "the modern social revolution"? Men have gone to Marx and Engels for more than a hundred years in search of an answer to this question, but they are still being turned away with a few vague words of prophecy. Here and there in their writings one is taken on a flight of exhortation or imagination, and in Marx's *Critique of the Gotha Programme* the momentous distinction between socialism and communism is made effectively. But that is all—there are no "recipes for the cookshops of the future" [27]—and it is hardly enough even for the friends of Marx and Engels, much less for their foes. We will have to be satisfied with these few facts and guesses about Marx's own expectations of the next stages of society:

Out of the wreckage and sacrifice of the proletarian revolution emerges the first stage of the Marxist future: *socialism,* a transitional period of indeterminate but not indefinite duration in which the proletariat, operating through the famous dictatorship, goes about the mighty task of rebuilding society on the principle of common ownership of all property in the means of production. In this stage, to put it crudely, the two classes of the present undergo a dramatic reversal of roles. The exploited become the exploiters, the exploiters become the exploited. In time, as the members of the bourgeoisie die off or are persuaded to see the light, the exploitation of man by man comes to an end. Before this can happen, however, stern measures must be applied, especially to suppress the lingering memories and desires of capitalism. To balance the effect of these measures, men must continue to be rewarded according to their contributions to the success of the dictatorship of the proletariat.

This dictatorship, it would appear, must substitute planning on a major scale for the haphazard methods of managing the economy in bourgeois society. Marx is distressingly silent about the question of planning under socialism—for one reason because he was irked by the grandiose claims of the Utopian socialists for their own brands of social technology; for another, because he was anxious to give no support to piecemeal reformers. Yet he and Engels both assumed that "the social anarchy of production" under capitalism would have to give way to "a social regulation of production upon a definite plan." [28] And if Marx was not a social engineer himself, every Marxist in power has had to be one. We may assert confidently that Marx assumes the necessity (certainly in the early stages of socialism) of central direction of production and distribution. Both must be made "rational," and how else can this great advance be secured except by conscious planning? We may leave the answer to Lenin, who learned the hard way that Marxists in power cannot rely on history to reconstruct society on a socialist basis.[29]

The next and last stage is *communism,* toward which history has been pointing ever since the first savages fell from grace by accumulating property for their own purposes. We already know most of Marx's prophecies for the golden age: a new race of men, from whose minds all memories of the alienated past will have disappeared; a classless society, in which all men will stand in the same objective relationship to the means of production and no man will have a fixed occupation; a collective economy, which will pour out products in abundance; an end to coercive government, and in its place the spontaneous association of like-minded persons for common purposes; an end to poverty and thus to all the frustrations and fears that corrupt human relations; the gentle domination of all public and private activity by "a really human morality"; and everywhere banners, handsome and presumably red, bearing the wondrous slogan "From each according to his ability, to each according to his needs." The banners will wave over universal beauty, for gone will be the slums and refuse heaps and ugly growths of bourgeois society.* Gone, too, Engels promises, will be "the antagonisms of town and country." The men of the future, who will be the first real men ever to have existed, will live and work in garden cities. Engels leaves no doubt that the great cities of the present must be dismantled before communism can reign forever. The dismantling "will take much time and trouble," but it will be done.[31]

---

* Arthur Koestler has told the story of a Communist writers' congress at which André Malraux, irritated by talk of the perfect world to come, asked

For a man who spent much of his time belaboring every specimen of Utopian, Marx was a fair specimen himself. If he was not
a Utopian in the sense of one who describes the structure and
functioning of the perfect society in perfect detail, certainly he
made a prophetic promise that would be hard to top. It is becoming increasingly hard for Communists to believe that the
promise will be fulfilled in any reasonable length of time, yet to
surrender it would be to break faith with Marx. As a result, the
Marxist millennium has about the same standing and purpose in
the Soviet Union today as does the Christian millennium in the
Western world: it cannot be believed; it cannot be discarded. I
doubt that Khrushchev would answer much differently in 1960 the
question put to Stalin by an American labor delegation in 1927:

QUESTION: Can you outline briefly the characteristics of the society
of the future which communism is trying to create?

ANSWER: The general characteristics of communist society are given
in the works of Marx, Engels and Lenin. Briefly, the anatomy of
communist society may be described as follows: It is a society in
which *a*) there will be no private ownership of the means of production but social, collective ownership; *b*) there will be no classes or
state, but workers in industry and agriculture managing their economic affairs as a free association of toilers; *c*) national economy,
organized according to plan, will be based on the highest technique
in both industry and agriculture; *d*) there will be no antithesis between town and country, between industry and agriculture; *e*) the
products will be distributed according to the principle of the old French
Communists: "from each according to his abilities, to each according
to his needs"; *f*) science and art will enjoy conditions conducive to
their *highest development; g*) the individual, freed from bread and
butter cares, and of the necessity of cringing to the "powers that be"
will become really free, etc., etc. Clearly, we are still remote from
such a society.[32]

Clearly we are, yet all true Marxists must cling to their belief
in what Tennyson called the "far-off divine event, to which the

---

impatiently, "And what about the man who is run over by a tram car?"
After a period of silence described as "painful," the answer came, "In a
perfect socialist transport-system, there would be no accidents." [30]

whole creation moves." * Marxist sociology, which holds out the promise of salvation on earth, appears finally as nothing more or less than secular chiliasm; it is a one-way ticket for an inevitable journey from Paradise Lost to Paradise Regained.[33] "It is all very well," Trotsky shouted, "for the priests of all religions to tell us tales of paradise in another world; we declare that we mean to create for the human race a real paradise upon earth." [34]

America has spawned some notable sociologists—Lester Frank Ward, William Graham Sumner, E. A. Ross, Thorstein Veblen, Arthur F. Bentley, W. Lloyd Warner, C. Wright Mills, and David Riesman, to mention a few of the best known—but as yet they have had little success in shaping our ideas about society to their findings or insights. The American social tradition is a kaleidoscope of contradictions. We talk a great deal about the classless society, yet we must admit under close questioning that such a society has never existed in America. We still love to toss about the slogans of rugged individualism, yet we know that the practice of such individualism by more than a few well-placed persons is disruptive of social stability. And certainly we manage to keep an uncomfortable distance between the way we preach and the way we practice the principle of equality. More disturbing than that, the kaleidoscope is only half-assembled. Our thoughts about society have been few and casual, as befits a people that has made a fetish of individualism. There are many questions about America that we have not even asked, much less answered, and this is one of those points at which the man who seeks to describe the American tradition must draw on the implicit workings of our customs

---

* Khrushchev reasserted his own faith in the advent of communism in his opening speech to the Twenty-first Communist Party Congress in January, 1959. In an oblique rebuff to the overenthusiastic claims for the advanced nature of the Chinese communes, he emphasized strongly the necessity of a long stage of socialist transition. He also made clear that "when we speak of satisfying the needs of the people, we have in mind not the whims and desires for luxuries but the healthy requirements of a culturally developed man."

and institutions rather than on the explicit words with which we are fond of praising them. What I am trying to say is that the real American social tradition is a benign reflection of the real American social structure. Its essence, which is Madisonian rather than Marxist, is roughly this:

Society is the sum of all the social units, and nothing more. From one point of view, it appears as a loose heap of freewheeling individuals; from a second, as a pattern of natural and voluntary groups; from a third, as a rough pyramid of social classes. Although no one of these views is any more "real" than the others (and all must be taken in order to get a clear picture of society), let us, out of deference to Marx, take the third, and so come up with these further observations:

Classes are an inevitable fact of social life, and what is inevitable is probably also necessary, not only for maintaining social stability but also for insuring social progress.

Classes in America are stages rather than castes. Our class system is a ladder, with at least six or eight rungs, up and down which heavy traffic moves constantly. (Here we have always been more sanguine than the statistics entitle us to be.)

Not only is there a vast amount of vertical movement between the classes, but the whole society is moving steadily upward in the scale of human existence. In specific terms, this means the steady growth, relative to all other classes, of an ever more prosperous and secure middle class.

The chief criterion of class distinction is achievement, especially economic achievement, although birth, wealth, taste, manners, power, and awareness all play their part.

The natural relationship of classes is a mixture of dependence and antagonism. There is friction in the joints, but not nearly enough to force us to talk of a "class struggle."

The best of all classes—in many ways, the only class that counts —is the middle class. The performance of any institution is to be judged finally in terms of how well it serves to expand or strengthen or reward this class.

A few additional details will emerge in the critique of Marxism to follow, but these, I think, are the basic points in the American social tradition. It would be hard to imagine a sharper confrontation between Marxism and the American tradition than exists in this field. Not even in the clash of materialism and idealism are the lines of battle more clearly drawn. These would seem to be the most compelling reasons for our inability to accept the lessons and exhortations of Marxist sociology:

First, Marx places far too much stress on economics as the decisive force in shaping social groups and patterns. It is simply not true that the institutions and tastes and habits and taboos of the American people are what they are and could be no different because of our mode of production. It is simply an exercise in definition, and not a very clever one at that, to say that a social class is fundamentally an aggregate of persons who perform the same broad function in the economy. History, psychology, cultural anthropology, and sociology all unite to affirm that both the origin and persistence of social classes can be understood only in terms of a plurality of causes, many of which defy economic determinism. Long before Marx, at least as early as James Madison, Americans knew well that men divided socially and politically on economic grounds, and certainly we should be the last people on earth to deny the power of production to influence our lives. But once again Marx has made one of the great determinants of social behavior the only determinant, and common sense bids us demur.

Second, we must demur, too, from the analysis of the class structure in Western society upon which he bases his revolutionary call to arms and his confident promise of a new society. When he talks of several kinds of bourgeois, several kinds of working-man, and of peasants and landlords and "third persons," we listen with interest and respect. When he insists that all these groupings are resolving inexorably into two, those who own and those who labor, interest turns to amusement, and respect to exasperation. There is no place in our thinking for this dialectical mania for shuffling all the complexities of social existence into a pattern of polar contradictions.

Third, even if we were to assume that his diagnosis was essentially correct, we could not take seriously his description of either of the two great classes. As the land of the bourgeoisie, a fact that Marx and Engels both acknowledged, what are we to say of the contempt he heaps upon us, our institutions, and our ideals? As the land with no proletariat (or so we like to think), what can we do but gasp when we hear of the role assigned to it? The fact is, as a hundred learned critics of Marx have pointed out, that the proletariat as Marx described it is a colossal myth, one of the most absurd if compelling in the Marxist armory (or whatever place it is in which men store myths). The Marxists themselves have never acted as if the proletariat were more than a useful abstraction, for always and everywhere it has been a select few—before the revolution a handful of intellectuals, after it a handful of bureaucrats—who have acted for and as the proletariat. The proletariat described by Marx does not and cannot exist; even if it did we would hardly care to put our destiny in its keeping.

Fourth, our history and tradition protest in unison against Marx's assertion that the class struggle is the normal condition of society and the motive power of history.[35] To the contrary, the pattern of class relationships in this country, as in many countries that come to mind, has been one of collaboration as well as of conflict. The advances of one class have brought benefits as well as injuries to other classes. We have long since abandoned the happy view of perfect harmony among classes, but this does not mean that we must now rush to the other end of the spectrum and embrace the bitter view of total war. One may find evidence of class antagonisms at many points in our history, but rarely has there been an antagonism that was not dampened eventually by the democratic process of give and take, if not dampened sooner by the flow of men from class to class. There is a wide gulf between the tensions and envies that can be found in even the healthiest society and the kind of "war to the knife" in which Marx saw the promise of revolution.*

History, we will admit, does some of its fastest moving under the impulse of struggle, but the direction of movement may be down just as easily as up, and the struggle is just as likely to be between sections or sects or parties or families or even persons as between classes. It does its most welcome moving, we like to think, through co-operation and compromise among groups that would not recognize the class struggle if it swept up and drowned them in hate. Although we agree with Marx that society is a process, we insist that evolution rather than revolution is the force that pushes the process in the right direction. All in all, it is hard not to agree with George Sabine that Marx's theory of the class struggle is "political poison." [37]

The next criticism is aimed at the Marxists rather than at Marx himself, although he was certainly an accessory before the fact. The fact is an unreasoning faith in social technology, a faith that would leave nothing in the social process (once Marxists are in power) to chance. Society, on this view, is a vast machine that can be stripped down, rebuilt, and then directed purposefully by men who take the trouble to probe it intelligently, that is, with the scientific tools of dialectical materialism. It is no accident that Marxist countries are in love with "plans," nor that the failure of these plans is blamed on stupid administrators rather than on the whims of nature, the perversities of peasants, or the inertia of the social process. As Communists love the blessed word "plan," they detest the cursed word "spontaneity"; and they will not give it any place

---

* I quite agree with Bertrand Russell that Marx's teachings have helped to bring on the class struggle he predicted, and with René Gonnard that this is a classic demonstration of the un-Marxist power of Marxist ideas. Toward the end of his life Stalin had occasion to insist that "the fierce class struggle" between bourgeoisie and proletariat did not necessarily mean "the disintegration of society, . . . a break of all ties between the hostile classes." [36]

in the progress of society. This is an important charge in the Marxist case against American pragmatism, which I shall review in Chapter VII. Marxism assumes that Marxists can know all there is to be known about society. "Given such knowledge," an American Marxist writes, "it is not necessary to proceed by guess work, by trial and error, by improvisation; one can proceed by prediction, planning and projecting." [38] Our way of life now makes room for social planning, but it makes no less room for "spontaneity."

We could go on indefinitely punching holes in Marx's sociology. We could review the inadequacy of his definitions of key words, drain the swamp of confusion into which he was led by the false simplicity of the dialectic, point to such fictions as "class will" [39] and such false predictions as the absorption of the middle class in the proletariat, ask embarrassing questions about the role of the peasantry, tell stale jokes about the classless society in Russia,* even cast up statistics to show that in many industrial countries the proletariat is a disappearing rather than a growing class. If we carried on too long, however, we might decide to chuck the whole business and conclude that Marx was not, after all, a first-rate sociologist. Yet such a sociologist he certainly was, if not as coolheaded scientist then as hot-blooded dramatist. Sociology, like all disciplines, needs an occasional man of genius to work with insights rather than with samples, with aphorisms rather than with statistics, in order to shake men out of their complacency, and it would be hard to think of anyone in history who did this more abrasively than did Marx in *Capital*. It needs, too, the man of

---

* According to official word, there are today in the Soviet Union no "antagonistic classes," only three "classes friendly to each other." Two of these are apparently full-fledged classes: the workers, who are *not* proletarians, and the peasants, who form "a completely new peasantry, the like of which the history of man has never known." The other is a "stratum"—the intellectuals, who are also "completely new" and unique, and "toiling." We have Stalin's testimony, enshrined in Article IV of the Soviet Constitution, that the "exploitation of man by man has been abolished, eliminated" in the U.S.S.R.[40]

genius to make a dramatic construction, however sparse in detail, for the transformation of society, and it would be hard to think of anyone since Plato who has shaken us more in this peculiar manner than did Marx in the *Critique of the Gotha Programme.* Even if his social ideas had not been so colossal a force in history, we would have to take him altogether seriously. Let me therefore cut short this critique by recording only one more point of contradiction between his way of looking at society and ours.

This point is simply the obsession of Marxism with classes— whether as tools of history, phenomena of society, or agencies through which the mode of production shapes the ideas, institutions, and aspirations of men. When a Marxist looks at a society— ancient or modern, agricultural or industrial, primitive or complex—he looks first and hardest for its class configuration, so hard indeed that he always manages to find what he expected to find. Then, having distinguished the exploiters from the exploited, having passed off all "third persons" as inconsequential, he proceeds to explain everything on the basis of class: the decisions of government, the strikes of unions, the sermons of preachers, the morals of bankers, the styles and trials of working girls, even the behavior of most individuals. The American, as I said before, tries to look at a society from any number of angles of vision. He may see it from one angle as a collection of individuals, from another as a layer cake of classes, from another as a web of organic and voluntary groups, from still another as an entire community with interests and loyalties that transcend class lines. In any case, the whole question of class is assigned a much more modest position in his ethics, his politics, and his social science. For neither classes nor the class struggle do Americans have one-tenth the awe that Marxists must have exactly because they are Marxists. In our opinion, an obsession with classes makes both the understanding and improvement of society far more difficult to achieve.

.

The most unacceptable result of this obsession with classes is the way in which it has blinded Marxism to the importance of two units of society that stand at opposite ends of the spectrum and yet are joined by what Lincoln called "the mystic chords of memory": the entire nation and the lone individual. The American tradition has too much respect for both nationalism and individualism to permit its followers to have much to do with Marxist sociology.

In Marx's teachings (as opposed to his prejudices and politics) there was no place for the nation.[41] One of the echoing slogans of the *Communist Manifesto* is, "The workingmen have no country," and no one can mistake Marx's intense desire to convince men that their primary allegiance was to their class, especially if it was the class of the future. The nation, he insisted, was an aggregate of interests and ideologies that was lodged well up in the superstructure of Western society, and it would come crashing to the ground when the substructure, the mode of production, had been converted to the universal purposes of the proletariat. Patriotism ranked not far below religion in Marx's chamber of horrors as one of the rankest illusions ever fostered by a ruling class in its own interests. (That he often behaved like a German patriot is amusing and revealing but in this instance beside the point.) It was an ideological stumbling block erected by the bourgeoisie to bar the road to revolution. With delight he predicted the end of "national differences and antagonisms," [42] an end toward which the practices of the bourgeoisie were already contributing and that would come at last, as all great ends come, with a sudden leap into a world without nations or national consciousness.

Lenin, who was as good a Marxist as a revolutionary Russian could be, carried forward the attack on nationalism.[43] He was consistent enough an internationalist and devoted enough a proletarian to accept the defeat of his own nation as a desirable turn of events. He was not a traitor; he was simply indifferent to the claims of emotional nationalism. It is one of those ironies of history which would be delicious if they were not so disastrous that the Soviet Union under Stalin and his successors has revived nationalism in its most virulent form, and that it has, moreover, dealt with the world in certain knowledge that "class hatreds have less explosive potential than the hatreds of nationalism." [44] Official Marxism still grants nothing, except in tactical situations,[45] to the nationalism of any country except the Soviet Union. Once again the Communists like to have it both ways. Just as they can make history and we cannot, just as their ideas have consequences and ours have none, just as their intellectuals can rise above class origins and ours cannot, so their country is a nation and ours is a bourgeois façade.[46]

For the time being, I think, we should take Lenin's word for the fact that "Marxism is incapable of being united with nationalism be it ever so 'just,' 'purified,' 'refined.' . . . Marxism puts in place of any and every nationalism its internationalism, the fusion of all nations into a higher unity." [47] And we must reply that while we, too, have dreamed of the brotherhood of man under the protection of a universal order, we think that the nations of the world must travel a far longer and different road from the one down which Marx and Lenin beckoned them. Even in the Great World Order there will be a place for love of country. In any case, our argument with Marx himself on the question of nationalism must go on indefinitely. We cannot avoid the judgment that he took a quite erroneous reading, not only of the force and tenacity, but of the historic mission and social benefits of enlightened nationalism. In their own tortured and, in this instance, un-Marxist way, the Communists of the Soviet Union appear to share this judgment.

Nor is there much more place in Marxism for the individual. Some of Marx's most brilliant interpreters, among them Karl Popper and Herbert Marcuse, have presented him as an individualist,[48] yet I do not see how an isolated phrase like "the free development of the individual," or a deep concern with the problem of alienation, or even an attitude of contempt for the bourgeois state makes him anything of the sort. He was, on any large view, a collectivist, a thinker who had a thoroughly social view of the claim to personal liberty, who obliterated ruthlessly the distinction between public and private man, who denied (with his master Hegel) that social institutions are means for the satisfaction of individual needs and aspirations, and who insisted that the behavior of any individual was determined almost wholly by his membership in a class. As he wrote in his preface to *Capital,* he preferred to "deal with" individuals "only in so far as they are the personifications of economic categories, embodiments of particular class-relations and class-interests." [49] A man who speaks thus of individuals, as he did in a hundred other passages, is not an individualist. The Marxist habit of studying individual successes or failures as socially-determined phenomena continues to deprive men of their dignity as well as of their responsibility.

Certainly Marx made collective action the primary force in the social process. As an old British Socialist, much quoted by Marxists, once put it neatly, the ethics of communism seeks not "the ideal society through the ideal individual, but conversely the ideal individual through the ideal society." It assumes that the good man, the worker, wants to "merge" his "individuality . . . in the collective existence" of his class.[50] It may also be argued that collectivism was Marx's end as well as his means. The tone of his few prophecies of the golden age of communism makes it hard to believe that anything we cherish as individualism—whether rugged, competitive, isolated, or co-operative—would be allowed to exist. Marx denied that he was one of "those communists . . . who wished to turn the world into one large barracks," [51] but it is much too easy to imagine his new world divided into a lot of small ones. Since there would be no contradiction between the wishes and views of any one man and the wishes and views of all, how could there be that desire for privacy that keeps each of us an individual, an individual not always *with* but sometimes *against* the community? The Marxist Utopia, it seems to me, would be a state of togetherness gone wild—a series of jolly collectives complete with group eating, group working, group dancing, and, who knows, perhaps even group sleeping. (If Marx were here today, he would be bound to say that, on this count at least, the Chinese were far better Marxists than the Russians.) Be that as it may, there is no room in his system for privacy; and privacy is still the essence of Western individualism. When it goes, individualism goes with it, and although we may nibble away at it carelessly ourselves with checks and tests and wire taps and mass techniques, at least we have a tradition that gives it a high value and us a guilty conscience about abusing it. We can only shudder at Stalin's definition of the "most valuable capital in the world: people—cadres." We can only laugh at Vyshinsky's testy insistence that "only in the land of socialism is man man's friend," that only under a collective system can men display real "friendship, collective support, organized aid, and unity." [52] For that kind of unity, we could never surrender our kind of individualism.

It might be thought unfair to Marx if I were to comment upon the state of individualism in the Soviet Union and among Marxists throughout the world, and so I will limit myself to the observation that life in a cadre or commune is not recommended for eccentrics who value their individuality.[53] I will conclude by setting up this particular confrontation between Marxism and the American tradition in a simple way: The Marxists deny that there can be any serious conflict of interests between the good man and the good society; we, even in our most social-minded moments, deny that such a conflict can ever be eliminated. For this reason we cling tenaciously to an idea that never did penetrate the old Russia. For this same reason they consider the whole question "undialectical" and out-of-order.[54] They cannot admit the existence of what we still cherish deeply: a sphere of individual activity that is "irrelevant to social or collective purpose and therefore exempt from social direction." [55] In Stalin's Marxist words:

There is not, nor should there be, an irreconcilable contrast between the individual and the collective, between the interests of the individual person and the interests of the collective. There should be no such contrast, because collectivism, Socialism, does not deny, but combines individual interests with the interests of the collective. Socialism cannot abstract itself from individual interests. Socialist society alone can most fully satisfy these personal interests. More than that, socialist society alone can firmly safeguard the interests of the individual. In this sense there is no irreconcilable contrast between Individualism and Socialism.[56]

It should not be hard to understand why American Marxists prefer Walt Whitman to Emerson and especially to Thoreau. The definition of Marxist individualism does not include, even for symbolic purposes, the escape to Walden Pond.[57]

In the last analysis, the differences between Marxist sociology and our social tradition appear as one more skirmish in the conflict between a monistic and a pluralistic way of life and thought. The American tradition takes society as it is and assumes all classes and almost all interests to be legitimate. Out of the mingled and jangled relations of the groupings in society there arises, thanks not least to the sanctions of a common tradition and common government, a state of social equilibrium in which most men can live without feeling too frustrated or cheated. Marxism denies the reasonableness of society, certainly as it has been constituted up to now, and singles out only one interest, more precisely one class, as legitimate. In this class it places all responsibility for the future of the race; any interest or group or class that defies or even questions it is branded an outlaw to be hunted down. As Marx himself was the first to admit, he discovered the importance neither of classes nor of the class struggle. But he was the first, both as social scientist and social revolutionary, to call for the struggle to be prosecuted single-mindedly until history had swallowed up all the wonderful varieties of social existence in One Big Interest. Even if such a society could be built, I doubt that any of us would care to live in it.

FIVE · MARXIST SOCIETY: THE INSTITUTIONS

In the last chapter we looked out over society from Marx's angle of vision, which compels the observer to fix his gaze almost exclusively on classes. In this chapter we shall survey it from several other angles, and thus remind ourselves again that there is a good deal more to any society than its class structure. To tell the truth, I am proposing a most un-Marxist exercise in empirical sociology, for I would like to look first beneath the class structure at the mode of production, then above it at such institutions as the family and the schools. An observer who tried faithfully to honor the Marxist scheme of sociological values would, it seems to me, work from the mode of production up to the class structure, then on above that to social institutions. I may be foolhardy to suggest that the "base" and the "superstructure," a venerated distinction in Marxism, may be looked at together.* For in suggesting this I must assume that the

* It has not been necessary to my special purposes to go at all carefully into this obscure area of Marxism, but it might be useful to give Plekhanov's precise account of the layers in the grand Marxist scheme of life and society, which turn out to be five (from bottom to top):

"1. The state of the forces of production;
2. Economic relations conditioned by these forces;
3. The socio-political regime erected upon a given economic foundation;

way men are organized to produce and distribute the means of life is not really much more basic than the way they are organized, let us say, to produce and raise children, and that the latter (the family) may radiate back to the former (the economic system) just as much influence as it receives. In any case, naive as it may appear to all Marxists, I propose to lump a number of social and economic institutions together in this chapter, and to consider all of them as interrelated means through which men follow their social natures and pursue their social purposes.

With a bow to Marx, let us begin at the base, for it is past time that we listened to his famous case against capitalism. I would think it unwise to break down the structure of capitalism into its many parts and to analyze them one by one in Marxist terms. Marx himself rarely bothered to do this; his study of capitalism, like his assault upon it, was aimed at the whole system. As the whole was corrupt, so, too, were the parts, and he was far more interested in describing and damning the operations of capitalism in general than in analyzing or salvaging any technique in particular. Indeed, the impossibility of salvaging any part of the capitalist structure for use in the society of the future was one of his basic assumptions.

Before we hear Marx on capitalism, there are three preliminary points to get clearly in mind. First, we should not concern ourselves with the fact, however decisive it may appear to us, that he was attacking the capitalism of 1860 and we are defending the "capitalism" of 1960. To orthodox Marxists there is not and cannot be any substantial difference between the two. Marx always denied the possibility of political or ethical reform of the inequities of capitalism. He would have described the great changes that have taken place since his day as mere sops thrown to the workers to postpone the inevitable assault on the bourgeoisie. The Marxists

---

4. The psychology of man in society, determined in part directly by economic conditions, and in part by the whole socio-political regime erected upon the economic foundation;
5. Various ideologies reflecting this psychology." [1]

of the twentieth century put more faith than did Marx in the capacity of political authority to control and reshape the economy, but they are no less certain than he that capitalism, no matter how much it may be prettied and propped up, is basically rotten. Everything Marx found to despise in the unreformed capitalism of his day is found by his followers in the reformed capitalism of this day. So long as a society is not socialist all the way through, so long as it makes room for private property in the means of production, it is a grim citadel of bourgeois capitalism marked out for destruction—if not sooner by storm then later by decay. Some countries in the West are grimmer citadels than others, but the case against the worst is the case against all so long as they have not passed into the first stage of Marxism.

Second, we are still dealing with Marx as sociologist rather than as economist, as social rather than economic critic of the capitalist mode of production, because that is the only way he can be dealt with fairly and reasonably. In some circles Marx the economist is still taken seriously, as he certainly took himself, but most economists would now nod assent to Lord Keynes's observation that Marx's economic theory is "not only scientifically erroneous but without interest or application for the modern world." [2] It is Marx the sociologist whom we must confront. We have no quarrel with the economist; he has long since been carried off the field on a shield heaped high with holy relics. We should not overlook his genuine contributions to our understanding, let us say, of business cycles, or economic growth, or monopolies, or the nature of labor as a commodity, nor can students of economics pass many of his observations and insights safely by. But I am convinced that most of his economic theory is irrelevant to modern problems and was indeed unnecessary to his own purposes, that his case against capitalism comes through more effectively if this theory is simply ignored, and that, in any event, he always was an imaginative sociologist masquerading as an occult economist. Marx arrived at his insights into the nature of capitalism almost intuitively; most of them were voiced well before he had worked out the economic theory that is supposed to support them. It was unfortunate, I am tempted to add, that Marx did not devote the man-hours poured into *Capital* to the histories of Rome and Byzantium or to the class structures of feudal France and republican America. Or would any book that he might possibly have produced have been converted in time into what E. H. Carr has labeled *Capital:* a "talisman"? [3]

Third, we are also dealing with the essential Marx, Marx the revolutionary anticapitalist, the one of all the many Marxes who embodies most significance for history and most danger for us. For more than a hundred years the compelling drive of Western radicalism has been hostility to capitalism and all its works; [4] and Marx remains a major source of inspiration to those who feel themselves cheated materially or spiritually in the distribution of the fruits of this economic system. When Marx rails against bourgeois exploitation of the toiling masses, it is the real Marx to whom we are listening. This helps to explain the peculiar intensity of Marxist attacks on the United States. We are hated not merely because we are the chief power arrayed against the Soviet Union, but also because we are the most successful and least apologetic operators of an economy based upon private ownership of the means of production. A Marxist must be, by definition and on principle, an all-out enemy of American capitalism.

Let us turn now to Marx's analysis of capitalism, to those hundreds upon hundreds of pages in which he attempts to unravel the tangled web of institutions, laws, customs, and relationships that radiate out from the all-shaping center of private ownership of the means of production. [5] In so doing let us recognize once again the ambivalence of his attitude toward this system. On one hand, as I tried to make clear in the last chapter with the help of the *Manifesto,* he has considerable admiration for the material accomplishments of capitalism. Indeed, with a little judicious cutting and some quoting out of context, we could run up a cheerful advertisement for unrestrained capitalism out of the first part of the *Manifesto*—something suitable for printing in *Business Week* and circulating to the membership of N.A.M. Capitalism, moreover, is a necessary stage in the dialectical progress of mankind to the promised land of communism; and toward those evils that are clearly necessary we all, even such as Marx, bear an attitude of wry tolerance. On the other hand, Marx hates capitalism with what I can only describe as a Marxist passion. Some of his and Engels' most striking pages are given over to an attack on it as a mode of production that has become totally evil. This, then, is the essential nature of the Marxist analysis of capitalism: it is an attack spurred by a deep-seated conviction that capitalism is a predatory system. And it is launched in a series of powerful waves at all the evils Marx claimed to have discovered in the England of his day.

His first and most direct attack is *social* in impulse and purpose. Marx hates capitalism for what it does to men as members of the community. Drawing on the ancient Western tradition of social protest, he assails the bourgeois economy for the way it exalts the fortunate few at the expense of the oppressed many. In the process of cheating the mass of men out of the just fruits of their labors, the bourgeoisie has made an "endless horror" of the society over which it rules. "Accumulation of wealth at one pole," Marx writes in *Capital,* is "at the same time accumulation of misery, agony of toil, slavery, ignorance, brutality, mental degradation, at the opposite pole." [6] Worse than that, in the words of an American Marxist, capitalism is "by its very nature a prolific breeder of crime." [7] Hundreds of pages in the writings of Marx and Engels are filled with savage descriptions of the ills of humanity under capitalism, the worst of which, by all odds, is the iron process through which man is converted by the needs of capitalism into a commodity, an adjunct of the machine, a beast of burden robbed of all dignity and humanity. It would, alas, take many pages of quotes to give the full, acid flavor of the passion with which they describe the lot of the workingmen of their time, and I can only recommend to the curious reader that he look into Chapters 10 or 15 or 25 of Volume I of *Capital,* and into Engels' *The Condition of the Working Class in England* and *The Housing Question.* There he will find a chamber of human horrors, a brutal catalogue of despair and degradation and disease, of suffering and cruelty and beastliness, of "barbarous indifference" and "nameless misery" and "social warfare," of broken men and withered women and pinchfaced children. And he will not soon forget it, especially when he remembers that the evidence they gathered, however selectively, was largely true of one stage of the industrial revolution.

It is not a pretty picture Marx draws of capitalism—"dripping from head to foot, from every pore, with blood and dirt" [8]—and he renders it even uglier by predicting that the lot of the workers and their families will grow steadily worse as the "Law of Capitalist Accumulation" runs its inevitable course and shaves the rate of profit on capital investment. The embattled capitalist, who cannot help himself, must force the worker to give him more and more hours for less and less pay.

> The worker becomes the poorer the more wealth he produces and the more his production increases in power and extent. The worker becomes a cheaper commodity the more commodities he produces. Hand in hand with the exploitation of the objective world goes the depreciation of the human world. Labor creates not only commodities; it creates itself and the worker as a commodity. [9]

As the proletariat sinks deeper, it will draw down with it not only those who are struggling frantically to stay afloat in the petty bourgeoisie, but also many of those who have sat for a time in the seats of the mighty. Marx explains the sharpening struggle within the bourgeoisie itself with his "Law of Concentration of Capital"; he dramatizes it in the celebrated phrase, "One capitalist always kills many." [10] And from that point he proceeds majestically to his "Law of Increasing Misery," [11] under which all the nonowners under capitalism are finding life ever more frustrating. If all this talk of "laws" seems confusing, let us pass on with this one-sentence statement of the Marxist criticism of capitalism on social grounds: Human existence and human relations are hell for all those who live under capitalism, and hell hath furies men have not yet imagined.

The second line of attack is *ethical,* an unexpected line for a Marxist to take. The fact is that Marx, who professes to be a scientist with no use for value judgments, introduces such judgments on a grand scale into his indictment of capitalism—and thus, in a sense, regains some of the respect he lost in posing as a scientist. He hates capitalism because it is exploitative, oppressive, and dehumanizing, but he also hates it because it is unfair, because it fosters inequality, because it cheats men out of a good part of what should come their way in return for their labors.

Central to this ethical attack, as indeed it is to the whole Marxist case against capitalism, is the celebrated "Theory of Surplus Value." I cannot, for a dozen reasons, enter into a detailed discussion of Marx's use and abuse of the concept of value, nor can I rehearse the amazing feat through which he conjures up the magic formula of surplus value out of the dull economics of the Ricardian theory of value.[12] I must limit myself to pointing out that Marx, following the classical economists, regards labor as the great value-creating force in the economy. Working single-mindedly from this key assumption, he goes on to make four other assumptions: 1) Under the increasingly mechanized conditions of industrialism, the man who labors can create far more value in any given period of time than is necessary to keep him and his dependents alive. 2) Under the ordinary conditions of capitalism, which have converted labor into a commodity to be bought and sold, the man who labors cannot hope to claim from his employer any more than a subsistence wage. Labor is the one really variable cost in the total input made by the employer, and in the struggle for survival he is under constant pressure to drive this cost downward. 3) The worker is therefore trapped without hope in a scheme under which he works a small part of the day for himself and a large part for his employer. 4) The second part, the value extracted without compensation from the unknowing or unwilling worker, is converted by the sale of the goods produced into the employer's profit. And so Marx puts his finger on the endemic curse of capitalism, surplus value, which in his view is nothing more than highway robbery. Indeed, "robbery" is a mild word for what he thinks of this whole fraudulent system. "Capital," he writes, "vampire-like, only lives by sucking living labor, and lives the more, the more labor it sucks." [13] This is much too simple a rendering of this cardinal doctrine of Marxist economics, but I trust that I have said enough to make clear Marx's contention, into which he poured all the "science" and all the passion at his command, that capitalism is a system in which most men are forced to labor meanly most of their lives so that a few men can live grandly in the luxury of parasitism. No one but a devout and purblind Marxist would take this theory seriously today, yet as a holy relic—as a "scientific" way of explaining the irreconcilable antagonism of bourgeois and proletarian, and a dramatic way of imputing primary significance to the latter and to his labor—it will continue to have great influence wherever Marxism penetrates. It may not be an "economic truth," but it is a "political and social slogan" that rings loud and clear in too many parts of the world.[14] It is Marx's way of crying out with Shelley to all the disinherited of the earth:

> The seed ye sow, another reaps;
> The wealth ye find, another keeps.

Marx's ethical attack on capitalism does not concentrate all its fire on the self-evident immorality of a system under which the men on top get something for nothing. It also sprays contempt on the pattern of morality under which, by appealing to a higher law, the bourgeoisie rationalizes its power and profits and position. Nothing angers Marx so much as the claim of the bourgeoisie to the approval of a universal ethic for the ideas with which it rules capitalist society. He and Engels blast the capitalists for "the selfish misconception" that transforms "the social forms springing from [their] present mode of production" into "eternal laws of nature and of reason," and they blast their own friends, too, for expecting that "twaddle" about morality and justice can help the workers to rise from their Slough of Despond.[15] I will deal at length in Chapter VII with the interesting question of Marxist morality; it is enough merely to note here that Marx despises the morality that celebrates industry, frugality, and self-reliance—not because any one of these qualities is evil in itself, but because they have all been used so dishonestly by the capitalists to maintain their economic and moral superiority. Marx hates capitalism for the hypocrisy it breeds and then feeds upon to live, and in hating it for this reason he passes a sentence of death that is essentially ethical in character.

In a closely parallel line of attack, Marx assaults capitalism on *esthetic* grounds. "Capitalist production," he writes, is "hostile to such aspects of spiritual production as art and poetry." [16] It has been the Marxists after Marx and Engels who have got the most mileage out of this criticism, but enough savage comments can be gathered from *Capital* and the *Manifesto* and *Anti-Dühring* to prove that the masters, too, condemn capitalism for the ugliness and vulgarity it has left everywhere in its wake. It fills the landscape with factories that exude stench and filth, raises mansions for the rich that are as vulgar as the hovels of the poor are mean, strips all decency and sensitivity from human relations, and condemns every form of creative self-expression—painting, sculpture, architecture, poetry, music—to a state of slavery to bourgeois whims. Through all the canon of Marxism there runs a rancorous assumption that capitalism is a dirty, vulgar, sinister way of life under which men who prize beauty and good manners and noble thoughts cannot hope to create or even bear to live.

Far more important is Marx's condemnation of capitalism on

economic grounds. By this I do not mean his analysis of the unjust workings of any system based on private ownership of the means of production, but rather the bold conclusion he draws from his empirical observations of bourgeois society: that capitalism is to be condemned as an economic system because it has run its appointed course, that from this time on, in Lenin's words, socialism alone can "make a gigantic development of the productive forces *possible.*" [17] Its successes, which Marx acknowledges, have been real enough, but it can no longer keep pace with the advances of technology and thus satisfy the needs of modern man. It has, indeed, in William Z. Foster's words, "outlived its historic mission." [18] The anarchy of its ends and irrationality of its means prevent the realization of material well-being among the mass of men. It is wasteful of natural resources, especially of the workers who are its greatest resource; it is incapable of making rapid and general use of the innovations it brings about in the techniques of production; and it is notoriously unstable, a system destined to oscillate with increasing violence between prosperity and depression. Although it can produce goods far beyond the capacity of nonsocialist society to absorb and use, it is organized only poorly to fill the real needs of men. And it is simply not equal to the demanding task of producing goods for men under socialism. These are only a few of the counts in Marx's bill of indictment against capitalism as an economic system, but they should be enough to demonstrate that he has not the slightest confidence that it can achieve the efficiency or stability necessary for an economy of true abundance. And that, be it remembered, is the economy that holds his fancy. As Eduard Heimann has pointed out, a "prime assumption of Marxism" is "the universal validity of large-scale production." [19]

It might be useful to recall what I had to say in Chapter III on the subject of alienation, for this is still another wave in the attack on capitalism: the *psychological*. One of the things Marx hates most about capitalism is what it does to the spirits of men.

Indeed, there are times when he seems to feel that the workers are worse off psychologically than they are materially, and that a rise in their standard of living, which might follow a rise in the fortunes of the bourgeoisie, would serve only to increase their misery. He sums up this particular criticism of capitalism in the doctrine of "fetishism," which is best understood as an extension of the concept of alienation.[20] The lot of modern man, he says, is no better than that of an African fetish-worker, who forgets that his wooden image is the work of his own hands and lets it assume command over him. Modern man, too, seems to have forgotten that the machines he has built and the goods he has produced were intended to serve his human ends, not to reduce his labor to the status of just another commodity.[21] Man is a slave to inanimate objects over which he must once again assume mastery. He can never hope to do this in a bourgeois economy.

Finally, Marx and his followers attack capitalism for *political* reasons—because it distributes both the power and freedom of society in grossly unequal amounts, because it makes a mockery of the practices of representative government, and because it projects the contradictions of capitalism into the international sphere and leads inevitably to imperialism,[22] colonialism, and war. I shall touch upon most of these points in Chapter VI.

For all these reasons—social, ethical, esthetic, economic, psychological, and political—Marx hates capitalism as malevolently as any man has ever hated any system of material production. He is therefore much relieved by his promise to himself that capitalism cannot survive much longer under the incessant pounding of its own inner contradictions. "In all countries of Europe," he wrote in his Inaugural Address (1864) to the First International in London,

it has now become a truth demonstrable to every unprejudiced mind, and only denied by those whose interest it is to hedge other people in a fool's paradise, that no improvement of machinery, no appliance of science to production, no contrivances of communication, no new colonies, no emigration, no opening of markets, no free trade, nor all these things put together, will do away with the miseries of the industrious masses; but that, on the present false base, every fresh development of the productive powers of labour must tend to deepen social contrasts and point social antagonisms.[23]

Nothing can improve the lot of the masses; nothing can prevent the sharpening of the class struggle; nothing can save capitalism from self-immolation. In one of the most famous passages in *Capital* he predicts the end:

Along with the constantly diminishing number of the magnates of capital, who usurp and monopolise all advantages of this process of transformation, grows the mass of misery, oppression, slavery, degradation, exploitation; but with this too grows the revolt of the working-class, a class always increasing in numbers, and disciplined, united, organised by the very mechanism of the process of capitalist production itself. The monopoly of capital becomes a fetter upon the mode of production, which has sprung up and flourished along with, and under it. Centralisation of the means of production and socialisation of labour at last reach a point where they become incompatible with their capitalist integument. This integument is burst asunder. The knell of capitalist private property sounds. The expropriators are expropriated.[24]

And that is the end of capitalism. What follows is a two-stage progression through socialism to communism about which Marx and Engels, as I have noted before, told us next to nothing, certainly about the way in which the economy might be organized for production and distribution. If we scrape together all the snatches of prophecy in their writings, we get a picture with at least these vague outlines: common ownership of all property in the means of production, including land; an economy of abundance based on an advanced technology (Marx and Engels were no machine-hating Luddites);[25] production for common use rather than for private profit; and production "under the conscious and prearranged control of society," a "society . . . organized as a conscious and systematic association."[26] The economies of socialism and communism would be planned economies, each in its own way, but who would do the planning and on what principles, Marx never did say, except to coin phrases about associations of "free individuals who work with jointly owned means of production, and wittingly expend their several labor powers as a combined social labor power." [27] He was too suspicious of the state, too irritated by the pretensions of the Utopians, too consumed by the urge to smash capitalism to go beyond these vague prophecies,[28] and Engels was not much more helpful, even in the chapter in *Anti-Dühring* devoted specifically to this subject.* Even Lenin had to complain in 1922:

> Not a single book has been written about the state capitalism that exists under communism. It did not even occur to Marx to write a word on the subject, and he died without leaving a single precise statement or irrefutable instruction on it. This is why we must get out of the difficulty entirely by our own efforts.[29]

Marx, it would seem, was a more faithful son (or even brother) of the classical economists than we have hitherto realized, for he seemed to assume that the plans of all the little collectives spread over the landscape would somehow be co-ordinated by a "hidden hand." His vision of the communist economy seemed to rest, if it rested anywhere at all, on the discredited notion of the self-regulating economy. Be that as it may, we now have the examples of Russia, China, Yugoslavia, and the satellites to teach us most of what we need to know about the planned economy of Marxism.

America is acknowledged the world over to be the leading citadel of capitalism, and the American tradition is no more bash-

---

* Another reason is that Marx expected the advance of technology to simplify the pattern of social life, thus rendering experts and expertise increasingly unnecessary. Lenin compounded this foolish expectation in his *State and Revolution*. Neither of them seemed to recognize that an advanced industrialism calls for more and more talented, trained, responsible, *specialized* men—and thus leads to the modern system of organized inequality of which the Soviet Union is an intriguing model.

ful than it should be in proclaiming the real and imagined virtues of our economy. This part of the tradition is the easiest to sound off about in the heat of political or industrial strife, the hardest to state soberly for general acceptance. Each of us carries his own image of capitalism in his mind, an image which is more likely than not to be dated 1896 or 1928 or perhaps even 1975. Each of us nurses a clutch of pat phrases like "equality of opportunity" or "the free market" or "the profit motive" or "people's capitalism" with which to explain in simple terms a social phenomenon of the most complicated order. Yet there is, I think, a growing consensus among thoughtful Americans about the guiding principles of our economy. I state these in admittedly ideal terms, at the same time insisting that the reality of the American economy comes close enough to the ideal to free us from the charge of harboring an ideology.

The ownership and management of economic enterprise are located largely in private hands.

Private property, including property in the means of production, is widely distributed under laws that secure the rights of individuals and, at the same time, guard the interests of the community.

The power of economic decision is widely diffused, especially through the encouragement of competition, but not of civil war, and the discouragement of monopoly, but not of large-scale production.

A condition of law, order, and opportunity exists under which men are able to accumulate capital and are willing to risk it.

The interests of workers are protected and served through a variety of techniques and institutions, especially through regulatory legislation and the processes of free collective bargaining.

Government intervenes in the operations of the economy to 1) regulate public businesses and natural monopolies; 2) restore and enforce competition; 3) perform economic services in fields unsuitable for private activity; 4) protect the interests of workers, farmers, consumers, small businessmen, and other groups at a natural disadvantage in a free economy; 5) stabilize the business cycle; and 6) direct the economy generally to higher and juster ends, with the burden of proof resting on those who counsel intervention.

The full powers of research, technology, managerial efficiency, and political stimulation are used to further economic progress, which is defined as the production of more and more goods at less and less cost, and their distribution to more and more people.

Individual initiative, which is spurred by many cross-cutting motives including profit, prestige, security, adventure, and power, is still the mainspring of this progress.

These are the elements of our economy in which most Americans now seem to take special pride. It is still by most definitions, and most assuredly by Marxist definition, a "capitalist" economy. This particular confrontation of Marxism and the American tradition is therefore sharp and irreconcilable. In this instance I am speaking, let it be clearly understood, of the critical Marxism that stems from Marx himself rather than of the "creative Marxism" of the Soviet Union. I am reluctant to get bogged down in a statistical comparison of the real wages of a steelworker in Gary and a steelworker in Magnitogorsk, however devastating to Communist claims such a comparison would be. I am even more reluctant to juggle the question of how much (or little) Marxism can be discovered in the techniques of the Soviet state. At the same time, I am anxious to resist turning this confrontation into an easy victory for capitalism by concentrating too narrowly on Marx himself, for he committed more intellectual trespasses in this area than in almost any other. His description of capitalism was a narrow caricature outdated even as he drew it; his predictions about the centralization of capital, or the dire fate of the workers, or the decline of the middle class have fallen flat. Worse than that, his economic theory was a hodge-podge of obscurity and passion, and his encompassing monism (in this instance, his obsession with the single fact of private property) blinded him to some of the great realities of politics and society. What interests me, as I trust it interests all thinking Americans, is the revised Marxist case against our capitalism; and for that we should go to those evolutionary Marxists outside the ranks of Communism who, drawing inspiration directly from Marx, attack us not for failing to imitate the Soviet Union but for refusing to vote ourselves into full-scale socialism. I have talked at length with several of these critics of American capitalism. I have read and reread those passages in the Marxist canon with which they bolster their argument. And this, as I understand it, is the sum of their Marxist case against capitalism. These are their key assumptions about our economy, indeed about any economy that is not fully socialized:

Capitalism cannot create an economy of true abundance.

Capitalism has a corrupting and ultimately destructive influence on political democracy.

Capitalism has an equally corrupting influence on taste, manners, behavior, and human relations.

Capitalism bestows wealth and power only on the capitalists; the workers cannot prosper individually or wield influence collectively so long as the means of production remain in private hands.

Capitalism cannot be "reformed," that is, made substantially more stable or efficient or just or humane by political action.

In denying each of these Marxist judgments upon all non-Marxist economies, Americans make much, as of course they should, of the record of their economy over the past quarter-century. We do not have to claim perfection, which we have no right to do in any case, nor do we have to fight dogma with dogma. For in recognizing clearly the distance we have yet to travel to achieve the most humane and stable economy to which men may reasonably aspire, we can also recognize the amazing distance we have already come. It would, in any case, profit us little to take these five assertions and pick them carefully apart, chiefly because each of them is wrong on its face. Consider, for example, the last charge in this bill of indictment, which, if it could be proved, would be enough all by itself to sentence capitalism to death. The truth is that political action, beginning even before Marx's time, has never ceased working profound influence upon the capitalist economies of the West. The capitalism against which Marx railed, not without reason, has long since vanished from the scene in America. It has been "reformed" without being socialized, and Marx's dogma of the impossibility of social reform through political means has, like many of his other dogmas, been refuted by events in the real world. Thanks to its own persistent virtues, to the efforts of reformers, and to the aspirations of millions of managers, workers, and investors, American capitalism has never flourished more vigorously than it is flourishing at this moment.

Our economy has its problems and imperfections (the reader can surely list four or five large ones without my prompting), but it is yet to be proved that these arise primarily out of the conditions of capitalism. The root causes of our economic discontents must also be sought in the persistent frailties of men, in the irregularities and inefficiencies characteristic of large-scale social organizations, and above all in the imperatives of an advanced industrial society, whether capitalist, socialist, or communist. Our Marxist critics, like Marx himself, have been extremely lax in failing to distinguish the ill effects of industrialism from those of capitalism, whether these be visited upon the beauties of nature or the spirits of men. By failing to make this distinction a century ago, Marx fell victim to the fraudulent assumption that the evils of modern civilization would be swept into oblivion by the demise of capitalism. By failing to make it today, the Marxist critics of American capitalism have compounded the fraud. It may be true that the human condition is more troubled than it should be, but common sense dictates that the reasons for this are to be sought in industrialism rather than in capitalism, in the existence rather than in the ownership of the factories that dot our landscape. We would do well to profit from this monumental confusion in the Marxist mind as we continue our own search for a healthy society. Beyond that we have little to learn from Marx the critic of capitalism. Although he may not have intended it, his case against capitalism was essentially a case against industrialism, and that case, as Americans and Russians alike will bear witness, is no longer before the court. The industrial society is here to stay.

We could spend the rest of our lives arguing with the Marxists over the merits (and demerits) of our real economy and their imaginary one, and the debate would end with each side no less convinced than it is today of the rightness of its system. I must therefore elect to move on to other aspects of Marxism and the American tradition, tossing one more idea into the arena even as we bid it farewell. In the end, I think, we have the better of almost any argument with the Marxist political economists because our system comes to grips realistically if not always effectively with a problem of which theirs, as we have learned already, seems hardly conscious: the problem of *power,* of what it is and how it works, of who is to wield it and on what conditions, of what it can accomplish and how carefully it must be limited. We are fond of our economic arrangements, not merely because they seem to do such a good job of production and distribution, but because they divide and disperse the power of economic decision. To turn the matter around, we distrust the arrangements of Marxist socialism, not merely because they seem to promise such a poor-to-average job of production and distribution, but because they put too much power in too few hands under too few restraints. The centrally owned and planned economy is worse than inefficient and unproductive; it is dangerous. It calls blithely for a concentration of power over the lives of men that anyone raised in the American tradition of human nature and political reality could not tolerate for a moment. Neither Marx nor Engels ever faced up squarely to the problem of power in the economic sphere, and their Communist followers have demonstrated harshly enough for

our satisfaction what can happen in a system in which by definition the problem is assumed not to exist. This, in the final reckoning, is why we could never accept the Marxist prescription for
economic bliss.

Let me conclude these two chapters on Marx's socio-economic
teachings by presenting his thoughts about several notable institutions of American society. To each of these our tradition accords
a place of respect and even sanctity; for each, certainly as we
know them, Marxism has severe contempt.

The first is the church, or more properly the churches, whose
spiritual and social contributions to the American community are
so immense that one could not imagine what our way of life
would be like without them. This, of course, is exactly what Marx
likes to imagine: a society without religion and the institutions
that support it. His scorn for religion as the quintessence of idealism is matched by his hatred of it as the most reactionary of social
forces. In his opinion, as we learned in Chapter II, the churches
are the symbol and bulwark of an imperfect social order, and they
will drop from sight and even from memory as the order progresses
dialectically toward perfection. For the time being, they must be
exposed and opposed. They come not to comfort the spirits of
men but to drug them, not to reform the evils of society but to
propitiate them, not to bless the quest for truth but to frustrate
it. Whatever the Soviet Union may concede to the Metropolitan
of Moscow or bestow upon the Dean of Canterbury, orthodox
Marxism makes no secret of its plans for the churches. They are
not, to put it mildly, the plans of most Americans, even of those
who prize this part of our tradition for its support of their indifference.

Marx's plans for the family are a little more difficult to decipher.
The *Communist Manifesto* is sprinkled with comments such as
these:

On what foundation is the present family, the bourgeois family, based? On capital, on private gain. In its completely developed form this family exists only among the bourgeoisie.

The bourgeois family will vanish . . . with the vanishing of capital.[30]

And Engels, who worked from Marx's notes after his death, writes in *The Origin of the Family, Private Property and the State:*

The modern individual family is founded on the open or concealed domestic slavery of the wife, and modern society is a mass composed of these individual families as its molecules.

In the great majority of cases today, at least in the possessing classes, the husband is obliged to earn a living and support his family, and that in itself gives him a position of supremacy, without any need for special legal titles and privileges. Within the family he is the bourgeois and the wife represents the proletariat.[31]

On the other hand, they laugh out loud at the bourgeois nightmare of communism as a "community of women," and sound like a team of revivalist preachers in their onslaught against adultery and prostitution and in their defense of monogamy and the purity of women. Nevertheless, out of the passion and piety of their comments upon the family and marriage we can extract this solid core of beliefs: 1) The family is located well up in the superstructure of society, which means that it is primarily a response to the requirements of the mode of production. 2) The bourgeois family, like bourgeois society, is basically corrupt, especially in the short shrift it gives women and children.* 3) The end of private property and coming of communism will produce a new kind of family in which all members will have genuinely equal rights. "However terrible," Marx writes,

and disgusting the dissolution, under the capitalist system, of the old family ties may appear, nevertheless, modern industry, by assigning as it does an important part in the process of production, outside the

---

* "The so-called freedom of the American woman is a myth," William Z. Foster has written. "Either she is a gilded butterfly bourgeois parasite or she is an oppressed slave." [32]

domestic sphere, to women, to young persons, and to children of both sexes, creates a new economical foundation for a higher form of the family and of the relations between the sexes. It is, of course, just as absurd to hold the Teutonic-christian form of the family to be absolute and final as it would be to apply that character to the ancient Roman, the ancient Greek, or the Eastern forms which, more-over, taken together form a series in historic development.[33]

Marx and Engels do not, as usual, tell us much about the future, but a few things seem certain. Monogamy, "far from disappear-ing," will "on the contrary be realised completely" for the first time;[34] man will seek out woman for her love rather than for her dowry; and adultery and prostitution will fade from the scene. Most important for our consideration, the family will apparently be stripped of its private character. In Engels' words:

> With the transfer of the means of production into common owner-ship, the single family ceases to be the economic unit of society. Pri-vate housekeeping is transformed into a social industry. The care and education of the children becomes a public affair.[35]

The goal toward which Marx and Engels look hopefully is "the liberation of the wife," and for that the "first condition . . . is to bring the whole female sex back into public industry." Lenin spoke to this point in 1919, in this instance certainly as a faithful Marxist:

> Notwithstanding all the liberating laws that have been passed, woman continues to be a *domestic slave,* because *petty housework* crushes, strangles, stultifies and degrades her, chains her to the kitchen and to the nursery, and wastes her labor on barbarously unproduc-tive, petty, nerve-racking, stultifying and crushing drudgery. The real *emancipation of women,* real Communism, will begin only when a mass struggle . . . is started against this petty domestic economy, or rather when it is *transformed on a mass scale* into large-scale so-cialist economy. . . .
> Public dining rooms, *crèches,* kindergartens—these are examples of the shoots, the simple everyday means, which assume nothing pompous, grandiloquent or solemn, but which can in fact emancipate

women, which can in fact lessen and abolish their inferiority to men in regard to their role in social production and in social life.[36]

We are bound to conclude, in the light of these observations and predictions, that the family in a genuinely Marxist society—which in this instance the Soviet Union certainly is not (but Communist China may well be)—would be thoroughly integrated into the life of the community. There is no more place for the private family than there is for the private man, and this is the point at which we must break cleanly with Marx and Engels. We have gone a long way since their time in the direction they counseled, which other men had counseled even before them. We have tempered the domination of the father; we have thrown all manner of protective laws and customs about the children; we have seen millions of women surge "back into public industry." Most of us would agree cordially with Marx's observation, "Social progress can be measured exactly by the social position of the fair sex (the ugly ones included)." [37] Yet we still pull up well short—thanks to our tradition, piety, and prudence—of any decisive action to wipe out the barriers between society and the family. So, too, do the people of the Soviet Union, who have done their best to prove that the family is not located in the superstructure at all, and who have made law and custom conform to their tenacious ways rather than to Bolshevik hopes.[38] The difference remains, of course, in the fact that orthodox Marxists must condemn these barriers or deny that they exist, while we cherish them not only for the sake of the family itself, but as a natural bulwark against the total society.

The Marxist solution to the question of education mingles radical purpose and conservative method in such a bewildering formula that it is hardly possible to set up a meaningful confrontation in this vital field. Marx and Engels had little to say on the subject. Here and there one stumbles across a sentence that shows their determination to rescue education from the corrupting influence of the bourgeoisie, to reverse the trend toward specialization by setting up the "whole man" as the ideal product, to introduce free public education "for all children," to integrate education with "industrial production," and generally to have the schools take a significant part in the building of the new society.[39] But in this matter they left the Communists of the twentieth century even freer than usual to do as they pleased.

This is exactly what the Communists have done, and the retreat from progressivism to old-fashioned pedagogy in the Soviet schools is a fascinating chapter in the history of education. Once Soviet pedagogues talked cheerily of "spontaneous education" and "the withering away of the school" and "learning through doing"; now they are committed to a theory of education that puts sweeping trust in formal, even formalized methods of instruction. Many sober-minded American educators feel that the Communists have gone much too far with their shift "from a highly experimental, extremely permissive system, in which the basic assumption was an idealized conception of the child, to a traditionalistic approach which places a high emphasis on discipline and obedience." [40] Those who still insist on identifying Dewey's progressivism with Stalin's Communism should devote an hour or two to George Counts's presentation and critique of Soviet pedagogy in *I Want to be Like Stalin*.[41] Despite many apparent agreements in method and even purpose, there can be no real peace between Marxism and the American tradition in the field of education—for a reason that Marx himself would have been the first to acknowledge. Education in the Communist countries is directed purposefully toward Communist ends. In the words of the orthodox:

> The Soviet school cannot be satisfied to rear merely educated persons. Basing itself on the facts and deductions of progressive science, it should instill the ideology of Communism in the minds of the young generation, shape a Marxist-Leninist world outlook and inculcate the spirit of Soviet patriotism and Bolshevik ideas in them.[42]

> Education in the U.S.S.R. is a weapon for strengthening the Soviet state and the building of a classless society.[43]

Education in America is directed, somewhat less purposefully, toward American ends. Since the Communists' chief end is a society organized on the basis of One Great Truth, control of education is centered decisively in those who are recognized as the guardians of this truth; and there is small place for variety, experiment, or local self-direction. Since our chief end is a society hospitable to a pluralism of values, control of education is dispersed widely; and there is a large place (some critics think too large) for variety and decentralization. The importance of private schools and colleges in the American system is an honest measure of the wide gap between our ideas and theirs. The private school as we know it would be unthinkable under orthodox Marxism. For them the final purpose of education is to create a new being called Soviet Man; for us it is to take man as he is and to help him toward the delights and disciplines of liberty. We need plenty of lessons in how to do this better, but we could hardly accept them from either Marx or Lenin or Stalin.[44] They can serve as grim warnings to those Americans (of whom we have a larger share than our tradition calls for) who like to think that we, too, possess One Great Truth with which our children should be relentlessly indoctrinated.

If organic groups (*Gemeinschaften*) like the church, family, and school are to be swallowed up in the collective society of which Marx dreamed fondly, what fate awaits voluntary associations (*Gesellschaften*) like labor unions, fraternal orders, and private charities? No kinder fate, if the truth be known, than swift oblivion—with the party rather than history wielding the broad ax of doom. I hardly think it necessary to linger upon the Marxist attitude toward fraternal associations or even philanthropy, which Engels damned as "self-complacent," "pharisaic," and "degrading." [45] Let me concentrate on the place of trade unions in the Marxist scheme.

Marx and Engels had scant respect for unions. They could not believe that the workers would reap any lasting benefits from them, and they supported them chiefly as crude weapons of the class struggle, which were to be cast on the scrap heap as soon as keener ones were forged. A union was a training ground for revolution, a breeder of class consciousness, or it was nothing at all. They could not foresee the powerful workers' organizations of Britain, France, and the United States. We go to them in vain for enlightenment on the position, power, responsibility, and functions of the modern union. They give no instruction; worse, they offer no defense. Toward the end of their lives they caught a glimpse of what the trade unions of Britain might become and do, and it unsettled them badly. They could have no patience with organizations that proved the proletariat to be either less miserable or less revolutionary than they had proclaimed it to be, that attempted to reform capitalism by bargaining and legislating, and that defied the whole pattern of their predictions for social and political development. If they feared unions in the present, they ignored them in their plans for the future. Nothing that we would recognize as a "free" trade union had any place in their calculations for socialist or communist society. The union, even under a democratic socialist system, is essentially a private, non-governmental center of power, and for such an organization the collective society can leave no room.

Whatever doubts might have existed on this score were resolved once and for all by Lenin. He saw clearly and said repeatedly that "pure and simple trade unionism" meant "the ideological enslavement of the workers to the bourgeoisie." [46] The very concept of a "free" union, a workers' association that is not an arm of the state, is intolerable to Marxist-Leninist minds. The conversion of Soviet trade unions under the first Five Year Plan from more or less independent organs for expressing workers' interests to completely dependent organs for regulating labor was, under the circumstances of a Marxist-Leninist society, an inevitable step. [47] "The trade unions," Bukharin had warned almost at the beginning of Bolshevik power, "must develop in such a way that they will be transformed into . . . instruments of the State authority; they must be 'statified.' " [48] If there are more hypocritical words than those lavished on trade unions by American Communists, I have not heard them.[49] Unions as we have known them would and could have no place at all in their America.

I have saved my few thoughts on private property until the last, for the clash of opinion between Marxism and the American tradition over the place of this institution in the well-ordered society provides a fitting climax to these two chapters. Private property in the means of production appears to Marx and Engels as both the cause and symbol of the ills of nonsocialist society. To the extent that we continue to cherish it as an essential of personal liberty and social well-being, we are at bluff odds with their prescriptions for the present and their prophecies for the future.

I am as tired of saying what I am about to say as my readers are of reading it, but once again I must proclaim the disturbing fact that neither Marx nor Engels is very exact or expansive in describing an institution of key significance in their analysis.[50] They make only a feeble attempt to distinguish between personal property and "property in the means of production," between property for bare existence and property for vulgar display, or between property as right and property as power. Most of their harsh words are aimed at private property in the means of production, which is the means of exploitation, the cause of alienation, and the source of corruption. It is the technique through which some men appropriate the labor of other men and cheat them of a fair return on the value they produce. As such it must and will be wiped out by the proletarians, who are to seize these means and place them in the keeping of the whole community while preparing the way for the final transit to communism. In Vyshinsky's orthodox words:

The dominance of the socialist system of economy and socialist property signifies the creation of an economic basis of society wherein private property is abrogated, instruments and means of production become the property of the entire nation, and man's exploitation of man—and the possibilities thereof—are completely and forever abolished.[51]

The total unwillingness of Marx and Engels to compromise with the bourgeois present is dramatized by their insistence on the socialization of productive land. Just what they thought would be left as private property for the individual under communism is impossible to say with certainty, although one might imagine the citizen of the future owning a modest house, furnishings, books, clothes, tools, and even a small plot of land,[52] or one might imagine him owning nothing but a toothbrush—if he were willing to share it. An aura of collectivism, and thus of collective living, pervades most of Marx's vague prophecies of life under communism, and I am inclined to think that he would expect and welcome the end of all personal property (certainly of property passed from one generation to the next) as the condition for the flowering of the truly human person. Still, I said at the beginning of this book that we should look at Marx in the most favorable light, and I will therefore leave this question undecided. Let us agree that he would have been willing to tolerate if not to look kindly at the amount and kinds of personal property that one may own in the Soviet Union today.

Even if we say this, we are not saying much to close one of the hugest gaps between Marxism and the American tradition. Our tradition, as we have learned already, is committed heavily to private ownership of productive property. It makes a special place for the Post Office and T.V.A. and Oak Ridge, but it is profoundly hostile to socialism as a total way of life. We have learned the hard way that the ownership of productive property is a form of social power subject to gross abuses, but we insist, in defiance of Marx, that we can eliminate most of these abuses through public regulation. If we were to turn to socialism as a corrective to them, we would open ourselves to a whole new array of abuses whose size and sorrow can only be imagined by observing Marxism in action.

Our commitment to property goes deeper than that, although we have been bashful about proclaiming it in recent years. The American definition of liberty has always included the right to acquire, hold, use, and dispose of private property, as well as to enjoy the fruits that can be fairly reaped from it. Whether natural or civil, whether given or earned, whether personal or social, the right of private property is a fundamental of the American tradition. Among the points we have made effectively in its defense are these:

Property makes it possible for a man to be free.* It gives him a place on which to stand and make free choices; it grants him a sphere in which he may ignore the state.

Property makes it possible for a man to develop in mind and spirit. Tools, house, land, clothes, books, heirlooms—all these are important for man's growth to maturity.

Property is essential to the existence of the family, the key unit of society.

The desire to acquire and hold property is essential to social progress, since it is a major spur to productive work.

Property is an important technique for the diffusion of economic and political power.[54]

One could think of still other points that might be made in defense of private property, but these should be enough to demonstrate its place in the American tradition. We make no case for its abuse or neglect, or for its existence in grotesque forms and exaggerated concentrations. We are prepared to assert the necessity of broad regulation of its uses in the public interest. We must acknowledge that we, too, have been careless in failing to distinguish between personal property and "property in the means of production." But we cling to the notion, at which Marxists can

---

* On this point, in effect, we strike agreement with Marx, who insisted that men without property must be the "slaves" of those with it.[53]

only laugh or rage, that property of both kinds is essential to human liberty and social progress. It is not a privilege granted to men simply because it would be too much trouble to exterminate. It is a right that expresses one important part of their needs and nature, and as such it rests in the foundation of the good society. The Marxist must deny this or be counted an imperfect Marxist.

We are not yet done with the sociology of communism, for as sociologist, Marx was also concerned with the state—with its present role in preserving capitalism and with its future role in destroying it. Let me ease the transition from these chapters to the next by quoting from one of Marx's most famous letters, which he wrote to his friend Weydemeyer in 1852. It looks back to catch the essence of his view of society; it looks ahead to catch the spirit of his design for politics:

And now as to myself, no credit is due to me for discovering the existence of classes in modern society nor yet the struggle between them. Long before me bourgeois historians had described the historical development of this class struggle and bourgeois economists the economic anatomy of the classes. What I did that was new was to prove: 1) that the *existence of classes* is only bound up with *particular, historic phases in the development of production;* 2) that the class struggle necessarily leads to the *dictatorship of the proletariat;* 3) that this dictatorship itself only constitutes the transition to the *abolition of all classes* and to a *classless society.*[55]

SIX · THE MARXIST STATE

Marx is a tough nut for political scientists to crack and chew. He is always numbered among the giants of political theory, and teachers pay him all the respect they pay Plato or Machiavelli or Hobbes or Rousseau. At the same time, he was not, properly speaking, a political theorist at all. The whole tendency of his observations on government was to deny its significance and ultimately even its necessity—and what kind of political theorist, we are bound to ask, would want to do that? Lenin was neither the first nor last to discover that Marx is a poor guide to the use of political power. The Marxists of today have made their own peace with his theory of politics (or rather of no-politics) by ignoring some of his peremptory commands.

It was Lenin who made a political theorist out of Marx, which he did by making a political practice out of Marxism. Leninism, Stalin wrote, "is Marxism in the epoch of imperialism and of the proletarian revolution." [1] It is Marxism carried willy-nilly into the area of political strategy and tactics—in Russia and China, in France and the United States, in Indonesia and Guatemala. I will have much to say about Lenin's additions to Marx and Stalin's to Lenin in the evolution of the Communist theory of the state,

for this is one area in which the Marxists after Marx wer~
to do some creative thinking of their own. It sh~
state here that Lenin added a great ~
least something of importance to Lenin. une result of this development has been an even larger amount of confusion than we
have been persuaded to accept as part of the price of studying
Marx. The cardinal question—how much responsibility for the
political theory of Lenin and Stalin can we properly attribute to
Marx?—is the toughest part of the nut, and political scientists will
be chewing on it for generations to come. Before we can chew on
it ourselves, we must make a special effort to distinguish the
Marxism of Marx from the Marxism of the Marxists, and that is
what I now propose to do.

The political theory of the old Marx, if not of the new Marxists,
can be mastered with the least fuss by projecting it onto the pattern
laid out in Chapter I: the four successive stages of description,
prediction, prescription, and prophecy. Let us first hear what
Marx and Engels had to say about the government in each of these
stages, then learn what happened to their teachings in "the epoch
of imperialism and of the proletarian revolution." For the clearest
exposition of these teachings we turn to *Anti-Dühring* and *The
Origin of the Family, Private Property and the State*. Once again
we are reminded of "the importance of being Engels."

In describing the governments of their time, Marx and Engels
sound like classical Liberals who have the courage of their convictions. The essence of classical Liberalism, as we know from
living with Jefferson, was a profound distrust of the state. Marx
and Engels, who had reason to hate most of the states under which
they lived, shared this distrust with men whom they otherwise opposed lustily. Throughout their writings, even in their most private
correspondence, there runs a "red thread" of hatred for political
authority. It was the authority of the bourgeoisie, of course, which
stirred their anger, but like most political thinkers they moved

effortlessly from the specific to the general, and thus ended up in a posture of hostility to the very idea of government. The main features of this posture, the basic assumptions of the Marxist theory of the state,[2] are these:

First, the state is not a "natural" but a man-created institution. It does not necessarily exist wherever men associate for common ends. Man is by nature a social but not a political animal; his needs and aspirations demand the existence of society but not of government. "The state," Engels insists, "has not existed from all eternity. There have been societies which managed without it, which had no notion of the state or state power." [3]

Second, the state arises out of the class struggle, which itself arises with the establishment of private property. "The state," Engels writes,

is a product of society at a particular stage of development; it is the admission that this society has involved itself in insoluble self-contradiction and is cleft into irreconcilable antagonisms which it is powerless to exorcise. But in order that these antagonisms, classes with conflicting economic interests, shall not consume themselves and society in fruitless struggle, a power, *apparently* standing above society, has become necessary to moderate the conflict and keep it within the bounds of "order"; and this power, arisen out of society, but placing itself above it and increasingly alienating itself from it, is the state.[4]

The state, therefore, is simply an instrument of class rule, the means through which the ruling class in any society exploits all other classes in behalf of profits and power.

As the state arose from the need to keep class antagonisms in check, but also arose in the thick of the fight between the classes, it is normally the state of the most powerful, economically ruling class, which by its means becomes also the politically ruling class, and so acquires new means of holding down and exploiting the oppressed class. The ancient state was, above all, the state of the slave-owners for holding down the slaves, just as the feudal state was the organ of the nobility for holding down the peasant serfs and bondsmen, and the modern representative state is the instrument for exploiting wage-labor by capital.[5]

There may come times in the life of a society, Marx concedes in *The Eighteenth Brumaire,* when the state appears as an equilibrating rather than exploiting force.[6] And in *The Origin of the Family* Engels gives several examples:

Exceptional periods, however, occur when the warring classes are so nearly equal in forces that the state power, as *apparent* mediator, acquires for the moment a certain independence in relation to both. This applies to the absolute monarchy of the seventeenth and eighteenth centuries, which balances the nobility and the bourgeoisie against one another; and to the Bonapartism of the First and particularly of the Second French Empire, which played off the proletariat against the bourgeoisie and the bourgeoisie against the proletariat.[7]

The key words in the first and third passages just quoted are "apparently" and "apparent," which leave us with the clear understanding that Marx and Engels regard these periods as "exceptional." Even at the height of such periods the state remains essentially an instrument of class rule. Engels concedes this point in his very next sentence:

The latest achievement in this line, in which ruler and ruled look equally comic, is the new German Empire of the Bismarckian nation; here the capitalists and the workers are balanced against one another and both of them fleeced for the benefit of the decayed Prussian cabbage junkers.

When the capitalists have finally come to power in Germany, Engels seems to say, there will be no doubt for whom and for what purpose the Prussian state exists. Then it will be seen that it is an illusion to think of government seriously as an instrument for managing the pursuit of the common interests of society, not least because, as we have learned already, there are no such interests in bourgeois society.

Next, the basis of the state, to put it as gently as possible, is force. Talk of "the consent of the governed" is nonsense, for "an essential mark of the state consists in a public power of coercion divorced from the masses of the people." [8] The whole structure of law is based on this hard fact of political life. The law is an instrument of the ruling class, and its sole purpose is the protection of private property. It achieves this purpose primarily through the threat and application of force to men who could not possibly have consented to its enactment in even their most resigned moments. The same may be said of the power of taxation: it, too, rests upon force and not consent.[9]

In his *Civil War in France* Marx speaks of the state as a "parasite feeding upon, and clogging the free movement of, society" [10]— a phrase written in anger, yet expressing honestly another key assumption in his theory of the state. Surely it follows from everything we have learned that government, whether it is the possession of a dying or a rising ruling class, is a foreign growth on the body of society. It feeds on the society, indeed it sucks its blood; and in return it gives the society exactly nothing of value.

Finally, the state is lodged in the superstructure that rises upon the economic base, which means that the mode of government bears a direct relation to the mode of production. "The specific economic form," Marx writes in *Capital,* "determines the relation of rulers and ruled." [11] And in his preface to *A Contribution to the Critique of Political Economy* he adds, "Legal relations such as forms of state are to be grasped neither from themselves nor from the so-called general development of the human mind, but rather have their roots in the material conditions of life." [12] Of all institutions, bad or good, the state is the most sensitive to changes in the mode of production, especially as their influence is transmitted through the class struggle. The bourgeois state, Engels writes, "is on the whole only a reflex, in comprehensive form, of the economic needs of the class controlling production." [13]

•

Working to and from this general theory of the state, Marx and Engels come to two conclusions of special interest to us. The first is that the latest and "highest form of the state, the democratic republic," is a travesty compounded of hypocrisy and oppression.[14] It is a gaudy façade behind which the bourgeoisie goes about its appointed business of exploiting the workers.

All institutions of parliamentary democracy are designed to keep the people at a safe distance from the seats of power. Constitutions are strings of traps set along the dreary road to reform, into which even the most astute radicals are sure to stumble. Bills of rights are clever devices calculated to give "formal" freedom to the multitude and to reserve "effective" freedom to the bourgeoisie. Legislative assemblies are pageants in which any representatives of the proletariat who may gain admittance are either ignored, slandered, or seduced by the minions of "parliamentary cretinism." Presidents and premiers and ministers are members of a grand "committee for managing the common affairs of the whole bourgeoisie," not of the whole people.[15] Elections are another kind of pageant in which no real division of opinion and interest is permitted to develop; the parties that contest them are all servants of the dominant bourgeoisie. They squabble eternally over "place, pelf, and patronage,"[16] but never over the issues that are of real concern to society. On such issues they maintain a united front in behalf of the ruling class. In short, the constitutional democracies of the West are governments of, by, and for a small minority of the people, the bourgeoisie, which means that they are just one more efficient instrument of "the dictatorship of capital." All activities of the bourgeois state, however innocent some of them may appear at first or even second glance, are expressions of the bourgeois need to rule.

This instrument, Marx admits, has been rendered somewhat more popular and thus somewhat less efficient by the drive toward universal suffrage. But the bourgeoisie is merely being more subtle in its methods of control. While it grants the vote to the workers with a reluctant hand, it keeps the other hand firmly on the levers. of effective power. If "the democratic republic," Engels asserts,. "no longer officially recognizes differences of property" in de-- termining the rights and privileges of individuals in political life;. this does not mean that the balance of power is shifting to the mass of people.

Wealth here employs its power indirectly, but all the more surely. It does this in two ways: by plain corruption of officials, of which America is the classic example, and by an alliance between the govern- ment and the stock exchange.[17]

This reference to America is only one of many similar observa- tions scattered through the writings of Marx and Engels. They know full well that the United States has pushed far beyond the old countries of Europe in its surge toward universal suffrage and popular participation in politics, but the only significant result, in their opinion, has been the conversion of American democracy into the gaudiest, most clever façade of all. In his introduction of 1891 to a new edition of Marx's *Civil War in France,* Engels com- pares the public men of Grover Cleveland's United States to those of Napoleon III's France.

Nowhere do "politicians" form a more separate, powerful section of the nation than in North America. . . . We find here two great gangs of political speculators, who alternately take possession of the state power and exploit it by the most corrupt means and for the most corrupt ends—and the nation is powerless against these two great cartels of politicians, who are ostensibly its servants, but in reality exploit and plunder it.[18]

Although Engels appears to be toying again with the notion of the politicians as a separate interest rising above the class struggle, he makes clear elsewhere that the "two great gangs of political speculators," the Republicans and the Democrats, are themselves all members or servants of the dominant bourgeoisie, which holds on doggedly to the power of the state no matter which gang hap- pens to be at the trough for the moment. In America, as in all capitalist countries, the state is the servant of the ruling class. The institutions of parliamentary democracy and the ideas of Liberalism are weapons forged on the anvil of capitalist production to the specifications of the bourgeoisie.

Marx's second conclusion flows from his commitment to historical materialism rather than from his observations of the bourgeois governments of his day. This commitment to a theory of economic causation of social and political events, stiffened by a profound dislike of the reformers of his day, inspires him to deny that government can ever be of primary importance in the life of society—except perhaps at a time of profound social upheaval, and then only to spark the "leap" to a new stage of history. It is the mode of production, not the power of government, that directs the lives and pursuits of the contending classes, and the power of government can never be equal to the task of genuine social and economic reform. The futility of political activity and the inadequacy of political authority form a double-barreled assumption that lies at the core of Marx's theory of the state. This is one of those occasions, not half so rare as some people might think, when Marx seems to agree unreservedly with the laissez-faire economists.

One consequence of this assumption is to deny that economic forces are amenable to legislative correction and administrative control, and thus to deride as mere "palliatives" the piecemeal efforts at reform of the farsighted or conscience-stricken members of the bourgeoisie. Another is to question the capacity of the political process to effect peaceable adjustments among the contending interests in society. And a third is to assert that the onward struggle of a class or group in the field of politics can move only a little distance ahead of its progress in the field of economics. Finally, Marx is encouraged to reaffirm his conviction that the reality of man lies in his labor and not in his political aspirations or activities. One of his pointed criticisms of political democracy is that it concerns itself with matters of secondary importance, and that in so doing it ignores the true nature of man, the animal that is social and economic but not political.[19]

A word or two might be added on this question of Marx's attitude toward the possibility of social reform through the use of political authority. In general, he and Engels had neither sympathy nor patience with that "part of the bourgeoisie . . . desirous of redressing social grievances"—"economists, philanthropists, humanitarians, improvers of the condition of the working class, organizers of charity, members of societies for the prevention of cruelty to animals, hole-and-corner reformers of every imaginable kind." For one thing, these men were pushing for reform only "in order to secure the continued existence of bourgeois society"; [20] for another, they had no more chance than anyone else in this society to make changes in the superstructure that were not reflections of changes in the base.[21] Neither evolution nor revolution could come "from above." Marx's conviction that only a genuine proletarian revolution would cure the ills of bourgeois society had much to do with this attitude of contempt for the persons, doctrines, and hopes of the reformers of the nineteenth century, for he was certain that such a revolution had to come "from below." He considered political reform inadvisable largely because he considered it impossible.

It is true, of course, that he gave support from time to time to trade unions and political organizations of the workingmen of England, France, Germany, and the United States. He did this, however, not out of any confidence that the workers would gain concrete benefits from such activity, but in the expectation that it would quicken their class consciousness and thus prepare the ground for revolution. Late in life Engels was to concede, in the famous letter to Bloch chastising the extreme economic determinism of the young Marxists,[22] that politics could have some influence on economics, and that, in effect, the power of government to alter the conditions of social and economic life was not entirely negligible. But even in this attempt to redress the balance of forces that men had found proclaimed in his and Marx's writings, Engels left the final and "decisive" role to economics. No teaching of classical Marxism seems more deeply rooted in the writings of the masters than that of the primacy of economics over politics—in the course of history, in the structure of society, in the behavior of man.

Marx's prediction of the immediate future of bourgeois democracy holds cold comfort for the ruling class. The façade behind which the bourgeoisie operates is growing more rickety with the passage of each year, and the juggling and corruption that have been going on quietly for generations are now brutally visible to all who have eyes to see—and sense enough to use Marxist lenses in their glasses. More and more members of the proletariat are becoming resentfully aware of the nature of bourgeois democracy; more and more members of the bourgeoisie itself are being driven into the ranks of the awakening proletariat. The class struggle is rising in fury; and, as it grows more vicious, it takes on increasingly the marks of a political struggle. Thus, for a moment at least, Marx looks almost benignly upon the "democratic republic," for he recognizes it as the last necessary stage before the proletarian revolution. In his *Critique of the Gotha Programme* he talks scornfully of that "vulgar democracy, which sees the millennium in the democratic republic and has no suspicion that it is precisely in this last state form of bourgeois society that the class struggle has to be fought out to a conclusion." [23] And Engels puts the ambivalence of their attitude toward the bourgeoisie, an attitude that considers it both historically necessary and historically doomed, in a few blunt words:

Fight on bravely, then, dear gentlemen of capital! We need your help; we need even your rule upon occasion. You must clear from our path the relics of the Middle Ages and of absolute monarchy. You must abolish monarchy, you must centralise, you must change all more or less destitute classes into real proletarians—recruits for us. Your factories and trade connections must lay the foundations for the liberation of the proletariat. Your reward shall be a brief period of rule. You shall dictate laws, and bask in the sun of your own majesty. . . . But remember—the hangman's foot is upon the threshold.[24]

The "brief period of rule" is even now coming to an end; the hangman's foot is over the threshold. And the hangman is the proletariat, politically conscious and politically organized. Marx predicts the entrance of the proletariat, in full force and under astute management, onto the stage of politics for the first time. Politics is important only in an age of revolution, and the last of such ages is upon us.

Marx does more than predict the rise of the proletariat to political power. He prescribes it, and he does it with that air compounded of scientific confidence and moral passion which gives all his calls to arms their peculiar appeal. His political prescriptions, such as they are, are directed exclusively to the leaders of the proletariat. He tells them what to do in each of the three successive situations in which they will find themselves in the next few years: 1) democratic disintegration; 2) proletarian revolution; and 3) proletarian consolidation. The nations of the world, each in its own time, will move from one period to the next in obedience to the iron laws of history, but Marx is anxious that the inevitable be made as quick and heroic as possible.

In the first period, upon which France, England, and the United States are already well embarked, the chief business of the proletariat is to prepare for and advance the coming revolution. This calls for the support of all programs and the exploitation of all events that aggravate the contradictions of capitalism and deepen the corruptions of democracy. Like all the Marxists who have followed him, Marx was faced with the question of how far Communists, the politically organized and scientifically oriented leaders of the proletariat, should go in co-operating and compromising with other apparently progressive groups. Like all of them he answered straightforwardly: just as far as is necessary to serve the all-consuming purpose of proletarian revolution. Co-operation with another group or class is permissible if it contributes to the weakening of the bourgeoisie, but the co-operation is never that of equal or like-minded partners. The proletariat is the chosen people of history, the only class with a future, and it enters into bargains and associations on its own terms, for its own purposes, and with its own mission firmly in mind.

Marx and Engels made all this clear in their *Address to the Communist League*,[25] in which they advised their friends in Germany how to act in the confusion following hard upon the unsuccessful revolution of 1848. The situation was one in which the proletariat had much to gain by working in concert with the dissatisfied middle class. The exiles in London told the leaders how to reap maximum benefit for the cause:

> The relation of the revolutionary workers' party to petty-bourgeois democracy is this: it marches together with it against the section which it aims at overthrowing, it opposes the petty bourgeois in everything by which they desire to establish themselves.
> The democratic petty bourgeois, far from desiring to revolutionise all society for the revolutionary proletarians, strive for a change in social conditions by means of which existing society will be made as tolerable and comfortable as possible for them.

After listing the demands through which the petty bourgeoisie hoped to improve and secure its position (cheaper government, a shift in the tax burden, abolition of feudal land laws), Marx and Engels went on:

> These demands can in no wise suffice for the party of the proletariat. While the democratic petty bourgeois wish to bring the revolution to a conclusion as quickly as possible and with the achievement at most of the above demands, it is our interest and our task to make the revolution permanent. . . . For us the issue cannot be the alteration of private property but only its abolition, not the smoothing over

of class antagonisms but the abolition of classes, not the improvement of existing society but the foundation of a new one.

From here they moved on to give specific advice on how to organize openly and secretly, how to goad the bourgeoisie to more radical steps, how to compromise on small points without abandoning the main goal. And how were Communists to behave toward democratic colleagues when a great victory had been achieved by united efforts?

From the first moment of victory mistrust must be directed not against the conquered reactionary party, but against the workers' previous allies, against the party that wishes to exploit the common victory for itself alone.

And they ended with an appeal to the German proletarians not to allow themselves "for a single moment to be led astray . . . by the hypocritical phrases of the democratic petty bourgeois." No matter how much they might choose to co-operate and compromise, they could not forget that they did it for one purpose only: "the permanent revolution." This piece should be required reading for all men (and all nations) who enter into association with Communists for common political ends. Lenin was never truer to Marx than when he criticized his comrade Axelrod in 1899 for having talked of "support for and alliance with" the democratic opposition to Czarism. "In my opinion," he wrote, *"utilize* is a much more accurate and appropriate word than *support* and *alliance."* [26] To the American eye, indeed to any eye not fogged by a doctrinaire mistrust of Western values, the amorality of Marxism in the area of political compromise is shockingly visible. Yet this remains one of the hardest lessons for the men of the West to keep fresh in their minds.

In the period of revolution the duty of the proletariat is clear on the face of history: to organize the ranks for armed action, to seize the machinery of the state, to smash this machinery into pieces that can never be glued together again, and to prepare for the tasks of the socialist transition by instituting the "dictatorship of the proletariat." The first and second of these prescriptions for revolutionary action require no elaboration, but a word might be said about the third. One of the bones of contention among revolutionaries of Marx's time was the question of how many features of the bourgeois form of government could be converted to proletarian use after the seizure of power. We should therefore note carefully that the only amendment Marx ever cared to make to the *Communist Manifesto* (in the Preface to the German edition of 1872) was designed to call a halt to this debate. "The working class," he wrote in echo of his *Civil War in France,* "cannot simply lay hold of the ready-made state machinery, and wield it for its own purposes." [27] All parts of this machinery are contaminated by bourgeois use and bourgeois ideology; they must be destroyed utterly along with the men who have operated them.

The fourth prescription for the period of revolution is also the key prescription for the period that follows it. It is here, in the proposal of a "dictatorship of the proletariat," that we come upon one of the most celebrated teachings in the political theory of Marxism. One cannot be much of a Marxist if one does not call and work for the dictatorship of the proletariat, and we must be quite clear in our minds what Marx meant by this phrase.

Marx is not much help to us. He expressed the idea of the dictatorship as early as the *Communist Manifesto* and as late as his last letters, but in all his writings one comes upon this exact phrase, which he seems to have borrowed from the French revolutionary Blanqui, only three or four times. [28] The most significant statement is in the *Critique of the Gotha Programme:*

> Between capitalist and communist society lies the period of the revolutionary transformation of the one into the other. There corresponds to this also a political transition period in which the state can be nothing but *the revolutionary dictatorship of the proletariat.*

As Lenin was later to testify, Marx gave few details about the structure and functioning of the dictatorship of the proletariat. "Without resorting to Utopias," he wrote in 1917, "Marx waited for the *experience* of a mass movement to produce the answer to the problem as to the exact forms which [the] organization of the proletariat as the ruling class will assume." [29] But he did say enough so that we can be reasonably sure of the essence of his teachings about the nature, purpose, and structure of this unique form of government.

It is by nature what all governments are by nature: oppressive. The only real change from past governments is in the identity of the oppressors and the oppressed. For the first time in history the normal pattern of authority is to be reversed in favor of the majority and against the minority. But it will be just as much a dictatorship, just as clearly an instrument of class rule, as all past governments have been. It will be the antithesis not of democracy but of "the dictatorship of the bourgeoisie," and its nature must therefore remain essentially coercive. "So long as the proletariat still *uses* the state," Engels wrote to August Bebel in 1875, "it does not use it in the interests of freedom but in order to hold down its adversaries." [30] "The dictatorship," Bukharin added in words that Marx might have used, "is the axe in the hands of the proletariat." [31]

The purpose of the dictatorship of the proletariat is to use coercive power boldly and imaginatively to prepare the way for the transition to communism. To this great end it must defend the proletariat against counterrevolution, root out the bourgeoisie from its positions of power, sweep away the rubble of the bourgeois state, socialize the means of production by "despotic inroads on the rights of property," and educate the people in modes of behavior suitable to the new society. If it accomplishes these great feats it condemns itself to death, as we shall shortly learn, but it will have completed a mission far nobler than that of any government in history.

The structure of the dictatorship of the proletariat is a matter of some conjecture. Despite certain concessions made by Engels to revisionist sentiment after Marx's death, we know that the dictatorship is not organized on the pattern of the bourgeois democracies, most of whose elaborate paraphernalia of courts and councils and commissions are to be swept into oblivion. But we are left well up in the air about even the broad features of the dictatorship—not half so far up, to be sure, as we would have been left if there had not been a popular uprising in Paris in 1871. For the uprising gave birth to the famous Commune, under which the workingmen of Paris and their allies governed much of the city and fought off the troops of Thiers for ten weeks,[32] until at last they were drowned in blood. The Commune has always occupied a sainted place in Marxist mythology; it has been hardly less important for the Marxist theory of the state. On the twentieth anniversary of the Commune, Engels wrote in defiance of the weak-kneed in his camp:

> Of late, the Social-Democratic philistine has once more been filled with wholesome terror at the words: Dictatorship of the Proletariat. Well and good, gentlemen, do you want to know what this dictatorship looks like? Look at the Paris Commune. That was the Dictatorship of the Proletariat.[33]

I doubt that it would profit us much to accept this invitation and review the sad history of the Paris Commune, especially since learned men, including learned Marxists, still cannot seem to agree just what its leaders intended it to be and do. What must interest us is the pattern of institutions and arrangements that Marx and Engels professed to have found in it, for in praising them they went a long way toward describing the government that would carry mankind from capitalism to communism. They admired the Commune particularly for five vast changes it seemed to work in the scheme of political authority: 1) *concentration,* since the Commune itself was "a working, not a parliamentary body, executive and legislative at the same time"; 2) *centralization,* since it intended, according to Marx if not to most other people, to organize "even the smallest country hamlet" on the same principles, and to retain exclusive responsibility for the conduct of national affairs; 3) *popularization,* since the suffrage was made universal, officials were paid workers' wages and rendered subject to recall, and the standing army was replaced by the "armed people";[34] 4) *simplification,* since it made a brave attempt to reduce the complexities of government to an elementary pattern of institutions and a comprehensible set of rules; and 5) *"proletarianization,"* since the working class alone was politically enfranchised.

The Commune did other things to please Marx and Engels, such as disestablishing the Church and making a stab at public education; but the changes in the pattern of government were its chief accomplishments, whether real or simply imagined by Marx. His one additional change in the pattern would have been to obliterate all traces of bourgeois influence, all carry-overs of ideas and techniques from the past. Marx's only real criticism of the Commune (other than his irritation over the smallness of its stage)[35] was that it was not ruthless enough in smashing the bourgeois machinery. One of the lessons of his *Civil War in France,* the work in which he grafted the memory of the Commune onto the mystic body of communism, was that the failure of this first dictatorship of the proletariat could be traced to a squeamish or careless attitude toward certain relics of bourgeois democracy.[36]

This discussion of the Paris Commune raises a question of great interest to non-Marxists: Was Marx a democrat? I wish to put off a final answer to this question until the last chapter, but we can take a large bite out of it here by fixing our attention on Marx's prescription for a dictatorship of the proletariat in the transitional stage of socialism. It is certainly possible to argue that this dictatorship, as he conceived it, was an instrument of what is generally styled "Jacobin democracy." It was, that is to say, the "democracy" of Saint-Just and Babeuf—of the concentration and centralization of authority, of the plebiscite and the mass meeting, of the unchecked majority and the helpless minority, of the sacrifice of liberty to equality, and of the pursuit of the One Great Interest. It was not the democracy we know, and which Marx quite openly despised: the democracy of representative government, dispersed authority, checks and balances, constitutional guarantees, two or more parties, hotly contested elections, and the ultimate reconciliation of most interests. The Commune has appealed to Marxists of all generations precisely, as Trotsky put it, because it was "the living negation of formal democracy." [37] Yet it was, surely, a government conceived as servant of the mass of the people, one in which, so Marx believed, the interests of the great majority would be served for the first time in history. Marx assumed that the men chosen to carry on the dictatorship would somehow be held responsible to the proletariat; he assumed, too, that there would be an active political life marked by free discussion. We may think him foolish for not understanding that this form of government is a standing invitation to the servants to become the masters, and that free discussion is not really free when restricted to those who share the One Great Interest. Yet we cannot deny that this part of his thought is a ticket of admission to a circle of men we admire for their aspirations if not for their prescriptions: Condorcet, Turgot, Helvetius, Sieyès, and, at least in one of the many poses he struck for our instruction and amazement, Jean Jacques Rousseau.* May we therefore conclude that, in the kindest light we can bring to bear, Marx the political strategist was a hard-shelled Jacobin democrat? [38]

Beyond the call for the dictatorship lies the prophecy that sets off Marx all by himself among the giants and even lesser giants of political theory: the state is destined in the fullness of time to pass from the scene of history. This startling prophecy is a natural

---

* While I am on the perplexing subject of Rousseau, I am bound to say that it would be hard to think of a more dramatic projection of the General Will than the class will of the proletariat as it infuses the promised dictatorship.

extension of Marx's theory of the origin of the state in class antagonisms. The state has always been an instrument of class rule; when there are no more classes, there will be no need for the state. It is all just as simple as that. I quote the famous passages in which Engels prophesied for Marx:

At a definite stage of economic development, which necessarily involved the cleavage of society into classes, the state became a necessity because of this cleavage. We are now rapidly approaching a stage in the development of production at which the existence of these classes has not only ceased to be a necessity, but becomes a positive hindrance to production. They will fall as inevitably as they once arose. The state inevitably falls with them. The society which organizes production anew on the basis of free and equal association of the producers will put the whole state machinery where it will then belong—into the museum of antiquities, next to the spinning wheel and the bronze ax.[39]

Whilst the capitalist mode of production more and more completely transforms the great majority of the population into proletarians, it creates the power which, under penalty of its own destruction, is forced to accomplish this revolution. . . . *The proletariat seizes political power and turns the means of production into state property.*

But, in doing this, it abolishes itself as proletariat, abolishes all class distinctions and class antagonisms, abolishes also the state as state. . . . As soon as there is no longer any social class to be held in subjection, . . . a special repressive force, a state, is no longer necessary. The first act by virtue of which the state really constitutes itself the representative of the whole of society—the taking possession of the means of production in the name of society—this is, at the same time, its last independent act as a state. State interference in social relations becomes, in one domain after another, superfluous, and then dies out of itself; the government of persons is replaced by the administration of things, and by the conduct of processes of production. The state is not "abolished." *It dies out* (*Er stirbt ab*).[40]

More poetic translators have rendered *stirbt ab* as "withers away," and I agree with them that the sense of Marx's and Engels' prophecy is captured most neatly in the phrase "the withering away of the state." Whatever the niceties of translation, the sense of their thought is too clear to miss. As Bukharin put it, "There cannot be a state without classes. A classless state is a round square." [41] It may be argued that "the withering away of the state" is based on a naive view of the uses of political power, that it is a Sorelian myth designed to inspire the proletarian revolution, and that Marx, in any case, was simply trying to take the wind out of the sails of his anarchist friends and rivals.[42] Yet I do not see how anyone can misread his genuine confidence that most of what we call "government"—legislatures, administrative bodies, civil service, courts, police, army—will fade into oblivion and be supplanted by a kind of confederated *Gemeinwesen*,[43] a network of freely associating communities by which all are served and in which all participate, not as political but as social beings. If this is the most absurd part of his entire theory of state and society, it is also the most appealing. However much we may blame him for failing to notice the statist tendencies inherent in his teachings, and thus for the blight of Soviet totalitarianism, we must admire his own refusal to glorify the state in any way. It is popular to say that he was not an anarchist, for he gave the state one last mighty task to perform before it withered away.[44] But in one sense, a highly important sense, he was one of the great anarchists in the history of political theory—great in vision, great in failure.

I wish it were possible to halt at this point and to confront Marx and Engels with Adams and Jefferson, for I would thereby spare my readers much confusion and myself much trouble. But we must face together the hard fact that the Marxist theory of the state began to have real influence on the affairs of men only after the death of its authors, and that this theory thereupon underwent several drastic changes. I hardly think it necessary, or perhaps even fair to Marx and Engels, to describe the governments that hold sway today in the Communist countries. My concern is with the changes in theory during the past half-century, the years in which men who thought of themselves as devout Marxists seized and wielded political power on a scale unmatched in all history. Two of these men, Lenin and Stalin, are of particular interest to us because of the theories with which they sought to square their actions with the words of the masters.[45]

The first thing to be noted is that the Communists of the twentieth century have had no trouble repeating all the catchwords and catcalls of political Marxism, especially those aimed at bourgeois democracy. Let us hear, for example, from Lenin's *State and Revolution:*

In capitalist society, under the conditions most favourable to its development, we have more or less complete democracy in the democratic republic. But this democracy is always bound by the narrow framework of capitalist exploitation, and consequently always remains, in reality, a democracy for the minority, only for the possessing classes, only for the rich. Freedom in capitalist society always remains just about the same as it was in the ancient Greek republics: freedom for the slave-owners. . . .

Democracy for an insignificant minority, democracy for the rich— that is the democracy of capitalist society. . . .

Marx splendidly grasped this *essence* of capitalist democracy, when, in analysing the experience of the Commune, he said that the oppressed were allowed, once every few years, to decide which particular representatives of the oppressing class should be in parliament to represent and repress them! [46]

I could spice this passage with a thousand similar quotations from Stalin, Trotsky, Bukharin, Khrushchev, Vyshinsky, and a host of lesser men, but it should suffice to prove that the new Marxism has not retreated one inch from the conviction of the old that bourgeois democracy is nothing more than a screen for "the dictatorship of capital." [47] The futility of political reform, the similarity of all non-Communist parties, the humbug of constitutional processes, the impossibility of effective freedom—all these Marxist strictures against our kind of democracy, as well as the warning that the whole machinery must be smashed into rubble,[48] are on the lips of the faithful today. The followers of Marx, like

Marx himself, have nothing but contempt for the law and institutions of Western democracy—even when they make good use of them. Our law is a "subtle and poisoned instrument which defends the interests of the exploiters"; our institutions are a "machine to crush and to repress the toilers"; our state is a "dreadful octopus, entwining and exhausting with its multiple tentacles the living body of the people." [49] It is "a league of robbers," a "union of the master class, formed to safeguard exploitation." [50]

It is one thing to hurl the slogans of the master at the despised enemy, quite another to put his principles to work in the real world of political power. Lenin always thought of himself as a faithful Marxist, and he did his best, in a series of situations for which Marx was a careless mentor, to keep the faith. In the painful process of learning how to bring off a revolution and then to reap its fruits, Lenin added at least four cubits to the Marxist theory of the state, or, to put it another way, took four long steps toward Bolshevism.

First, he gathered Marx's scattered comments on the necessity of a proletarian party, especially his words of advice to the Communist League,[51] and expanded them into a theory of organization that today forms the hard core of Communist doctrine. Marx's party, to the extent that he described it, was a Western-style workers' party. In a revolutionary situation it was to act in a revolutionary manner; the Communist leaders, "the most advanced and resolute section" of the working class movement, were to give firm direction to "the great mass of the proletariat" in the struggle against the bourgeoisie.[52] But it was, nevertheless, a democratic party in the two key senses of mass membership and responsible leadership, and it was only vaguely identified with the dictatorship of the proletariat.

Lenin's party, as he described it before the revolution in *What is to be Done?* (1902) [53] and after in *"Left-Wing" Communism* (1920), was something quite different, although not so different as to be un-Marxist. Its most important, and to many old Marxists frightening, characteristics were these: 1) a narrow membership, in Lenin's words "a small, compact core, consisting of reliable, experienced and hardened workers"; [54] 2) a smooth-functioning, action-oriented organization not accustomed to wait for the "spontaneity" of the masses to point out "what is to be done"; 3) a high level of discipline, to which all members must submit gladly; 4) a passionate devotion to doctrine, of which the party and not the masses must be the guardian and interpreter; and 5) a relationship to the masses of stern parent to beloved but inexperienced children. The party of Lenin was not a "rear-guard of opportunists" but "a genuine vanguard of the most revolutionary class." [55] It was a "citadel," as Stalin wrote in 1905, "whose doors open only to the worthy." [56]

When Lenin wrote *What is to be Done?*, he was bent on making a revolution in Czarist Russia, and he could be excused if not praised for placing so much emphasis on the necessity of an autocratic party. But in *"Left-Wing" Communism* and other late writings he carried this party out of the world in which Marxists conspire against tyranny and into the world in which they occupy the seats of power. This shift was made official in a resolution adopted at the Second Congress of the Third International in 1920:

> The Communist Party is a part of the working class, namely, its most advanced, class-conscious, and therefore most revolutionary part. The Communist Party is formed of the best, most intelligent, self-sacrificing and far-seeing workers. . . . The Communist Party is the organized political lever by means of which the more advanced part of the working class leads all the proletarian and semi-proletarian mass in the right direction.[57]

To lead the mass in the right direction before, during, and after the revolution: this is the historic assignment that Lenin gave to the party. As he gave it in fact, so he gave it in theory, and thereby

added the one element that expels all democratic tendencies from
Marxism and transforms it into Bolshevism: the close-knit, iron-
disciplined, doctrinally pure party of dedicated revolutionaries
who are ready to lead the proletarian masses at all times and in
all places.[58] If the party is responsible to the masses at all, it is
only before the throne of history. Indeed, in the sense that counts
most, the party *is* the masses. Needless to add, wherever it comes
to power it is the only party permitted to function. It is by definition the party of the proletariat, which means that all other parties
are parties of the bourgeoisie; * and for the power of the bourgeoisie, as we know, the proletarian revolution is a sentence of
death. In a Communist state there is no more room for two parties
than there is for two governments.

This takes us directly into Lenin's second addition or corrective:
the new life he gave to the concept of the dictatorship of the proletariat. This concept, about which Marx the antistatist had been
so casual, had fallen into neglect in the years since his death,
especially among German Marxists; and it was Lenin, first somewhat obliquely in *State and Revolution* (written in August-September 1917), then with conviction in *The Proletarian Revolution and
the Renegade Kautsky* (1918), who put it back in circulation.
He did more than this; he made it an object of uncritical devotion.
"A Marxist," he wrote in *State and Revolution,* "is one who
extends the acceptance of the class struggle to the acceptance of
the *dictatorship of the proletariat."* [60] By admitting and then almost boasting that this dictatorship was a state, by assigning to
it the specific tasks of suppressing the bourgeoisie and educating
the proletariat, by assuming that these tasks would take a very
long time, and finally, in *The Proletarian Revolution,* by describing
it as a "proletarian democracy . . . *a million times* more democratic than any bourgeois democracy," [61] Lenin readmitted the
state to Marxist respectability. *State and Revolution* is full of

---

* In Foster's words, "The Socialist party is a specialized section of the
capitalist machinery for exploiting the toiling masses." [59]

delightful and utterly naive passages* about the simplicity of proletarian government and the withering away of the state,[62] but there is little doubt that Lenin gave the state a place of honor that would have dismayed Marx and Engels.[63] Trotsky was at one with Lenin in his insistence that "the road to Socialism lies through a period of the highest possible intensification of the principle of the State," [64] and so, too, was Bukharin in putting off the stateless society an "epoch," elsewhere defined as at least "two or three generations." [65] "Just as a lamp," Trotsky wrote,

before going out, shoots up in a brilliant flame, so the State, before disappearing, assumes the form of the dictatorship of the proletariat, i.e., the most ruthless form of State, which embraces the life of the citizens authoritatively in every direction.[66]

The third step toward Bolshevism followed hard upon the first two: identification of the party with the dictatorship of the proletariat and thus, no matter how one turns it around, with the state. Lenin, who tried to be both a good Marxist and a successful revolutionary, did not come to this position without much backing and filling. Yet before his death he was able to make this identification with unusual frankness.[67]

Finally, out of the hot arguments with friends and enemies, the anxious genuflections to Marx, and the chilling plunges into reality, there arose in Lenin's political consciousness a new and quite un-Marxist feeling for the uses and delights of political power—"power won and maintained by the violence of the proletariat against the bourgeoisie, power . . . unrestricted by any laws," [68] power "democratically centralized" in the hands of those who know how to use it in behalf of the proletariat. "The continuous and ubiqui-

* The closest thing in American thought to Lenin's naïveté is Andrew Jackson's first annual message to Congress. Jackson asserted that "the duties of all public officers" were or should be "so plain and simple" that all "men of intelligence" could easily prepare for their performance. Lenin went Jackson one better by defining a "man of intelligence" as "anybody who can read and write and knows the first four rules of arithmetic." (John Quincy Adams would doubtless have remarked: "Well, that disqualifies Jackson.")

tous search for power" is the driving force of the Communist party under bourgeois democracy; [69] the persistent and total use of power is its duty under the dictatorship of the proletariat. It is doubtful if any men at any time in history have thirsted for power more passionately or slaked their thirst more greedily than have the Communists, and it was Lenin who transformed this thirst from a sin to a virtue. "The state, my dear people," he said in 1917,

is a class concept. The state is an organ or apparatus of force to be used by one class against another. So long as it remains an apparatus for the bourgeoisie to use force against the proletariat, so long can the slogan of the proletariat be only—the *destruction* of this state. But when the state has become proletarian, when it has become an apparatus of force to be used by the proletariat against the bourgeoisie, then we shall be fully and unreservedly for a strong state power and centralism.[70]

By keeping this promise Lenin toppled the antistatism of Marx over on its side. It remained only for Stalin to stand it on its head, and thus to make Bukharin's "round square" a square square.

It would be a weariness if not indeed a mortification of the flesh to give a full account of Stalin's political theory. Suffice it to say that he was a better Leninist than Lenin was a Marxist, and that he carried each of the new departures—the autocratic party, the full dictatorship of the proletariat, the unity of party and state, and the veneration of power—to new heights of totality and brutality.[71] In particular, he minced no words on the role of the party:

In the Soviet Union, in the land where the dictatorship of the proletariat is in force, no important political or organizational problem is ever decided by our soviets and other mass organizations without directives from our party. In this sense, we may say that the dictatorship of the proletariat is substantially the dictatorship of the party, as the force which effectively guides the proletariat.[72]

The party today, thanks to Lenin, Stalin, and their heirs, is the driving force of Soviet society,[73] in the words of the Soviet Constitution the "vanguard of the working people in their struggle to build communist society" and the "leading core of all organizations of the working people, both public and state." In one sense, it *is* the society, and Soviet thinkers sound a note of sheer mysticism in making an organic connection—even an identification—of the party with the state, the party with the people, even the party with truth and reason. Unfortunately, this mystic view is grounded on a harsh reality, for the party does serve as a commanding, directing, inspiring elite for the Soviet masses. It controls the whole process of election,[74] permeates and directs the military and economic bureaucracies, dictates taste and manners and morality, rules over the arts and sciences, and "guards the purity" of Marxist-Leninist ideology "as the apple of its eye." It is centralized and disciplined within,[75] monopolistic and autocratic without. It sits squarely on the support, real or alleged, of the masses, but it remains faithfully Leninist in its attitude that they are unenlightened, unpredictable children who must be led into the future by men "of a special mold." [76] The cult of the party has risen in intensity since the death of Stalin, and it has never exercised a more complete dictatorship over the whole life of the Soviet people.

To return to Stalin himself, it was left to others, to foes like Trotsky and to friends like the editors of *Pravda,* to identify the dictatorship of the party with the dictatorship of its central committee, and the dictatorship of the committee with the dictator himself.[77] Stalin did not leave to others, however, the final responsibility for standing Marx's antistatism on its head. He took his time, in theory if not in practice, and he became especially adept at parrying the obvious question why the Soviet state was growing steadily in size and power rather than withering away. For some years he talked of the important tasks of educating the proletariat and suppressing the bourgeoisie, with only occasional hints of a larger role for the state.[78] In 1939, he made his famous shift to the theory of "capitalist encirclement," which promises the withering away of the Soviet state only when the "danger of foreign military attack has disappeared" and a period of "socialist encirclement" has set in.[79] No matter how he looked at the problem, he admitted, he could not foresee the end of the state before an "entire historical epoch" had passed.[80]

In the end he became an honest man, still more honest in fact than in theory, but honest enough so that we may now speak fairly confidently of the disappearance of antistatist suspicions and anarchistic aspirations from the orthodox Marxist theory of the state. The prophecy of the stateless society is still heard in the Soviet Union, but it is the kind of prophecy in which no one can really believe, even in his Marxist heart. "The problem of the 'dying away' of the state," Vyshinsky wrote in behalf of Stalin, "is a purely theoretical problem," [81] something for Marxist dialecticians to play with in their happy hours—which are, incidentally, more plentiful since Stalin's death. The state is back in full force, not merely as an instrument to suppress the obstinate bourgeoisie, educate the awakened proletariat, and defend the socialist citadel against aggression, but as the benevolent creator of "the economic and cultural prerequisites" of a truly communist society. As it moves from one success to another, it may substitute persuasion for coercion in many of its administrative and even judicial activities, but this can hardly be interpreted as a "withering" of its powers.

The key thrust in this successful campaign to carry the state beyond mere respectability to veneration was struck somewhat obliquely in Stalin's tract *Marxism and Linguistics* (1950), in which the Soviet state was given credit for bringing about a "revolution from above" in reorganizing the whole basis of Russian agriculture [82]—a boast that would have laid Marx out cold. The way had already been paved by dozens of lesser theoreticians; and, needless to add, Stalin's boast was followed quickly by demonstrations of enthusiastic support from other theoreticians, journalists, academicians, and pamphleteers throughout the Soviet Union. Indeed, the demonstrations were so enthusiastic that Stalin himself had to issue a warning two years later (in his *Economic Problems of Socialism*) to go slow in proclaiming the Soviet state as the mightiest force for social progress in all history.[83] But he had done his work well, for since his death there has been no sign of retreat from the new theory of the Soviet state as the great engine of socialist society, a state that may encompass but also rises above the dictatorship of the proletariat. To anyone so obtuse as to recall Engels' remark that the state is the sign of a society "cleft into irreconcilable antagonisms," the Stalinist and post-Stalinist answer is that the classical Marxist analysis is still applicable to bourgeois states but not to the Soviet Union.[84] The government of the U.S.S.R. is a "new kind of state" that Engels, Marx, and even Lenin could not have been expected to foresee.* It is the first state in the memory of man engaged in service to an entire people. It is the first state that is not merely an element in the superstructure of society, that is not oppressive but benevolent in nature and purpose, and that is a shaping hand of economics and thus a prime mover of history. As a fact, it arises out of class harmony rather than class struggle; as a symbol, it stands for justice rather than oppression.[86]

This is much too brief an account of the great revolution in the Marxist theory of the state, especially when we realize that some of the most sacred teachings of Marxism had to be reinterpreted drastically to accommodate it. I will say more about this amazing shift in my final chapter. It should be enough to point out here that the new theory of the state in the Soviet Union is a flat repudiation of the classical Marxist assumption of the supremacy of economics over politics. While not all the details have yet been filled in, the main outlines of the new political theory are even now hardening into dogma under the approving eye of Khrushchev and his theoreticians. Political power in Marxism will never again

---

* Yet Lenin played his part here, too, when he wrote after the revolution: "Politics cannot but have precedence over economics. To argue differently means forgetting the ABC of Marxism." [85]

be depreciated or considered ultimately superfluous. Political power, it now seems, is the dominant power in a Marxist society, and as such it is equal to any task it is called upon to perform— not just in a time of revolution,[87] but at any time in the life of a socialist or perhaps even communist society. As for "state haters," they, according to Vyshinsky, are "unprincipled traitors and doubledealers." [88] Harsh words to pin on the ghosts of Marx and Engels! *

This excursion through the political theory of Marxism old and new has been a long one, and we may be pardoned a sigh of relief as we turn back to look briefly upon the American political tradition. Although much of it remains implicit in our working institutions rather than explicit in our sacred texts, this is the one part of the American tradition about which there is today the most general agreement—except, of course, among the dwindling remnant that still swears allegiance to the severe antistatism of William Graham Sumner. Let me try to state my own understanding of the American consensus on the origin, nature, purpose, basis, structure, and conditions of government.[90]

Government may be said to have its origin in the nature of men, who are political as well as social and economic animals. Like the family and tribe out of which it probably arose, it is society's prescriptive answer to a timeless human need that is felt in common by all members of the community. A core of government, although not all the trappings, is a "natural" phenomenon of civilization.

Government is both a positive blessing for which men can give seemly thanks to wise Providence and, to a lesser extent, a necessary evil for which they can blame their own moral insufficiencies.

---

* Vyshinsky, to be sure, is no longer a man to be quoted in polite circles in the U.S.S.R. Whatever may have happened to his reputation, however, the doctrine he expounded in *The Law of the Soviet State* is still pure and orthodox. His heresy, like Trotsky's, was political—and a mild case at that.[89]

Even if men were angels, some political authority would be needed to adjust the complexity of angelic relations and to do for the citizens of heaven-on-earth what they could not do as individuals or families. In any case, no time-honored instrument that has proved so essential to man's liberty and security can be considered inherently and irrevocably evil.

Government is something like fire. Under control, it is a useful servant; out of control, it is a ravaging tyrant. The danger of its getting out of control is no decisive argument against its generous use. Held within proper limits, it answers all these common purposes:

It defends the community against external assault and internal subversion.

It is a symbol of unity, a focus of allegiance that turns a lumpy mass of men and groups into a community.

It establishes and administers a system of justice, which alone makes it possible for men to live and do business with one another.

It protects men against the violence they can do one another; by the judicious use of force, it ensures "domestic tranquillity."

It secures the rights of men, including the rights of property, against the assaults of license, anarchy, and envy.

It adjusts conflicts among the groups that contest unceasingly for power and security, thus acting as the major equilibrator in the balance of social forces.

It promotes public and private morality, without which freedom cannot long exist. It does this by protecting organized religion, by supporting the means of education, by enacting laws against vice, and by offering an example of justice and rectitude.

It aids men in their pursuit of happiness, chiefly by removing obstacles in the path of individual development.

It takes important, often decisive responsibility for the economic and social health of the community.

Finally, it acts as a humanitarian agency in cases of clear necessity. It relieves human suffering by acts of charity, and in more developed communities it may guarantee each citizen the minimum material requirements of a decent existence.

Government serves many purposes but not all. It cannot on principle act as a proper substitute for other institutions such as the family and the church; it cannot in fact take over and direct effectively the instruments of production. Even in its own areas of operation it cannot be entirely, much less consistently successful. The frailties of the race, the rights and interests of men, the obstinate co-existence of other human groupings, and the unpredictability of nature are all drags on the effective performance of the functions of government.

The basis of government is the consent of the community, which means simply that the best kind of government is a democracy: a system in which the liberties and welfare of the people form the chief object of political concern, and in which the final power of decision rests, in one way or another, with this same people. Those governments that place this power in a man or group or class or party are wicked, unnatural, and doomed to destruction. Democracy, too, must have its leaders, but there must be ways to keep them in touch with, and responsible to, the settled opinions of the community.

The structure of government is grounded on certain manifest truths about the mixed nature of men. The fact that men can be wise and just, that they can govern themselves and other men fairly, is reflected in provisions for popular elections and for popular participation in the decision-making process. The fact that they can be unwise and unjust, that they can be hurried into rash decisions and corrupted by the taste of power, is reflected in arrangements that divide and check the total authority of government. Of these the most important are: the *separation of powers,* the distribution of political authority horizontally among a series of independent offices and agencies; *federalism,* the distribution of authority vertically among two or three levels of government; *checks and balances,* the provisions that guarantee mutual restraint among all these centers of power; *constitutional restraints,* the written laws and unwritten customs that reduce the discretion of public servants to the lowest level consistent with the effective operation of the political machinery; and *representative government,* the system under which the laws are made at a level once removed from the people, that is, by representatives elected to serve a limited period and held directly responsible by their electors.

The great services of all these arrangements, which bear the generic label of *constitutionalism,* are that they force men to think, talk, and bargain before they act, and that they institutionalize the processes through which public policy is made, administered, and enforced. The rule of the majority is the essence of democracy, but the majority must be coolheaded, persistent, and overwhelming, and it must be forced to recognize those things it cannot do by right or might. Without limitations there can be no constitutionalism; without constitutionalism, no democracy.

Finally, democracy flourishes strongly only when social and spiritual conditions are favorable. Some of these conditions are a healthy political system, in which two or more parties contest seriously but not savagely for power, and thus provide both a spur (the majority party) and a check (the opposition) to the process of government; a network of associations not beholden to the state, through which the legitimate interests of society may express and defend themselves; a productive economy, which guarantees a broad distribution of property and gives most men a "stake in society"; a sound pattern of morality, under which men may put trust in other men; a sound system of education, which raises men who can live decent lives and make prudent decisions; and, most essential, a faith in the rightness and fairness and competence of democracy, a faith that spreads wide and deep among the people.

I have made this statement of our political tradition in a "characteristically American" vein, that is, in ideal terms. I am aware of the gap between ideal and reality in our application of many of these principles. I am aware, too, that our political history has been a long battle to suppress our own urges toward Jacobin democracy. And I suspect that several principles of our tradition may need extensive reshaping in response to the pressures of an advanced industrial civilization. Yet I consider this a fair statement of the principles of good government to which we will be giving our allegiance for a long time to come, one that presents the American tradition in a light neither brighter nor darker than it deserves. Viewed in this light, most of the points at which Marxism and the American political tradition are in opposition are so visible to the naked eye that it would be a waste of time, not to say an insult to intelligence, to tick them off one by one. If ever there was a system of political institutions designed to exasperate the Marxists of this world, it is the "smokescreen for the dictatorship of capital" that operates in Washington and all over America through "ideological fictions" like the separation of powers and "Babbitt ideals" like federalism.[91] If ever there was a set of political ideas calculated to quicken the Marxist talent for abusive ridicule, it is the "apology for decay and oppression" I have just done my best to present. Marxism has no respect at all for our constitutional democracy, and I feel sure that my readers can be counted on to understand the reasons why. For my own part, I should like to single out the fundamental reasons for the inability of any constitutional democrat to accept the teachings of Marxism about politics and government, to list the points at which Marx and Engels and all their followers left the path of political reality to go astray in the fields of error.

The first of these points I discussed at some length in Chapter III: the flaw in the Marxist view of the realities and potentialities of human behavior. No orthodox Marxist, from Marx himself through the latest apologist for the Soviet state, has ever grasped the implications of the universality of man's desire for power, nor ever stopped to observe or imagine the changes that can come over even the noblest members of the race when power without restraint or responsibility is placed in their hands. Marx's prescription for the dictatorship of the proletariat, like the dictatorship that has actually emerged in one Communist country after another, is based on the assumption that some men can be trusted to wield absolute power over other men without succumbing to the corruptions of greed or ambition or pride or even spite. To us this assumption, whether it be made out of indifference or conviction, appears absurd and dangerous. We are not yet prepared to base our own prescriptions for good government on the notion that all men are perfectible and a few men, whether Communists or Republicans or professors of political science or graduates of West Point, already perfect.

The second point is a corollary of the first. In failing to make room in his system for the psychology of power, Marx also fails to grasp the essentials of what we may call its sociology, that is, the way in which political power is structured and manipulated in society. We have already noted how strangely blind he is to the realities and ambiguities and perils of economic power, at least under socialism; and he is, if anything, even less conscious of the play of forces in the political arena. The most unacceptable result of this indifference, certainly from our point of view, is the gaping absence in his thought of any appreciation of the uses and merits of constitutionalism, a gap that has been filled by the Bolsheviks with their autocratic doctrine of "democratic centralism." [92] What we think is the first prerequisite of a sound system of government —the diffusion and restraint of authority through the techniques of constitutionalism—Marx and the Marxists consider either counterfeit or irrelevant. We may shudder at what we hear from Hobbes or Machiavelli about the uses of power, but at least we hear something. We may squirm when we read Madison or John Adams on the abuses of power, but we know that they are grappling honestly with a universal problem of government. It would be hard to find a figure in the whole history of political thought who has less to say than Marx on either aspect of the problem of power, indeed who gives less appearance of knowing that the problem even exists. Our aim has always been to *institutionalize* the uses of political power, that of the Marxists to *personalize* it, and their aim is a direct legacy from Marx and Engels. Marx or no Marx, it continues to amaze us that the repeated purges of Soviet officials for "abuses of authority" has never led to even a whispered reconsideration of the necessity of constitutionalism.

It is no wonder, then, that we fall out with the Marxists irreconcilably over the importance to human liberty of the instruments of "mere formal freedom." As Karl Popper writes, "This 'mere formal freedom,' i.e., democracy, the right of the people to judge and to dismiss their government, is the only known device by which we can try to protect ourselves against the misuse of political power; it is the control of the rulers by the ruled." * And since it is admitted today, in both the Soviet Union and the United States, that political power can go far to control economic power, "political democracy is also the only means for the control of economic power by the ruled." In our opinion, the Marxists have grossly undervalued the efficacy of what Lenin called the "hackneyed forms of routine parliamentary democracy" [94] as the means of making the state the servant and guardian of the entire people. No small part of the world's present grief may be traced to the distressing truth that Marx never understood what institutions and rules were essential to the proper conduct of popular government. He was altogether right in pointing out that the trappings of democracy can be used to serve the selfish interests of a ruling class, altogether wrong to insist that they can never be used to serve the common interests of an entire society.

The truth is that Marxism has never been able to get the role of political authority in proper perspective. It has never really attempted to answer the question posed by Edmund Burke, whom Marx saluted as that "celebrated sophist and sycophant," [95] of "what the state ought to take upon itself to direct by the public

---

* There are other known devices, but the hyperbole serves its purpose.[93]

wisdom, and what it ought to leave, with as little interference as possible, to individual discretion." [96] This, needless to say, is a central question of politics, and we condemn the Marxists for their refusal even to think about it. Marx himself errs in the direction of granting the state too little competence; the latter-day Marxists, who share his sentiments on the futility of bourgeois politics, err in the direction of granting it too much. Marx was a peculiar sort of anarchist, the Marxists are straight-out statists; and for neither of these polar positions can we have respect. We can show sympathy for the old Marxism, since we, too, were once classical Liberals who suspected that the power of government was both evil and useless. We were, to be sure, far better Liberals in theory than we were in practice, yet it cannot be denied that we now give a larger assignment and thus a larger measure of respect to government than we did twenty-five or fifty or a hundred years ago, and that anarchy is no more than a fleeting thought in which Americans indulge once a year when they file their income tax returns. Marx himself, we feel, is never more mistaken than when he derides the capacity of government to serve the general welfare —to humanize industrialism, to reduce class and group tensions, and generally to improve the lot of all men. We think we have proved what he denies: that government can manage efficiently and direct equitably the pursuit of at least some of the common interests of society.

At the same time, we have remained well this side of veneration for the state, and toward the new Marxism we therefore bear nothing but uncompromising hostility. The Stalinist state is so foreign to our way of thinking that we find it almost impossible to decide just where to begin to attack it. We deny the new Marxist theory of the state (which we rightly call totalitarianism) for its assumptions that all citizens are public men who share the One Great Interest, that all authority must be concentrated and all restraints liquidated, and that politics is supreme not only over economics but over every other area in which men pursue their ends: religion, culture, education, and social life. Whether politics should and must have command over economics, or economics over politics, is a question that Americans can debate indefinitely. The one thing of which we are certain, and which prevents the debate from turning into a brawl, is that the command of each over the other should be limited in scope and operation. As for the supremacy of politics over, let us say, religion and culture, we deplore this with all our might. Despite the pretensions of certain congressional and state legislative committees, there is still no place in American democracy for the "politicalization" of all human affairs.

This indictment of Marxism for gross errors in the area of politics could go on indefinitely. I should account for our dissent from the Marxist notions that the essence of all politics is struggle, that compromise between genuinely contradictory interests is impossible, that political parties are a fraud in bourgeois democracy and unnecessary in Soviet democracy,[97] and that consent is no explanation at all of the legitimacy of political authority; but I think it sufficient for our purposes merely to state this dissent. I shall have something to say in the next chapter about still another major charge we level against the political theory of Marxism, that it is blatantly elitist. We may cut off this discussion here with two lops of the sword: first, by restating the other major charges, which are the misreading of human nature; the indifference to the perils of power; the consequent neglect of constitutionalism; the contempt for the instruments of formal democracy; and the inability to put politics and political authority in their proper place; and second, by affirming that, in the final reckoning, we see little to choose between Marx and Stalin, between the old and new Marxist theories of the state. It is all very well to talk, as I have talked myself, about the anarchism of Marx. But the truth is that Marx, though he was an anarchist in his hatred of the bourgeois present and his hopes for the communist future, was an authoritarian in his plans for the proletarian revolution. He pushed

power out the front door in a weakened condition, then let it
march in the back door in renewed vigor. Bakunin, Marx's rival
in the First International and an all-out anarchist, was probably
the first to detect the authoritarian strain in Marx, whom he
branded a "fanatical state-worshipper." Writing of the "privileged
minority" that would in fact wield power in a "proletarian government," he prophesied accurately:

> That minority, the Marxists say, will consist of workers. Yes, per-
> haps of *former* workers. And these, as soon as they become rulers
> or representatives of the people, will cease to be workers and will
> begin to look upon the entire world of manual workers from the
> heights of the State. They will no longer represent the people, but
> themselves and their own pretensions to rule the people. . . . But
> these selected men will be ardently convinced, and at the same time,
> learned socialists. The term "scientific socialism" . . . proves that the
> alleged People's State will be nothing else but the quite despotic rule
> over the popular masses by a new and not very numerous aristocracy
> of real or spurious savants.[98]

And in another context he said:

> It is easy enough for Marx to soar theoretically into a rational
> concept of freedom, but the instinct of freedom is absent in him; he
> is from head to foot an authoritarian.[99]

Bakunin was both more personal and more severe in his assessment of Marx than we have reason to be. Still, there can be no
doubt that the authoritarian strain infects the one part of his
political theory we have to take seriously: his plans for the dictatorship of the proletariat. Marx, I repeat, was a Jacobin democrat,
and Jacobin democracy, as Burke and John Adams told us even
before history taught this lesson (which it has now taught a
hundred times over), is a standing invitation to tyranny. He may
have been altogether sincere in his belief that the proletarian system of concentrated, centralized, and unrestrained authority would
do its job speedily and then pass into oblivion, but sincerity is
still no excuse for folly. The one question that even the most gen-

teel apologists for Marx will never answer to our satisfaction is how he could have expected the leaders of the proletariat to be the first ruling group in history to decide that the people could get along without them and to abdicate their positions of power. By opening the door to naked power in the period of proletarian rule, Marx opened it for all times and to all comers. The Jacobin democracy of Marx has become the people's democracy of Ulbricht and Kadar, and who will deny that he was an accessory before the fact?

SEVEN · THE MARXIST TEMPER

$\mathbf{M}$arxism is more than a collection of judgments and prophecies about the course of human events. It is also a way of making judgments and prophecies, and one has not tasted or even imagined the true flavor of Marxism until he has learned for himself that the judgments are almost always wrathful and the prophecies sanguine. The ideas of Marx and his heirs are a fearful challenge to American democracy; the challenge is rendered all the more fearful by the way in which these ideas are generated and expressed.

It is with this final aspect of Marxism, not *what* its oracles and acolytes happen to think about human nature or social classes or the state, but *how* they think it, that I am concerned in this chapter. We are dealing, of course, with something very fuzzy and "unscientific," something difficult to isolate and even more difficult to analyze. It is impossible to draw a sharp line between what a man thinks and how he thinks about it, between what a man believes to be the truth and how he found it. It is confusing to talk about an aspect of Marxism (or, for that matter, of the American tradition) that is a blend of things mental and spiritual and moral. Yet the aspect is there—whether we call it mood, tone, humor, mental set, moral bias, cast of mind, or, as I

193

prefer, *temper*—and we must probe it as carefully as we can. Only thus will we make our final reckoning with Marx and the Marxists.

In the pages that follow I propose to observe the orthodox Marxists as they go about their intellectual and moral business. This is not a study in character. I am not especially interested in proving that Marxists are less likely than democrats to exhibit such qualities as honesty and kindness. I am certainly ready to concede that convinced Marxists, like convinced Americans, are spread all along the spectrum of character from baseness to nobility. It is the common temper of these men, the intellectual habits and moral bias that all Marxists seem to display, into which we must now inquire. Such an inquiry will serve the larger purposes of this study well. It will acquaint us better with the original model of all Marxists, Marx himself; and since no one can say he understands Marxism until he knows Marx intimately, this fact alone makes the venture worthwhile. More than that, it will furnish a vital connecting link between Marx and Lenin and between Lenin and all the Marxist-Leninists who have come after. It was not so much Lenin's pious devotion to Marx's teachings that made him, in the opinion of many scholars, a thoroughgoing Marxist; it was, rather, the sameness of their ways of dealing with men and ideas and events.[1] If ever a man displayed the Marxist temper more consistently than even Marx himself, that man was Lenin, whether in Shushenskoye or Geneva or Petrograd or the Kremlin. Most important, it is exactly here, in the obscure but commanding realm of the mind and spirit, that the confrontation of Marxism and the American tradition reaches its climax. The American temper is, if anything, a more pervasive element of the American tradition than the Marxist temper is of Marxism, and no contrast we have yet set up is as significant as that which I am about to describe.

How does the Marxist think? How does he give his thoughts to the world? With what predispositions does he judge our way of life to be corrupt and doomed? With what passion does he call upon the proletariat to smash it into rubble? In what mood does he prophesy his great society of the future? What, in short, are the elements of the Marxist temper, and how sharply are they at odds with the cast of mind that we recognize and cherish, even when we fail to display it, as "characteristically American"? These are the questions I hope to answer in this chapter.

The most striking feature of the Marxist temper, certainly to the eye of the non-Marxist observer, is the *quest for certainty.* This is, of course, a universal urge of the human species: the fear of doubt, the dislike of contingency, the appetite for the absolute. Men of every culture in every age have found it intolerable to live with uncertainty, and with glad shouts of surrender they have rushed to embrace the infallible word of priests or kings or philosophers. But few men in all history have surrendered so completely to the lure of the absolute as have the Marxists, led in this as in most such matters by Marx himself.

The Marxist, for reasons sociological as well as psychological, has not merely roamed far and wide in search of certainty. He has found what he was looking for, and the fanfare with which he proclaims the infallibility of his beliefs is a measure of the need that sent him upon the search. He has hungered and thirsted after certainty, and his hunger has been filled and his thirst slaked by one of the richest diets of intellectual absolutism in the history of civilized man. Most men are content to be certain about a few things; the Marxists profess to be certain about all things. Most men cling to their few certainties as matters of faith; the Marxists proclaim their many as matters of fact. Their philosophy has told them, in the words of an American Marxist, "that the world and its laws are fully knowable, that our knowledge of the laws of nature . . . is authentic knowledge having the validity of objective truth, and that there are no things in the world which are unknowable, but only things which are still not known." [2] So long as they remain true Marxists, they seem never to entertain any of the doubts either about themselves or about the cosmos that beset most other men. Their feeling of certainty, as we have learned, projects into the future as confidently as it does into the past. In the Marxist mind there is a close connection, even an identity between the certain and the inevitable. Few men in history, perhaps not even Jeremiah and Nostradamus, converted certainty into the coin of prophecy more assertively than did Marx, and his Communist heirs have spent this coin with a lavish hand.

The fact that their quest for certainty has been uniquely successful is a source both of strength and weakness to the Marxists of this world. On one hand, they move into combat with the spokesmen and statesmen of liberal democracy armed with a self-assurance that makes them the most formidable of foes. Their faith, based on the bedrock of "fact," is something we cannot match in scope or intensity, that is, in the number of things we believe to be true or the dead-sureness with which we believe them. This puts us at a distinct disadvantage in the struggle for the respect of the uncommitted men of the non-Western world. It is hard to stand up successfully to men who are convinced that they are the chosen instruments of history. At the same time, however, the Marxist is especially vulnerable to the kind of intellectual cataclysm that can fall with a crash upon the True Believer who admits only one little doubt into the citadel of his absolutism. A disillusioned Marxist is not a happy sight. If the quest for certainty was often a compulsive pilgrimage, the flight from certainty becomes a demoralized rout that is hard to halt short of some other haven of false certainty. Even the serenely confident Marxist is less stoutly armed than he appears at first glance. Lacking what Hunt calls a "theory of uncertain judgments," incapable of allowing for "situations in which any one of a number of different views may reasonably be held on the evidence available," [3] he falls victim to the rigidity of mind that is usually the price of self-professed infallibility. He cannot bend to the challenge of uncertainty, and under pressure he must therefore break with reality. Such is the fate of the man whose mind deals always in certainties, never in possibilities or even probabilities, and such was the fate of the man who hardly ever dealt in anything else, Karl Marx. The Marxists after Marx have tempered their doctrinal rigidity with operative flexibility. To the extent that they have done this at the expense of the purity of the Marxist absolute, however, they have been less than true to the demands of their faith. This is another way of saying that intellectual absolutism and manipulation of the human predicament do not fit easily together.

The Marxist longing for certainty comes to the surface in the Marxist cult of science. Religion has been the refuge of most seekers for the absolute in history; the Marxist, despising religion as the "heart of a heartless world," has found his own refuge in what we may fairly call "scientism" (which, of course, includes the "scientific" view of history). I am not speaking here primarily of the tremendous faith in physical science and the respect for scientists that pervade the social climate of the Soviet Union,[4] although this is in part a product of the Marxist assumption "that the world and its laws are fully knowable." I am speaking, rather, of the conviction shared by all dedicated Marxists that their understanding of history and society is strictly "scientific." It is a body of verifiable truths that are unassailable except by men blinded by bourgeois prejudice or bought off by bourgeois gold. "Dialectical materialism, the world outlook of the Marxist-Leninist party," a British Marxist writes, "is a truly scientific world outlook." "Dialectical materialism," an American Marxist echoes, "is logical, clear and practical because it is a true reflection of the external world." And Stalin proclaimed to all Communists who went to school with him:

The science of the history of society, despite all the complexity of the phenomena of social life, can become as precise a science as, let

us say, biology, and capable of making use of the laws of development
of society for practical purposes.

Hence the party of the proletariat should not guide itself in its
practical activity by casual motives, but by the laws of development
of society, and by practical deductions from these laws.

Hence Socialism is converted from a dream of a better future for
humanity into a science.

Hence the bond between science and practical activity, between
theory and practice, their unity, should be the guiding star of the party
of the proletariat.[5]

I shall have more to say about this passage in a moment, for
the connection Stalin makes between "the science of the history
of society" and the "party of the proletariat" is a key to the workings of the orthodox Marxist mind. What I am anxious to point
out here is that in this as in so many other matters, Stalin was a
faithful follower of the "founders of scientific socialism." Marx
and Engels, not their heirs, first claimed the status of science for
the Communist view of man, history, society, and state. The most
memorable claim was made by Engels himself. Standing at Marx's
graveside in Highgate cemetery, London, on March 17, 1883, he
paid the highest tribute that could be paid by one intellectual of
the Victorian age to another: "Just as Darwin discovered the law
of evolution in organic nature, so Marx discovered the law of
evolution in human history." [6] Marx himself took pains to label
his own socialism "scientific" and the socialism of even the best
of other men like Saint-Simon and Fourier "Utopian." Writings
such as the *Critique* and *Capital* are studded with allusions to the
fields of physics and chemistry. As Jacques Barzun writes of
Marx's arrival at his theory of value, "He thought of himself as
a kind of Lavoisier or Dalton having just isolated an element and
laid the foundation of a new science." [7] The fact that in his mood
and methods he was very far from being a scientist, even a "scientific historian," has given no pause to modern Marxists, who delight in saluting him as "the greatest man of science." Benjamin
Farrington, a British Marxist and scientist, puts his salute in this

extraordinary way: "Marx should rank not only as the founder of the science of history but as founder also of the history of science, for in his immense perspective they appear as two aspects of one process." [8]

From the belief that Marxism is the only scientific form of socialism to the belief that it is the only science of society is apparently as easy a step for the heirs as it was for the founder. Modern Marxists, again following Marx's own lead, proclaim without hesitation that theirs is a science that can be applied confidently to all social phenomena, not merely to "understand" the world but to "change" it. They echo Marx in asserting that "science is *always* connected with the changing of nature for human use, and with the understanding of nature *only* in so far as it can be used to change it." [9] The Marxist "science of man and of things human" is "not just a contemplative, interpretive science, not a mere statistical and classificatory one, but an operative science, a science that gives leverage for manipulation in accordance with long term purposes." [10]

If we put this statement together with the passage I quoted from Stalin, we come close to an understanding of the devotion to science (or better, of the "scientism") that is an essential element in the Marxist temper. Marxist science is not simply interpretive but operative, not simply operative but partisan. [11] It serves a genuine long-term purpose, indeed the highest of all possible purposes: the transformation of society through the activity of the party of the proletariat. It is, in short, an instrument of revolution, and only those who desire the revolution can call themselves true scientists. Marx and Engels found their science ten times truer than all other so-called "sciences of society" exactly because it was partisan, because it eschewed neutrality and breathed defiance of a doomed system. Marxists ever since have proclaimed the importance of class origins and attitudes in shaping science and the consequent supremacy of the one science that can serve the class destined to remake the world. In writing of the "class character" of science, especially social science, Nikolai Bukharin asked: "Why is proletarian science superior to bourgeois science? Why are red glasses better than white ones? Why is it better to look at reality through red ones?" And he answered his own questions:

> It is not difficult to understand . . . why proletarian social science is superior to bourgeois social science. It is superior because it has a deeper and wider vision of the phenomena of social life, because it is capable of seeing further and observing facts that lie beyond the vision of bourgeois social science. It is therefore clear that Marxists have a perfect right to regard proletarian science as true and to demand that it be generally recognized.[12]

The truth is, of course, that the quest for certainty has taken every Marxist from Marx to Mao out of the constricting area of science and into the broad realm of ideology. Marx was a hot-eyed reformer, not a coolheaded scientist. He was a partisan leader who cast his strictures and promises in pseudo-scientific form—perhaps, as H. B. Mayo suggests, "because of the prestige attached to science in the nineteenth century," [13] perhaps because he really believed he was a Darwin or even a Dalton. To those who can survey him at all critically he appears as an extreme ideologue, a man with a unique penchant for identifying the subjective wish with the objective fact. Marxists profess to despise ideologues before all other men, yet they are, if anything, even more guilty than their master of proclaiming an ideology and calling it a science, so guilty indeed that they have gone him one better by moving from the broad to the boundless, from ideology to quasi-religion.[14]

Many students of Communism have pointed to the close parallel between Marxism-Leninism and revealed religion.[15] So, too, have many disillusioned Communists, for whom it was a "God that failed." Almost every feature and concern of the religions of our age may be found in the Marxism of the Communists: the veneration of saints and prophets and martyrs, the invocation and exegesis of sacred texts, the hierarchy of priests and missionaries, the concern for the souls rather than the bodies of men and thus the urge to convert and crusade and persecute, the paraphernalia of conversion and confession and excommunication, the aura of mysticism that pervades the minds of the most faithful children, even the fostering of the myth of Eden and the promise of the millennium. Marxism serves almost every purpose for Marxists that religion serves for other men: it explains reality and man's part in it; it gives a higher sense of the purpose and meaning of life; it apparently provides one of the most gratifying "opiates" ever devised for men in trouble. If one wishes to search for every possible analogy, it even has a collective devil in the capitalists and a collective redeemer in the proletariat—a proper confrontation of absolute evil and absolute good in a collective faith.[16] Marxism has everything a religion should have except a devout belief in God, and that lack is filled, at least psychologically and sociologically, by a devout belief in History. God may have promised the Christian faithful salvation in another world, but History guarantees it to the Marxist faithful in this one. Lenin is said to have been irritated in 1908 when his fuzzy-headed friend Anatole Lunacharsky proclaimed Marxism to be a "natural, earthly, anti-metaphysical, scientific and human religion";[17] he would have been a hundred times more irritated by the deterioration of his "science" into a state religion almost Byzantine in its insistence upon ironclad orthodoxy.

We must not make too much of the analogy between Marxism and religion, especially any particular religion like Catholicism or Judaism.[18] We must also not make too little. If it is not a religion in the high sense of a supernatural "ethic transcending the relativities of power and class interest,"[19] it is one in the common sense of a simple faith for which millions of men will die gladly and without question. It is no whimsical accident of history but an ineluctable incident of Marxism that it should have worked an influence upon the twentieth century comparable to that of a new world-religion. To this un-Marxist end, to the replacement of a transcendent religion by an immanent pseudo-religion, the quest for certainty has brought the dedicated Marxist. He has forgotten, if he has ever even heard, the wise counsel that Proudhon wrote to Marx in 1846. To the latter's proposal of collaboration in the cause of socialism, Proudhon replied:

Let us by all means collaborate in trying to discover the laws of society, . . . but, for God's sake, after we have demolished all the dogmatisms *a priori,* let us not of all things attempt in our turn to instil another kind of dogma into the people. . . . Simply because we are at the head of a movement, do not let us ourselves become the leaders of a new intolerance, let us not pose as the apostles of a new religion—even though this religion be the religion of logic, the religion of reason itself. Let us welcome, let us encourage all the protests; let us condemn all exclusions, all mysticisms. But never let us think of any question as closed, and even after we have exhausted our very last argument, let us begin again, if necessary, with eloquence and irony. On that condition I shall be delighted to associate with you— but otherwise, no! [20]

Marx, as we know, was temperamentally deaf to pleas of this nature. Exactly because he was so deaf to the appeal to reason and tolerance, he will be remembered by history as the prophet of a faith rather than the founder of a science.

I hesitate to use the prickly word *dogmatic* to describe this first pervading element of the Marxist temper, yet I know of no other that so honestly sums up its inner nature and outer behavior. It is popular among hard Marxists to echo Stalin's cry that "Marxism is an enemy of all dogmatism," [21] to talk admiringly of Lenin's flexibility,[22] to quote Engels as authority for the belief that "nothing is established for all time, nothing is absolute or sacred," [23] and to nod agreement to the polite scolding of softer friends who warn them that "to be a dogmatic Marxist is to repudiate Marxism." [24] But the fact is that today one must be a dogmatic Marxist or really not much of a Marxist at all. Marx was, in the common sense of the word, one of the most dogmatic men who ever lived in the world of ideas, and the truculent temper of modern Marxism may be traced to the way his mind functioned as well as to the "scientific" truths it conjured up.[25] No Pope who ever reigned could hold a candle for intellectual and moral certitude to even the minor spokesmen of Marxism. This is one reason why the enlightened modern mind, which must manage to live with many dogmas, has unusual trouble living with Marxism. A more compelling reason is the realization that Marxist dogma, unlike all other dogmas, was formulated not before but after the rise of science and rationalism. While most of the world's thinkers have been moving away from what Bertrand Russell calls the "habit of militant certainty about objectively doubtful matters," [26] the men who think for the Communist world have holed themselves up in a citadel of dogmatism far more commanding than any that other men in other centuries were able to rear. This retarded dogmatism may well account, as Stanley Alderson suggests,[27] for the peculiar attraction of Marxism to the faithful as well as its peculiar repulsion to us. In any case, it is an interesting footnote to this account of the quasi-religious nature of modern Marxism. The Marxist is asked to believe unequivocally in a great many more things about the world he can see with his eyes than the Christian is asked to believe hopefully about the world he can only imagine. The Marxist is apparently capable of a far greater act of faith than any we have set ourselves. The test of the Christian's certainty is deferred until after his death; the test of the Marxist's goes on throughout his life.

Let me conclude by pointing briefly to several manifestations of this pervading air of dogmatism. The first is the Marxist habit of seeing all complexities and stating all differences in terms of black and white—I might add, of blackest black and whitest white. Albert Camus has noted that the essence of the act of rebellion is "an attitude of All or Nothing," [28] and the Marxists seem to express their vaunted dedication to the "permanent revolution" by thinking always in terms of starkest oppositions.[29]

The second is the Marxist contempt for the spirit and techniques of compromise.[30] The Marxist will occasionally give a point in intellectual exchange with the non-Marxist, but he enters such exchanges, as he enters negotiations about practical matters, first to utilize and ultimately to annihilate. A compromise on an issue that involves principle is either a coolly planned tactical maneuver,[31] which is the kind of compromise permitted to Marxists, or a sign of weakness and uncertainty, which is the kind of compromise indulged in by other men. It is, in any case, a quality for which Marxists have innate distrust, and men who deal with them, in Russia or out of it, must be prepared to agree with the American official described by Margaret Mead. Out of his long experience of negotiating with the Russians he could testify sorrowfully:

> We think of compromise as a natural way to get on with the job, but to them "compromise" is usually coupled with the adjective "rotten." They are puzzled by our emphasis on the desirability of compromise.[32]

The third manifestation follows directly upon the second: the identification of dissent with error, error with heresy, and heresy with sin. "To the advocate of Communism," F. J. Sheed writes, "the mere hint of a criticism produces an instant emotional reaction more proper to a religious than to an economic discussion. He does not pause to find out what the criticism means; much less to ask himself whether it might contain some conceivable point. Unable to believe that the questioner is in good faith, he simply asks himself what evil motive lies behind the question." [33] This ingrained refusal of the children of infallibility to deal reasonably with criticism or dissent reaches its peak in the Communist practice of unmasking an opponent rather than refuting him, of fixing attention upon his class origin rather than upon his arguments, of dismissing all criticisms from outside and even from inside the ranks of the doctrinally pure as expressions or vestiges of "bourgeois ideology." Nothing could be more revealing of this central aspect of the Marxist cast of mind than Berdyaev's observation:

Philosophical controversies, which in Soviet Russia are prolonged over years and are then printed, are problems debated not so much from the point of view of truth or error as from the point of view of orthodoxy or heresy, that is to say, they are theological rather than philosophical controversies.[34]

This, then, is the first ingredient of the Marxist temper: the relentless quest after certainty that makes a "science" out of an array of value judgments and a secular religion out of this science. "We reject every attempt," Engels wrote in *Anti-Dühring*, "to impose on us any moral dogma whatsoever as an eternal, ultimate and forever immutable ethical law."[35] Yet his colleague Marx had already begun to impose such a dogma on the forces of socialism throughout the world. Lenin was the best of Marxists when he wrote in 1913 that "the Marxian doctrine is omnipotent because it is true."[36]

It is hard to speak at all conclusively of a common American attitude toward certainty. Yet I think we may properly say that, for all the inanities and aberrations of our behavior as individuals, we display a collective temper with these marks: we want certainty in many things but expect it only in a few; we confine this expectation to the realm of the soul and (certainly this is true of most of us) leaven our convictions with a sprinkling of doubt; and we dress these convictions in the robes of other-worldly faith rather than of this-worldly fact. There is little in the American cast of mind that makes it friendly to absolutes, at least in the realm of politics and human relations. We have been a great people for appealing to "the law of nature," but that law has been a vague, shifting, and sparsely filled concept throughout our history. Toward knowledge of man and society the American temper is highly empirical: insisting with its great mentor John Locke that men remember "they may be mistaken,"[37] refusing to convert interesting hypotheses into iron laws of nature or history, leaving a door always open to criticism and correction. Toward science it is, in its best moments, prudently respectful: recognizing the power of science but confining it to areas in which its methods are truly operative, sparing its agents the indignity of insisting that they ignore or alter tested facts because of political considerations,[38] and putting emphasis on the kind of science that asks questions rather than makes pronouncements. We recognize that one result of science has been to increase the area of the unknown and perhaps even the unknowable; we leave open even the most solemn scientific "truths" to the challenge of further experiments and hypotheses.

The American temper is, above all, a standing reproof to dogmatism, and those who dogmatize about "objectively doubtful matters"—and there are plenty of such Americans to go around—are breaking faith with the tradition. The ideal American confines his moral certitudes, of which he has his fair share, to matters of faith; he assumes that he can live peaceably with men who "think otherwise" about the things of the soul and spirit. He is uncomfortable when he is found using only blacks and whites; he puts a high value (as did the great bourgeois Franklin) on the spirit and techniques of compromise; and he tries to value eccentricity and dissent at least as highly as loyalty and unity. In all things social and political he does his best to transcend his irrational nature and maintain an open, searching, reasonable mind. This is not an easy thing for any man to do, but the tradition of the open mind strengthens many Americans for the attempt.

The American has a word to describe the open mind in action. He calls the workings of such a mind *pragmatism,* a word he uses commonly to express an attitude of mind rather than to denote a full-blown philosophy. He does not let his pragmatism bully him, for he would be something more or less than a human being if he were able to put every principle and prejudice to the test of experience. Yet he does put a high value on what the great philosopher of pragmatism praised as "the attitude of looking away from first things, principles, 'categories,' supposed necessities; and of looking toward last things, fruits, consequences, facts." [39] And just because he does, he finds himself in the sharpest possible intellectual contrast with the Marxist. Lest there be any doubt on this score, let me quote from the article on the philosophy of pragmatism in the authorized American version of the *Short Philosophic Dictionary* used throughout the Soviet Union:

> *Pragmatism,* an idealistically inclined and reactionary tendency in contemporary bourgeois philosophy . . . denying the objectivity of truth and maintaining that the value of scientific theories is to be found, not in the fact that they actually reflect reality, but exclusively in the utility which they yield in this or that particular case. Though paralleled by similar tendencies on the continent of Europe, pragmatism is thought of primarily as an American philosophical movement associated with the names of C. S. Peirce, William James, and John Dewey. It is often thought of, indeed, as the distinctive philosophy of the United States. . . . Pragmatism is the sworn enemy of materialism, and especially of Marxism.[40]

As the "sworn enemy" of Marxism, pragmatism, both as formal philosophy and common attitude, has come under heavy attack from American Marxists. Men like Sidney Hook have tried in good faith to go St. Thomas Aquinas one better by seeking to make Marxism perfect with the aid of pragmatism, but the kind of assault launched by Harry K. Wells in his frankly titled *Pragmatism: Philosophy of Imperialism* is far more characteristic and revealing of the current Marxist cast of mind. It is true that certain methods of both Marx and Engels anticipated the pragmatist criteria of validity,[41] that Lenin's personal approach to scientific truth and indeed political strategy was highly instrumentalist,[42] and that Khrushchev, like all men in power, exhibits the worst features of what we may call "vulgar pragmatism." But no one of these men could have been a conscious pragmatist in the image of Franklin and his countless heirs. The founders of Marxism would have hated pragmatism as a method because it condemns the methods by which Marx arrived at all his great judgments and prophecies. Their heirs must hate it as a philosophy because it is a standing reproach to the kind of confident planning into which their "science" constantly lures them; because it is a flat denial of any kind of historical necessity; because it is essentially a theory of suspended judgments; and because, as Wells puts it directly, it combines "empiricism," "individualism," and "spontaneity" (not to mention "opportunism," "subjectivism," and "obscurantism") into a philosophy that makes a mockery of both materialism and the dialectic.[43] Most important, it is one of the most effective if crude attacks ever launched on intellectual absolutism of any stripe. Small wonder that Marxists like Howard Selsam must resort to name-calling and brand it "the distinctive philosophy of imperialism, the philosophy of the 'big stick,' the philosophy of the sheerest expediency, of practice without theory, movement without direction, getting-by, and the ultimate in American business creeds, 'nothing succeeds like success.' " [44] Or, as Wells puts it even more bluntly, pragmatism is the "world outlook of the capitalist class," the "brainchild of bourgeois ideologists," the "reinstitution of superstition," and a "dead-end philosophy of a dead-end class." As for that great pragmatist, John Dewey, he is the "high priest of bourgeois apologetics in the United States. He is the head salesman of theology." [45] So much, in the hard Marxist view, for the philosophy of the open, searching mind and thus, it seems clear, for the open, searching mind itself.

I would think it useful to conclude this contrast of the Marxist and American attitudes toward certainty with a passage from Dewey's memorable *Freedom and Culture,* for it puts the central issue in simplest terms. This is at least one aspect of the American temper at its most humble and hopeful:

It is ironical that the theory which has made the most display and the greatest pretense of having a scientific foundation should be the one which has violated most systematically every principle of scientific method. . . . It is of the nature of science not so much to tolerate as to welcome diversity of opinion, while it insists that inquiry brings

the evidence of observed facts to bear to effect a consensus of conclusions—and even then to hold the conclusion subject to what is
ascertained and made public in further new inquiries. . . . Freedom
of inquiry, toleration of diverse views, freedom of communication,
the distribution of what is found out to every individual as the ultimate
intellectual consumer, are involved in the democratic as in the scientific method.[46]

To this I would append Darwin's expression of the genuine spirit
of science—humble, open-minded, hesitant—especially since, as
I have said before, Marx admired him as much as he could any
man:

> I had also during many years followed a golden rule, namely, that
> whenever a published fact, a new observation or thought came across
> me, which was opposed to my general results, to make a memorandum
> of it without fail and at once.[47]

What could be further removed from the Marxist temper?

The second ingredient in the Marxist temper is the *urge to revolution*. The revolutionary spirit bound Lenin most closely to the
memory of Marx, and it continues to separate hard Marxists all
over the world from most other men, including most other socialists. Revolution is at the core of all Marxist hopes and in the fore-
front of all Marxist calculations. It is the cutting edge of history,
the high road to social salvation, the sure promise of the dialectic
of history. If one is not a revolutionary in spirit and purpose, one
is not a full-blooded Marxist. Rightly did Lenin reserve his fullest
contempt for those "opportunists within the labor movement" who
sought to water down the fires of Marxism, who tried to "omit,
obliterate, and distort the revolutionary side of its teaching, its
revolutionary soul." [48]

The revolutionary urge arises out of the feeling of indignation
that whips the Marxist conscience. The true Marxist is an angry
man, and angry he must remain until the last trace of capitalist

manners and morals and institutions has been swept away in the stream of history. Now I do not mean to say that every Communist, whether in Paris or Chicago or Calcutta, goes about his daily business in a fit of rage. He can be as serene and forgiving as the most gentle member of the Society of Friends. But when he thinks consciously as a Marxist, when he looks at the bourgeois-imperialist world all around him and contrasts it with the communist world promised by Marx, he is as wrathful as a man can be and still keep his wits about him. As for the successful revolutionaries of Moscow, their zeal has simply been redirected toward the world outside. "We were revolutionaries in opposition," Trotsky wrote in behalf of all Bolsheviks, "and have remained revolutionaries in power." [49]

This urge arises, too, out of the prime Marxist techniques for searching into the mysteries of this world, which turn out not to have been mysteries at all. That technique is, of course, the dialectic. The man who applies it to social relations is bound to think in terms of antagonism. The man who applies it to history is bound to see struggle as the chief spur of progress. If he seeks evidence of the workings of the Law of Transformation of Quantity into Quality, where can he find it more dramatically displayed than in the kind of cataclysm that leads to a new social order? Marx and Engels, as I pointed out in Chapters Two and Four, converted the Hegelian dialectic into a creed that made revolutions a necessary part of the scheme of progress, and the Marxists of the twentieth century have been extraordinarily faithful to the creed. For them the dialectic has been, in Alexander Herzen's words of long ago, "the algebra of revolution." [50]

In this instance, too, Marx was the true ancestor of all the Marxists. Whatever he may have been in the circle of his family (a devoted husband and kindly father), he was by common report a most disagreeable man in his dealings with other men. To give him his due, he was on fire with indignation at the poverty, suffering, degradation, and injustice that soiled Western society, and the fire heated his relations with all men, enemies and friends alike. Carl Schurz testified:

Never have I met a man of such offensive, insupportable arrogance. No opinion which differed essentially from his own was accorded the honor of even a half-way respectful consideration. He answered all arguments which displeased him with a biting scorn for the pitiable ignorance of those who advanced them, or with a libelous questioning of their motives. I still remember the cutting, scornful tone with which he uttered—I might almost say "spat"—the word *bourgeois;* and he denounced as "bourgeois"—that is to say, as an unmistakable example of the lowest moral and spiritual stagnation—everyone who dared to oppose his opinions.[51]

Just what made Marx such a fierce hater and arrogant polemicist and implacable fighter, it will always be impossible to say. (His genes and carbuncles are generally given most credit.) That he was all these things, a Jacobin of Jacobins, is the conclusive testimony of history. One of the revealing signs of his fighter's instinct is the way in which he cast most of his works in the form of attacks on specific persons—on Feuerbach, Proudhon, Karl Vogt, Karl Grün, Max Stirner, and Bruno Bauer, as well as on Palmerston and Louis Bonaparte. The attacks, I might add, are still not pleasant reading. One critic has called his onslaught on Proudhon, whom he should have loved, "the bitterest attack by one thinker on another since the celebrated polemics of the Renaissance."[52] I forbear to put in print what he had to say about other radicals who crossed him, like Lassalle and Bakunin, and will add only that it is one of the tasty ironies of history that his hatred of Russia came close to a mania. In the words of Engels himself, spoken at the graveside, "Marx was before all else a revolutionary. . . . Fighting was his element."[53] He was a revolutionary in mind as well as in spirit, in his cool calculations as well as in his hot explosions. He was a supreme dialectician, a man who thought about history and human relations in terms of inevitable conflict and essential disharmony. He tied the dialectic and the class struggle together so tightly that they have never really been separated. Trotsky was in good Marxist form when he warned that "the will to revolutionary activity is a condition indispensable to the understanding of Marxist dialectics." [54] He would have been in perfect form had he added, "and vice versa."

The orthodox Marxist temper of 1960 is a faithful reflection of Marx's temper in any year between, say, 1843 (when he went to Paris) and 1883 (when he died). It is angry, vindictive, and implacable toward all men and ideas that fail to follow the hard line of Marxist truth. Again I make clear that I am not speaking of the personal characteristics of this or that member of the Communist party in any of the fifty-odd countries in which it is known to operate. I am speaking, rather, of the kind of thinking and talking and writing in which he is bound to indulge if he becomes at all active as a Marxist polemicist. Marxist man, Jean Lacroix reminds us, is a "fighter," and we can "understand nothing of the psychology of the Communist" if we do not "begin by seeing that he is in a state of *total war* with contemporary society." [55] The most striking feature of much of the political, social, and even philosophical literature of Communism today is the venom that is poured on those "jackals," "hyenas," "spys and wreckers," "hooligans," and "gangsters" who dare to oppose the current orthodoxy. (The epithets used most often in the attack on Boris Pasternak were "pig," "Judas," and "snake.") As John Dewey pointed out, and as generations of democratic socialists know to their sorrow (or is it really delight?), the venom is "even greater against those who agree in some respects than towards professed representatives of capitalism." [56] This is, more than incidentally, an accurate description of Marx's own relations with the men and women who came into his life. There is something about the temper (as well as the tactical position) of the political extremist that makes him much angrier at those who dissent only a little bit from his orthodoxy than at those who will have nothing to do with it at all.

The urge to revolution in the Marxist temper finds its great analogue in the inevitability of revolution in Marxist doctrine. The assertion of the impossibility of fundamental social change in bourgeois countries except by revolution is at the core of Marxist orthodoxy. Although some Marxists have steadfastly denied the necessity of revolution out of conviction, and many more have occasionally denied it for tactical reasons,* I do not see how it is any longer possible to argue that Communists expect or even desire the transition from capitalism to socialism on a world scale by peaceful means. I state this as what it surely is—an opinion, not a fact—yet I do so with all the conviction that one can ever bestow on mere opinion.

Marx and Engels were both somewhat equivocal on this crucial point, especially in their later years. Marx, as is well known, made possible exceptions of England, America, and "even Holland" in an address to the Amsterdam section of the First International in 1872, wondering aloud whether in these countries at least "the workers may hope to secure their ends by peaceful means." [58] But the evidence for the contrary opinion—that Marx expected and wanted a revolution to seal the doom of capitalism—seems to me overwhelming. As M. M. Bober has summed up this evidence, Marx assumed the necessity of revolution for at least three reasons: because the exploiters would never give up their power over the exploited without a desperate struggle; because, in the words of Marx and Engels themselves, there was only one way to cut short the "murderous death agony of the old society and the bloody birth pangs of the new society"—"revolutionary terrorism"; [59] and because, most important, "the building of communism demands a change of heart on a mass scale, and only in the shock of revolution can this change be wrought." [60] "Only in a revolution" can

---

* I am not certain which of these explanations applies to Emile Burns, who tells us the lesson of Mao's China: that "education, persuasion, patience, respect for people—for their prejudices, and even for their status" are the "fundamental Marxist approach to the transformation of people." [57]

the proletariat, in the words of Marx and Engels, "succeed in rid-
ding itself of all the muck of ages and become fitted to found
society anew." [61]

To this roll I would add two further reasons for believing that
revolution is a historical necessity in Marxist doctrine: first, the
apocalyptic assumption of all the great Marxists that history demands blood as the payment for blood, that the prodigious suffer-
ings of men under capitalism can be expiated only by more suffering; and second, the related assumption that the course of history
grinds its way along in a dialectical pattern, with the great advances coming in the form of social cataclysms. If one believes
seriously in the dialectic and insists upon applying it to historical
development, one must look hopefully for the emergence of such
cataclysms,* which we could hardly expect to be untouched by
violence. The course of history, in the Marxist view, is punctuated
by bloody revolutions, and the bloodiest of all must spark the leap
from capitalism to socialism. Marxists have argued for several
generations about the social preconditions of successful civil war
and about the distinction between "permanent" and "uninterrupted" and "continuous" revolution.[62] They have never argued
for long about the necessity of revolution, not if they wished to
be accepted as orthodox Marxists. Lenin knew what he was doing
when he wrote in *State and Revolution* that the "exception made
by Marx is no longer valid," [63] and Stalin echoed him faithfully:

As far as the imperialist countries are concerned, we must regard
it as a universally applicable law of the revolutionary movement that
the proletarian revolution will be effected by force, that the bourgeois
State machine will have to be smashed, as an indispensable preliminary
to the revolution.

No doubt in the distant future, if the proletariat has triumphed in
the chief countries that are now capitalist, and if the present capitalist
encirclement has given place to a socialist encirclement, it will be

---

* One can, of course, be the kind of Marxist who simply "looks for" but
does not "work for" or even "advocate" revolutionary leaps into the next
stage of society. One would not, in such case, be much of a Communist.

possible for a "peaceful" transition to be effected in certain capitalist countries where the capitalists, in view of the "unfavourable" international situation, will deem it advisable "of their own accord" to make extensive concessions to the proletariat. But this is to look far ahead, and to contemplate extremely hypothetical possibilities. As concerns the near future there is no warrant for any such expectations.[64]

One gets the feeling that the proletarians of those last encircled capitalist countries will be rather disappointed and find their victory somewhat hollow—like a team that wins a coveted championship by default.

This leads to the prickly question whether Marxism is, as many of its critics insist, a "cult of violence." I do not wish to avoid taking a clear stand on so important an issue, yet I am bound to say that the answer, like the answer to most such questions, is both Yes and No, or rather No and Yes. Marxism is not Nihilism; it does not worship violence and regard it as an end in itself. Even when Lenin in his most revolutionary mood called for "the greatest ferocity and savagery" against "the exploiting minority," he was advocating violence as a means to an end. Yet Marxism does make a special place for violence, which is, as it were, a "necessary expedient" for the greatest of ends: the triumph of the proletariat. Marxist violence is *collective* violence, violence employed "not for personal subjective reasons, but to facilitate objective social processes."[65] Men who counsel its employment as confidently as do the Marxists must be judged to have a temper different from that of most men in the world. This judgment is about 60 per cent true of those who adhere to the Marxism of Marx, about 90 per cent true of those who proclaim the Marxism of Lenin. In the words of Nehru, another man who has learned about Communism the hard way:

Communism has definitely allied itself to an approach of violence. Even if it does not indulge normally in physical violence, its thought is violent, and it does not seek to change by persuasion or peaceful, democratic pressures, but by coercion and, indeed, destruction and extermination.[66]

One of Lenin's major contributions to the development of Marxism was the restoration of violent revolution to the place it had occupied in the writings of the young Marx. In 1918, Lenin chastized those "sugary writers" and "petty bourgeois types" who complained of the suffering caused by the Bolshevik revolution in these words:

> They had heard and admitted "in theory" that a revolution should be compared to an act of childbirth; but when it came to the point, they disgracefully took fright. . . . Take the descriptions of childbirth given in literature, when the authors aim at presenting a truthful picture of the severity, pain, and horror of the act of travail. . . . Human childbirth is an act which transforms the woman into an almost lifeless, bloodstained mass of flesh, tortured, tormented, and driven frantic by pain. But can the "type" that sees *only* this in love . . . be regarded as a human being? Who would renounce love and procreation for *this* reason? [67]

It can be argued, of course, that many Marxists have nothing to do with violence. They may be in no position to achieve their ends, or they may happen to achieve them through the collapse of the opposition. This does not mean that a tendency toward violent solutions is missing in their personal tempers. As Karl Popper has wisely written, "If a man is determined to use violence in order to achieve his aims, then we may say that to all intents and purposes he adopts a violent attitude, whether or not violence is actually used in a particular case." [68] Certainly the hard Marxist is determined to use it, without qualms and without regrets. His dogmatism blends with his urge to revolution to produce a kind of fanaticism for which force is second nature. The techniques of terror occupy a central place in the Soviet system not least because that system is operated by men who are determined Marxists.[69] For those who have fallen victims to the terror it must be comforting to have Vyshinsky's assurance that "proletarian revolutionary violence is democratic in the true sense of the word—both by its social essence and by the forms wherein it is realized." [70]

The American temper has never been noted, even in 1776 or 1861, for the revolutionary impulse. It is not easily roused to indignation, prefers harmony to struggle as an explanation of social progress, and avoids taking stands based on inflexible principle. Far from maintaining a dogmatic front in its dealings with men and ideas, it is more likely than not to be accommodating and tolerant—much too accommodating and tolerant, according to many Americans. We are supposed to have a special fondness for violence as a solution to our ills, but we resort to it, when we resort to it at all, carelessly and fitfully. The deed done, the violent American makes too many excuses for it to permit us to think of him as a man with a genuine penchant for violence in his nature. For all these reasons, and for the further reason that they have seldom had cause to argue bitterly with their system, only with the men who happened to be running it at a particular time, Americans are simply not revolutionaries in the classic sense of the word. They are traditionalists who make room in their tradition for steady progress in the condition of men. I am almost tempted to say, in contrast to my remark on the Marxist a few pages back, that if one is not an evolutionary in spirit and purpose, one is not an American.

This, too, might be judged a matter of opinion rather than of fact, but I think it distinctly more fact than opinion that all attempts of American Marxists to link up the Revolution of 1776 with that of 1917 in Russia and "the one still to come" in the United States are gross distortions of doctrine as well as of history.[71] Our great revolution was conceived by its makers as a war of political liberation. The men of 1776 went to war not to make the world over but to preserve a social and political order that they found, even in their fanciful moments, the best of all possible worlds. The famous American "right of revolution" that justified the actions of Washington and Jefferson was a severely limited concept that found no glory in violence and no virtue in subversion. Indeed, the Americans of 1776 talked of "resistance," not of "revolution." If I may quote the words with which, in another context, I have summed up the essential features of this right:

The right of resistance is the last refuge of a whole people unable to protect their lives, liberties, and properties by normal constitutional methods; it cannot be stretched to justify the *coup d'état* of a militant minority dedicated to the building of a new order. The people have a duty to be peaceful and law-abiding, and history demonstrates that they can be counted on never to resist except under overriding compulsion and to temper their methods to the nature and degree of oppression. The only possible outcome of a full reversion of power to the people is a new contract with new rulers under new terms of reciprocal obedience and protection. God granted men the right of resistance to help them preserve orderly government, not to induce them to fly from the tyranny of arbitrary power to the tyranny of no power at all. In short, resistance, the extreme form of which is revolution, is not so much the right as the solemn, unpleasant duty of a betrayed people.[72]

And if I may add the words of a man who has been in his time both a good Marxist and a better American:

In American socialist writing, it has not been unusual to try to vindicate the idea of socialist revolution in terms of the American revolutionary tradition. The two, however, have little to do with each other. The American, or rather the Anglo-American, revolutionary tradition is essentially the assertion of the right of revolutionary resistance to "tyrants," that is, to governments that overstep their proper limits and invade the "inalienable" natural rights of the citizen. . . . But the revolution of which socialism speaks is conceived as the "locomotive of history." It is essentially the new class, the proletariat, seizing power, as the agent of history, in order to inaugurate the new social order. Except for the fact that they both involve some sort of disturbance in the political status quo, there is no real connection between the two conceptions.[73]

There is, then, in temper and creed and memory, a razor-sharp contrast between Marxism and the American tradition in this mat-

ter of revolution. I do not mean to say that we faint at the sight
of blood or fail to recognize the possibility of progress through
cataclysm. To the contrary, we take as much pride as any nation
in our military tradition; we dislike those revisionists who aim to
prove that this war was "unnecessary" and that conflict "repres-
sible"; and we are certain that, in the long view of history, at
least three of our wars had beneficial social results. But we are
at bottom a people who put primary trust in peace and good order
and mutual respect among social classes as the prerequisites of
progress, and we therefore cherish the man who smooths rather
than shakes the earth—unless, of course, the earth-shaker is long
dead. As weak human beings in a menacing world, we too often
hate when we should love, and rage when we should be calm. But
at such times we know that we are not listening to what Lincoln
called "the better angels of our nature"; and always we know that
we cannot build the good society on those foundations. I once
wondered if there might be a strange affinity between the mystic
views that Lenin and Lincoln held of the agony of history, specifically, between Lenin's assumption that the shedding of blood
called for payment in blood and Lincoln's premonition, at his second inaugural as President, that God might ask that "every drop
of blood drawn with the lash shall be paid by another drawn with
the sword." The affinity, I am now convinced, is only apparent.
Lenin had hatred in his heart and Lincoln had pity; Lenin wanted
blood and Lincoln wept that it had to be shed; Lenin was plotting
like a faithful Marxist and Lincoln was crying aloud like an an-
guished Christian. They were different men of different tempers,
and in them may be found the decisive contrast between the two
different ways of life of which they are, Lenin for all Communists
and Lincoln for all democrats, the revered saints. In the final
reckoning, the gulf that divides them is the gulf between love and
hate, not as personal qualities but as approaches to life and explanations of the human predicament. I agree with E. H. Carr, a
man who has sought almost too eagerly to understand and be kind

to the Bolsheviks, that Lenin believed in the "creative properties of hatred." [74] Lincoln, I think we can say with conviction, put his own hopes in the creative properties of love. His memory and example must always make it impossible for Americans to embrace what has been truly described as "the first great system in human history to make hatred the principle of progress." [75]

Every great way of life and thought finds expression in a code of morals, a pattern of right conduct made up of maxims, customs, taboos, and habits. The code is rarely a model of internal consistency; it is not easily written down or efficiently enforced; and, if it is at all operative, it is general and flexible and reasonably permissive. It is, nevertheless, a table of commandments that leaves small room for doubt about the final distinction between right and wrong, and as such it provides an open window into the minds of men who do their best to honor it. It should come as no surprise to learn that the Marxists have their own morality, and we can learn something important about the Marxist temper if we look into it briefly.

The first thing we must note (and Marxists are anxious to have us note it) is that Marxism has nothing but scorn for the morality of the West, of which America is held to be the chief bearer in the twentieth century. Marx and Engels used words like "twaddle," "cant," "superstition," and "prejudice" to describe the moral preachings of both the capitalists, who were trying to hold the workers down, and the reformers, who were trying to help them up.[76] They insisted that all codes of morality were shaped to the needs of a particular class. "Men," Engels wrote, "consciously or unconsciously, derive their ethical ideas in the last resort from the practical relations on which their class position is based—from the economic relations in which they carry on production and exchange." They heaped ridicule on foes and friends alike who sought to palm off their own ideas of ethical behavior as "eternal laws of nature and of reason." Whatever purposes, good and evil, the dominant morality of the West had served in its time, that time was now past. Engels upbraided other socialists for basing their hopes on moral concepts that "do not take us an inch further." [77]

The heirs of Marx have been even harsher on our morality. Perhaps the worst sin, in Bolshevik eyes, of revisionists like Bernstein was their attempt to bring Kant to the support of Marx, to base the hope of a new society on ethical principles. Lenin found this kind of Marxism even worse than "twaddle," and he poured out his wrath on those who were such faithless children of the master. Since it might be argued that Lenin was not a man of the West to begin with, let me make this point with the help of an American Marxist, Howard Selsam, who has devoted an entire book to this problem. From his *Socialism and Ethics* we learn that "the traditional ethics is sick with the very disease of the world whose product it is." It is a cloak for prejudice, racism, bigotry, and exploitation; its conception of the good life has been left far behind by the onward rush of history. Worst of all from the Marxist point of view:

> The whole classical tradition of moral thought, valuable as many of its contributions are, has remained to this day preoccupied with limited questions of right and wrong centering around the conception of the virtuous individual, and has remained blissfully neglectful of the broader and wider idea of the concrete material and cultural welfare of mankind at large. . . . The fact is that ethics is still largely conceived in terms of individual *virtue* and that, in so far as our vast and complex social problems are recognized and dealt with, the tendency is to treat them as if they arose solely from individual moral shortcomings and could be solved by individual moral betterment. Behind this is the uncritical assumption that if only all men would be properly *ethical* in their activities and relationships all problems would thereby be solved.[78]

In these passages is caught the essence of the Marxist critique of our morality: this morality is individualist rather than collectivist, supernaturalist rather than naturalist, idealist rather than materialist. It must give way to "a new ethics . . . a new morality, freed from the taint of an exploiting economic class and of a ruthless acquisitive society."

It is difficult to say what rules the morality of the future is supposed to encompass, and therefore to understand in what sense it would be "new." The Marxists are at their fuzziest in discussing the code that should govern the comings and goings of ordinary men. Selsam surrenders to the spell of the unknowable more openly than do most Marxists when he writes that "ethics as we have known it will be so transformed as to be beyond the possibility of significant speculation." [79] He is not, however, breaking faith with the masters. Engels wrote wistfully in *Anti-Dühring* of the emergence of a "really human morality" rising above "class antagonisms and above any recollection of them." [80] Yet neither he nor Marx was any more accommodating than usual in drawing the outlines of the new society. As a matter of fact, there is considerable evidence for the belief that the great Marxists expected the good habits and seemly virtues of the present society—purged, of course, of their bourgeois character—to form at least part of the moral code of the communist future. In his address to the First International, Marx called for vindication of "the simple laws of morals and justice, which ought to govern the relations of private individuals." [81] Lenin predicted in *State and Revolution* that men and women under communism would "gradually *become accustomed* to the observance of the elementary rules of social life that have been known for centuries and repeated for thousands of years in all school books." [82] And Selsam writes so respectfully of "personal moral values—such as integrity, honesty, kindliness, generosity, cooperativeness, and just plain humanity," [83] that one is at a loss to say much more about the ethics of communist society than that men will really believe and practice what they have always known to be correct and decent, and that they will do so out of concern for the community rather than for themselves. Is it possible that the new morality will be simply the old morality dressed up in the Marxist robes of perfectibilism and collectivism?

Let us desist from giddy thoughts of an ethics suitable to men "ten feet tall," and turn to consider the more substantial issue of Marxist morality in the ages of proletarian revolution and socialist transition; for that, after all, is the morality with which the non-Communist world is likely to be confronted for some time to come. A great deal has been written in exposition and criticism and defense of this morality, but there is still no more effective and honest way to portray it than to quote Lenin's famous speech to the Young Communist League in 1920:

> The whole object of training, educating and teaching the youth of today should be to imbue them with communist ethics.
>
> But is there such a thing as communist ethics? Is there such a thing as communist morality? Of course, there is. It is often made to appear that we have no ethics of our own; and very often the bourgeoisie accuse us Communists of repudiating all ethics. This is a method of shuffling concepts, of throwing dust in the eyes of the workers and peasants.
>
> In what sense do we repudiate ethics and morality?
>
> In the sense in which it is preached by the bourgeoisie, who derived ethics from God's commandments. . . .
>
> We repudiate all morality taken apart from human society and classes. We say that it is a deception, a fraud, a befogging of the minds of the workers and peasants in the interests of the landlords and capitalists.
>
> We say that our morality is entirely subordinated to the interests of the class struggle of the proletariat. Our morality is derived from the interests of the class struggle of the proletariat. . . .
>
> The class struggle is continuing and it is our task to subordinate all interests to this struggle. And we subordinate our communist morality to this task. We say: morality is what serves to destroy the old exploiting society and to unite all the toilers around the proletariat, which is building up a new, communist society. . . .
>
> When people talk to us about morality, we say: for the Communist, morality lies entirely in this solid, united discipline and conscious mass struggle against the exploiters. We do not believe in an eternal morality, and we expose the deceit of all the fables about morality. Morality serves the purpose of helping human society to rise to a higher level and to get rid of the exploitation of labour.[84]

These astounding words have been echoed thousands of times by Communist polemicists throughout the world. Among the recent authoritative echoes in the Soviet Union itself are: "The only scientific definition of morality is the defense of the interests of the victory of Communism"; "in our time only what furthers the destruction of capitalism and the victory of Communism is moral"; and "the highest criterion of Communist morality is . . . self-sacrificing struggle for Communism." [85] The obvious corollary of this proposition is less often mentioned, but it is no less significant for an understanding of Marxist morality: the only scientific definition of immorality is the delaying of the victory of Communism.

If I may sum up by again quoting the American Marxist who has made this problem his special province, the actions of the working class

cannot be judged by the criteria that are the ethical expression of the capitalist class. This is not because the goals of the working class are good in and of themselves, but rather because they are the sole means to general human progress and the widest human good. Thus the Marxist does not examine each strike, each labor struggle or each revolutionary uprising of workers, farmers, or colonial people to see whether in every particular case the ethical canons of the bourgeoisie are observed. He examines them only in terms of whether they will or will not advance the cause of the oppressed masses.[86]

I think it important not to read any more wickedness or cynicism into these statements of Marxist-Leninist morality than is really there, for they are self-damaging enough simply as they stand, and as they have found practical demonstration in the past four decades. We can, in any case, come to these firm conclusions: that Communist morality turns out to be what the men in command of the party of the proletariat say it must be; that it puts severe demands of loyalty, self-sacrifice, courage, and discipline upon those who serve the party; [87] and that it calls upon them to be ready to take any action, however "unethical," that may advance the cause of revolution. At a time like this, when I might be ac-

cused of bourgeois prejudice, I am grateful that a man like Harold
Laski should have catalogued some of the practical applications
of the Marxist-Leninist morality. This was his sober judgment in
1948:

> The passion for conspiracy, the need for deception, the ruthlessness,
> the centralised and autocratic commands, the contempt for fair play,
> the willingness to use lying and treachery to discredit an opponent or
> to secure some desired end, complete dishonesty in the presentation
> of facts, the habit of regarding temporary success as justifying any
> measure, the hysterical invective by which they wrought to destroy
> the character of anyone who disagreed with them; these, in the con-
> text of an idolisation of leaders who might, the day after, be merci-
> lessly attacked as the incarnation of evil, have been the normal be-
> havior of Communists all over the world.[88]

What the Communist ethic adds up to is a denial of the age-old
attempt of moralists to distinguish means and ends, and to demonstrate the influence of the first upon the second. From a crude
point of view, the Communists seem to assert as boldly as any
men in history that their noble end justifies any sordid means they
may find necessary to adopt, and that the sordidness of the means
will not soil the end when it is finally attained. From a more subtle
point of view, however, they appear as men who consider this
distinction and all the problems it raises to be simply irrelevant.
"The question of a conflict of ends and means," a critic has written, "cannot be raised in a Party whose leadership claims that it
can foresee an inevitable future." [89]

It will be noted that I have been careful to use the words "Communist" or "Marxist-Leninist" to describe the morality of proletarian revolution and socialist transition, since I am not certain
that the blame can be laid fully at the master's door. Marx, for
all his demurrers, was one of the supreme moralizers of all time.
His strictures upon the world about him, far from being cool and
scientific, were moral judgments of the hottest kind. Indeed, it is
hard to imagine a concept in political economy more severely

ethical in nature than Marx's theory of surplus value. Small wonder that at least one Marxist has claimed that the master's "originating and basic attitude" was "moral and humanistic," or that Laski should consider the behavior of most Communists a denial of the true spirit of Marx and Engels.[90] Most of the evils Marx laid into indignantly were evils that we, too, profess to hate. It is hard not to concede a point to the revisionist Marxists, and think of Marx as a man who would have been shocked by Lenin's definition and Stalin's applications of Communist morality. Yet there is also much to be said for Barzun's point that although Marx "can be quoted to many purposes," the "prevailing cast of his mind, at least in public, leaves uppermost his scorn for moral obligation—a scorn which others have found only too easy to carry out in numberless concrete ways." [91] Lenin drew upon this aspect of Marx's public temper when he wrote of the "justice of Sombart's remark that in Marxism itself there is not a grain of ethics from beginning to end; theoretically, it subordinates 'the ethical standpoint' to 'the principle of causality'; practically, it reduces to the class struggle." [92] When can a system of thought be both moral and amoral at the same time and to the same ends? Apparently, when it is Marxist.

There is little that we need say about the principles and sanctions of the commonly accepted American morality. They are too well known to bear repeating; their clash with Marxism on the two persistent issues of individualism versus collectivism, and idealism versus materialism is too open to require any special description. Indeed, at almost every point our morality runs head-on into Communist morality, except when the spokesmen of the latter slip and speak of the qualities we admire as if they were universal and eternal—a most un-Marxist thing for them to do. We have learned over the years, from J. S. Mill as well as from Marx, that "wherever there is an ascendant class, a large portion of the morality of the country emanates from its class interests, and its feelings of class superiority." [93] We must admit that Americans of every generation have soiled our cherished morality by using it to cover up cruel and sordid practices. Yet we cannot concede that any hidden weakness has been revealed or permanent damage done by such abuses. To the contrary, they have served only to point up the fact that an operative code of morals must express the aspirations as well as the realities of human behavior. We persist in thinking that the fundamentals of our morality are essentially the same for all civilized men everywhere; that there already exists, as it has existed for centuries, a "really human morality"; that, in Hunt's words, "underlying the flux of history there is . . . a certain continuum to which all ethical judgments can be related, and which lead men to agree that Socrates was a good man and Nero a bad man, and that truth and charity are better than falsehood and malice." [94] As John Dewey wrote in explaining why he could never be a Communist, "fair play" and "elementary honesty" are "something more than 'bourgeois virtues.' " [95] Or if we may go deeper into reality by calling upon Dostoievsky, the moral order, as Raskolnikov proved, rests ultimately on a mystical element—on "a still, small voice" that silences "all the babel of human argument and counterargument." [96] We can never believe that our moral principles, however they may be shaped on the surface by time and circumstance, can have "no other basis" than the "concrete changing conditions of human life." [97] This is the first point at which we are at odds with the Marxists.

The second is the tangled question of means and ends. The Bolsheviks may refuse to consider the probability "that the chances of attaining certain goals may be lessened by the protracted, large-scale use of means which are at extreme variance to them," [98] but we may not, for ethical as well as for practical reasons. Even if we were to agree with both Hegel and Marx that actions which cannot be justified by the moral standards of the police court may ultimately be approved by history,[99] we would have to make our final choice for Hegel, who never went on to say that some men were therefore free to act as they pleased because history was bound to bless them. As Sidney Hook has pointed out, there is a close connection in the Marxist mind between inevitability and amorality. "The most fateful of the consequences of the belief in inevitability," he writes, is "its tendency to paralyze the nerve of moral responsibility. Political life abounds with temptations to use dubious means to advance political causes. And a view which sanctifies in advance the use of any means—for the good end, socialism, is sure to be realized 'sooner or later'—makes it easier to yield to these temptations with an easy conscience." [100]

Since American minds have no developed sense of the inevitable, they find it doubly difficult to think amorally. This may well be, as several of our tough-minded compatriots have complained, the Achilles heel of our diplomacy, but most Americans find it a small price to pay for a reasonably sound conscience. In any case, we make a distinction in our minds between means and ends, and in making it we see clearly that they can never be completely severed, just as they can never be completely merged. Means can corrupt ends as easily as ends can excuse means. One might go further to assert that means are more important than ends, that if one concentrates upon the former the latter will take care of themselves. In the end, we agree with a man who learned this lesson the hardest way of all, Milovan Djilas:

> Throughout history there have been no ideal ends which were attained with non-ideal, inhumane means, just as there has been no free society which was built by slaves. Nothing so well reveals the reality and greatness of ends as the methods used to attain them.[101]

And nothing so well reveals the unreality and wrongness of Marx's and Lenin's ends as the ruthlessness they counseled as the means for arriving at them. The discrepancy between evil means and noble ends is one that, in its best and most honest moments, our temper cannot bear. Theirs can, and that is a thing to remember.

•

There are other aspects of the Marxist temper that we could probe with equal care, but these three—the conviction of certainty, the urge to revolution, and the dedication to a morality of inevitability—are by all odds the most striking to the gaze of the American observer. Before I sum up the contrasts in mood and spirit between Marxism and the American tradition, let me mention briefly three lesser aspects. One is not very momentous and the other two far from unique to Marxism, but they are all interesting pieces that help to fill out the picture.

The first is the Communist practice of prefacing all praise or even explanation of their way of life with damnation of ours. This practice is a direct heritage from Marx (who was far more concerned to expose capitalism than to build socialism) and comes naturally to minds that see the world in blacks and whites. A classic product of the workings of this compulsive habit is Vyshinsky's celebrated *The Law of the Soviet State,* which was for many years the standard Soviet treatise upon the larger aspects of constitutional and administrative law.[102] Thanks to the downgrading of its author, the book is no longer used widely, but it still reads as an orthodox Marxist text. What astounds the American reader is the way in which it introduces each exposition of Marxist theory or Soviet practice with a hard slap at the West. Before Vyshinsky can discuss the Marxist-Leninist theory of the state he must dwell upon all the falseness and "pseudo-science" of the various bourgeois "theories"; before he can celebrate the Soviet scientific approach to law he must spend pages flaying Kant, Jellinek, Hauriou, Duguit, Gumplowicz, Krabbe, and Kelsen; and before he can describe the workings of the Soviet courts he must rehash the stories of Dreyfus and of Sacco and Vanzetti. His survey of the rights of Soviet citizens is studded with repeated contrasts to bourgeois practice as he moves from A (the right to work) through K (the right of asylum); and the whole thing is preceded by a lengthy diatribe against the "rights of citizens in bourgeois states."

This pattern was not peculiar to this peculiar man. *The ABC of*

Communism, a popular exposition written by Bukharin in the first years of the Bolshevist regime and (despite its authorship) still used widely by Communists in the most unlikely places, is equally concerned to expound Communism by first exposing capitalism. Khrushchev, to take an even more conspicuous example, is a slave to the habit. He rarely salutes a Soviet accomplishment or predicts a Soviet advance without taking his own cut at capitalism, and the Soviet press follows dutifully in his wake. It prefaced every boastful article on the Soviet election of 1958 by deriding some of the quainter practices of the American electoral system; it greets each new work of art created in the spirit of "socialist realism" with a few choice words about "the decomposition of culture" in bourgeois countries. The pattern has even found expression in basic documents. The Soviet constitution of 1923, for instance, began with the words:

Since the time of the formation of the Soviet republics, the states of the world have divided into two camps: the camp of capitalism and the camp of socialism.

There—in the camp of capitalism—national enmity and inequality, colonial slavery and chauvinism, national oppression and pogroms, imperialist brutalities and wars.

Here—in the camp of socialism—mutual confidence and peace and the fraternal collaboration of peoples.

I am not certain how much weight we should give this habit in our final estimate of the nature of Marxism, but we can go at least part of the way with Berdyaev in his analysis of Communism as "almost a Manichean dualism," a system of thought that must have an enemy as the chief point of reference.

The kingdom of the proletariat is the light kingdom of Ormuzd; the kingdom of the bourgeoisie is the dark kingdom of Ahriman. . . . The fanaticism, intolerance, cruelty and violence of the thorough-going type of communist is explained by the fact that he feels himself faced by the kingdom of Satan and he cannot endure that kingdom. But at the same time he depends negatively upon the kingdom of Satan, upon evil, upon capitalism, upon the bourgeoisie. He cannot live without an enemy, without the feeling of hostility to that enemy; he loses his *pathos* when that enemy does not exist.[103]

I am certain that we should not succumb to this habit ourselves. Our way of life must be justified by its own fruits. We gain no glory for our supposed virtues by listing them only after the supposed sins of the Communists. In any case, to be an unrelenting Manichean is not to be a levelheaded American. The "devil theory" of history or politics or war is not becoming to civilized minds. If we must be obsessed with the evils of any system, let us be obsessed with those we are trying to eliminate from our own.

A close relation of this aspect of the Marxist temper is the messianic complex. The Marxist, we have learned, is the supreme optimist of all time. He is convinced that the light he bears will penetrate and finally wipe out the darkness that still lingers over most of the world. His mission is to spread this light, both by example and activity; and no missionary has ever gone more piously to convert the heathen. The idea of mission is one of the oldest and most powerful in civilization. The Soviet Union is only the latest of a long line of peoples "chosen" by God or Fate or History for a destiny higher than their own well-being—the latest, and also the most convinced. Not even the prophets of Israel could match the followers of Marx and Lenin in their confident zeal. They have been singled out by history to do a necessary job, and they are doing it (or so they like to tell themselves) in the sure and certain hope that it will be done. In the words of an American militant:

The proletarian revolution is the most profound of all revolutions in history. . . . The hundreds of millions of workers and peasants, striking off their age-old chains of slavery, will construct a society of liberty and prosperity and intelligence. Communism will inaugurate a new era for the human race. . . . [It] will bring about the immediate or eventual solution of many great social problems . . . war, religious superstition, prostitution, famine, pestilence, crime, poverty, alcoholism, unemployment, illiteracy, race and national chauvinism, the suppression of women, and every form of slavery and exploitation of one class by another.[104]

And of a Czech philosopher:

We are struggling for the most perfect government of, by, and for the people, for a socialist democracy in which our children can live as citizens liberated from all terror and oppression and in which there will be no exploitation, no human degradation in subservience to wealth and capital. . . . These new generations will not even know of the problems that Hegel called those of the isolated "unhappy consciousness," neither will they understand the anxieties that filled Hamlet nor the dilemmas that harassed Faustus. A new Man will arise, the ruler of the earth and, in the atomic age, perhaps even the ruler of other planets—the ruler of a new history the curve of which will continuously rise toward higher degrees of spiritual and material civilization, thus overcoming all lower stages in harmony with the cosmic dialectics of being.[105]

Once we, too, had a strong sense of mission in this country,[106] especially during the years between Washington and Lincoln; but it was a pale thing contrasted with the messianism of the Soviets and of their friends all over the world. It called upon us primarily to serve as a testing ground for freedom. If the test was successful, if Americans were able to prove that men could govern themselves under "free principles," then free government would spread all through the world—as Jefferson said, "to some parts sooner, to others later, but finally to all." But we rarely supposed that we could spread freedom by any means other than the force of good example, and we always supposed that we might fail in the test. Neither of these suppositions has softened the profound Marxist sense of mission, which exalts the Soviet Union as "the shock-brigade of the world proletariat." [107] The mind of the dedicated Marxist is a study in messianism.

Finally, the Marxist temper is conspicuous for its elitism. For all their happy talk about the masses, Marxists put special trust in the charismatic few for the exploration of ideas and the solution of problems as well as for the governing of men. The quest for certainty is led by those few who never forget their "obligation to *be in advance of everybody,*" [108] who refuse to let "spontaneity" hold sway in the world of ideas. The revolutionary spirit is kept alive by the same few, who have the "advantage" over the "great mass" of "clearly understanding the line of march, the conditions, and the ultimate general results of the proletarian movement." [109] And the definition of conduct that "furthers the destruction of capitalism and the victory of communism" is placed firmly in the hands of the same few, who alone can predict and guide the inevitable course of history. Whether in the fanciful world of Marx's mind or in the real world of Khrushchev's Russia, the Communist party has final responsibility for seeking out and proclaiming the truth; and within the party there is a much smaller, more dedicated, and more farseeing group upon whose guidance, in the end, all progress depends. One cannot read far in the intellectual history of Communism without concluding that the need for an elite of consciousness, purpose, and intelligence is a persistent assumption of the Marxist temper. Nothing, I think, could be less true of the American temper, which has been, if anything, overly suspicious of the "natural aristocracy of virtue and intelligence" for which men as far apart in time and mood as John Adams and Admiral Rickover have cried in the wilderness.

This chapter has already spawned so many conclusions that I will say only these few words by way of summation: The Marxist temper, as the American sees it from his remote point of view, is zealous, dogmatic, revolutionary, violent, amoral, and elitist. It is supremely confident of the rightness and the ultimate triumph of the Children of Light, the proletariat; yet it is strangely obsessed with the sins and the staying-power of the Children of Darkness, the bourgeoisie. The American temper, in contrast, seems easygoing, pragmatic, tradition-directed, peaceful, moral, and democratic. It is supremely confident of nothing except the fact that no group of men, certainly not the Marxists, has a monopoly of truth. It is more Manichean than it used to be, but it is still far removed from obsession with ideas and forces other than those it calls its own. It is more apocalyptic, too, thanks to Spengler, Toynbee, and Marx himself, but it still cannot believe that America must bury Communism or be buried by it.

Perhaps the decisive difference between these two casts of mind, a difference about which Americans may be sad or glad or neither, is the plain truth that Marxism has a great purpose, a collective end, a historic destiny, and that the American tradition, certainly as we know it today, has none. The characteristic Marxist, when he is really a Marxist and not just a man with a wife and a job and perhaps a few carbuncles, knows that the world is moving on a predetermined course to an inevitable goal—which means that he, who is helping to reach that goal, has a purpose more profound than his own salvation and a meaning more transcendent than his own dignity. He is not and can never be one man alone; he is part of a collectivity with an end of its own. For him and for all his fellows the end, the victory of Communism, is clear and all-determining, and he cannot think or judge or even dream without being conscious of it.

The characteristic American, to the contrary, does not know where the world is going. He believes that his nation has meaning, as indeed it does, but he also knows that few of his fellows are likely to agree with his own version of our national destiny. He is, in any case, too much an individualist (a reactionary, bourgeois individualist, the Marxist says) to feel the urge to submerge his own hopes and fears in the higher purpose of a collective destiny, certainly of a destiny that is directed right down to the last left turn to glory by a charismatic elite. Out of the lives of millions of free, decent, duty-conscious individuals there may well arise, the American thinks, some greater purpose: peace on earth, progress for the race, glory for God. But essentially he is a man who, try as he might, can find no ultimate purpose in history, no consuming mission for his country, no cosmic plan for all men in which he can hide his own doubt and despair. Even if he can suggest a national mission—and who cannot if asked politely to give it a try? —he has no reason to believe that others share his view. Even if he can discover a pattern in our history, his undogmatic cast of mind leads him to suspect that America has moved forward in ways too peculiar and mysterious to have immediate relevance for other peoples. And even if he is a devout subscriber to the most demanding kind of religion, his God is more than likely to be a God who cares only for individuals. This must surely be the decisive point of contrast between the Marxist and American tempers: the one is dogmatically collectivist, the other searchingly individualist. If this leaves us the weaker camp in the great struggle for the minds of men—an easy assumption that is yet to be proved —we are at least following our own star and remaining faithful to the great and democratic tradition that made us the people we are.

EIGHT · AMERICA AND MARX

I hope," Marx once wrote in a mixed mood of jest and spite, "that the bourgeoisie as long as they live will have cause to remember my carbuncles." I expect that we will have cause, as long as we live; and we may give thanks that only rarely has he proved so keen a prophet. Marx is a giant who reigns in awe over the world—even over those parts that deny his sovereignty—as no man of ideas has reigned in all history.* He is, in his own words, a "specter . . . haunting" every country, every party, every interest, indeed every thinking man in the world, and not just because he is the father of Communism. Marx the thinker may be a man to reckon with long after Communism has joined the other legendary tyrannies in "the dustbin of history." For all his trespasses against reason, science, history, and common sense, he owned one of the mighty minds of the human race, and we may be prisoners of his words and categories and eccentricities as long as we were of Aristotle's. The prospect is appalling, but it lies before us, and we had better learn to live with it bravely.

* In this chapter I will concentrate, largely for reasons of art, on Marx himself at the expense of Engels. I do not mean to indicate any less respect than I have already shown for the latter's stature, for he was, I think, the best of all possible Marxists. It is simply a question of wanting to play the one light I have available on the one giant on stage. The reader is at liberty to add "and Engels" whenever he reads "Marx" in the text.

We in the West, especially in America, have most to learn, for upon us Marx unleashed the brunt of his attack, and upon us the attack continues in undiminished violence. Indeed, it almost seems as if he were as vibrantly and censoriously alive today as he was in 1848. We have no social arrangement—our welfare capitalism, the ascendancy of our middle class, the variety of our groups and interests—for which he can say one kind or even understanding word. We have no institution—church, family, property, school, corporation, trade union, and all the agencies of constitutional democracy—that he does not wish either to destroy or to transform beyond recognition. We have no ideals or ideas—from the Christian ethic through patriotism to individualism—that he does not condemn out of hand. The essence of Marx's message is a prediction of doom for the Western, liberal, democratic way of life. He announces that prediction not sadly but gladly, not timidly but furiously, not contingently but dogmatically; and so, of course, do his heirs. Lenin was once again a faithful child of Marx when he wrote, "In the end one or the other will triumph—a funeral requiem will be sung over the Soviet Republic or over world capitalism," and Khrushchev a faithful grandchild when he laid to rest all doubts about our future by promising happily, "We will bury you." He will bury us, he thinks, because we deserve to be buried, and because Marx promised that we will get what we deserve. Khrushchev harbors a quasi-religious conviction of the overpowering rightness of Communism and the overweening wrongness of Western democracy. He makes the sharpest possible confrontation of his system and ours, and he makes it, let us not forget, apocalyptically—that is, by predicting the total victory of the one and the total defeat of the other, whether the game be played on the battlefield, in the laboratory, or in the heavens.

It is time that we, too, made this confrontation far more sharply than we have made it in the past generation. Whether we, too, must come to an apocalyptic conclusion I am not yet ready to say, but I am certain that we must not fear to look orthodox

Marxism straight in the face. That is why I have attempted this small beginning by looking into the assumptions and motives which make that face so grim as it stares back at us and so hopeful as it scans the future. Let me collect and restate the many points of confrontation we have discovered, in the form of three deep-cutting, irreconcilable conflicts:

The first arises primarily in the realm of ideas: the head-on collision of monism and pluralism. Marxism is, as Engels said jokingly, "an all-comprising system" constructed by men of a "terribly ponderous *Gründlichkeit";* it is, as Lenin said solemnly, a "solid block of steel," a "prolific, true, powerful, omnipotent, objective, and absolute human knowledge." Marxism is the latest and greatest (and easily the most presumptuous) of all those celebrated systems of thought with which learned men, moved by the doubts and fears of the unlearned, have sought to interpret the world in terms of a single principle. It has an explanation of everything, and to everything it grants one explanation. The whole range of man's behavior is explained in terms of the business of making a living, the whole configuration of society in terms of the class structure, the whole sweep of history in terms of the class struggle, the whole phenomenon of classes in terms of private property; and all these primary forces, most notably property, are hung upon a hook fashioned from the "solid block of steel": dialectical materialism. The dialectic of Hegel and the materialism of Hobbes and Holbach are clamped together, if never really consolidated, to account for all things from "the dance of the electrons" to "the conflicts in human society." [1] Marxism, at least as theory, is a closed system in which all new facts and ideas are made to conform to the original pattern, which is itself a thing of breathtaking simplicity. [2]

The American tradition, to the contrary, is consciously pluralistic. Its unity is the result of a process through which unnumbered diversities of faith and intellect seek to live together in accommodation, if not always in harmony. Man, history, society, politics, nature—all are explained, to the extent that they can be explained, in terms of multiple causation. Our system of ideas is open to new thoughts and fresh evidence. It has its bedrock beliefs in the dignity of man, the excellence of liberty, the limits of politics, and the presence of God; but on these beliefs, even in defiance of the last, men are free to build almost every conceivable type of intellectual and spiritual mansion. For this reason, we find it hard to grant much respect to Marxism, a system that presumes to relate all thoughts and all wonders to a single determining principle. More to the point, we find it increasingly hard to grant it license, for too much evidence is now before our eyes that monism in the world of ideas leads to absolutism in the world of events. In order to survive, a truly monistic system must put an end to the great debates that have gone on for thousands of years,* give dogmatic answers to questions that men can never answer finally, and destroy all other systems, closed or open, that seek to understand something of the mysteries of life. The monism of Marxism makes it the ideology of ideologies, and we can never make peace with it. Those Americans who have themselves succumbed to monism are in palpable violation of one of our most cherished principles, and they could profit a great deal from the Communist example.

The second conflict arises primarily in the realm of institutions:

---

* The course of events in Red China over the past few years is a fascinating case study in the inevitable results of monism. In February 1957, Mao Tse-tung made his famous appeal to the Supreme State Conference in Peiping: "Let a hundred flowers bloom, let a hundred schools of thought contend." No sooner had Mao's garden begun to grow, however, than most of the new flowers were identified as "poisonous weeds," and rooted out savagely. As the *New York Times* said editorially, any flower may grow in Chinese soil if it meets these conditions: "First, views expressed must serve to unite and not divide the people. Second, they must benefit socialist transformation and construction. Third, they must help to consolidate the 'people's democratic dictatorship.' Fourth, they must help to consolidate 'democratic centralism.' Fifth, they must strengthen the leadership of the Communist party. Sixth, they must benefit international Communist solidarity and that of 'peace-loving peoples.' " This hardly leaves much room in the garden for even slightly mutant blooms.[3]

the head-on collision of collectivism and individualism. Marx, we
have learned, seems more concerned with abstract men in the
real mass rather than with real men in the abstract mass. He talks
of classes rather than of individuals, of systems rather than of
persons; he seems to have no respect at all for private man. His
prescriptions are based on an honest assumption that all conflicts
between the interests of any one man and the interests of all
society, between what a man owes himself and what he owes his
fellows, can be eliminated by social reconstruction. On both "the
individual withdrawn into his private interests" and the family
with even a symbolic fence between itself and the community he
pronounces a sentence of doom; and he does it in the best of faith
because he cannot believe that any man or family will feel the
need to hold something of value aloof from the proletarian or
classless community. His prescriptions are therefore, as we have
seen, thoroughly collectivistic. No man, no group, no interest, no
center of power is to defy the dictatorship of the proletariat in
the period of socialist transition or to remain outside the harmonious community in the endless age of communism. That age would
surely be marked, as I wrote in Chapter IV, by a state of "togetherness" that would obliterate every barrier between man and mankind. Collectivism is Marx's means, and it is also his end. It may
be gentle, comforting, and unforced—once the dictatorship has
passed—but it is still collectivism with a vengeance.

The American tradition is doggedly individualistic. It makes
room for the state, for society, and for natural and voluntary groups;
and only a few men on the fringes of the tradition have ever denied
the intensely social nature of man. Yet it leaves a wide sphere to
private man, the private family, and private groups even in its
most socially conscious moments, and it insists on a meaningful,
lasting contradiction between the interests of this sphere and those
of the common weal. Lacking the monistic urge to have all things
in order, it understands that freedom is an eternal paradox. It is
prepared to live indefinitely with the division of each person into

an "individual" and a "citizen." If this leaves all thinking men in a state of ceaseless tension, the tension must nonetheless be borne as part of the human condition.[4] Marx tries to resolve it, and that is where he goes off the track, or rather down the wrong track. We try to live with it, and that is why we go bumping along on the right track. There have been times, to be sure, when we hurried down it much too blithely. We have lost sight of the free group in our anxiety to celebrate the free individual; we have made too much of competition and too little of co-operation as engines of social progress. But fundamentally our tradition is a challenge to collectivism at both levels; a challenge in behalf of the free individual, a challenge in behalf of the free group. The full measure of this giant confrontation should be understood as a collision of collectivism with both individualism and social pluralism.

The last confrontation is both ideological and institutional: the not quite head-on, yet resounding enough collision of radicalism with conservatism and liberalism. Marxism is, by almost any standard, the supreme radicalism of all time. It is radical in every sense of that sticky word: because it is revolutionary, because it is extremist, because it proposes to dig down to the roots of all things. It insists that the political and social institutions of the West are oppressive and diseased, the values that support them rotten and dishonest; it bids us supplant them with an infinitely more just and benign way of life. So complete is its commitment to the future, so unwilling is it to suffer delay, that it is prepared to force entry into this future by subversion and violence. Its attitude toward the social process is simple and savage: it means to disrupt it as thoroughly as possible in defiance of all rules of the game. The rules, in any case, are monstrous cheats, which may be ignored, manipulated, or turned against their makers—whatever course seems most likely to serve the cause of revolutionary radicalism. The Marxist is a man with a blueprint for rebuilding society, and the first three items on the sheet of instructions that goes with it read: smash the foundations of the old society into rubble; cart the rubble away; start to build a new foundation with new materials that have never been used before.

The American tradition, like most successful traditions with a broad appeal, is a casual blend of conservatism and liberalism. It is conservative in all the useful senses of that sticky word: because it is cautious and moderate, because it is disposed to preserve what it has inherited, because it puts a high value on tradition as a social force and prudence as an individual virtue. It does not encourage, to put it mildly, an attitude of bitter criticism among its children; it is committed to a discriminating but dogged defense of the American system against radical change. Yet it is liberal, too, in most senses of that stickiest word of all: because it is open-handed and open-minded, because it really expects the future to be better than the past, because it is interested first of all in the development of free men. Product of a history of ceaseless change and growth, it makes a large place for progress through conscious reform and prescriptive innovation. It breeds optimism rather than pessimism about the next hundred years, even in the teeth of the Marxist challenge. Some Americans interpret their tradition as a stamp of approval on things as they are, others interpret it as a summons to restless experiment; but all (or almost all, because the tradition also makes room for the men on the fringes) have little use for the kind of radicalism Marx proclaims. While there is still room for Utopia in the American dream, short cuts to it are looked upon as roads to ruin. The American mind has been sold some amazing prescriptions for specific ills; it has never been sold a panacea, and probably could not be.

Each of these major aspects of Marxism—monism, collectivism, radicalism—feeds upon the others. They are all of the same variety; no one of them can flourish without the nourishment of the other two. The monistic mind cannot brook dissent and must move to obliterate it with collectivist solutions. The collectivist solution cannot succeed unless infused by the radical spirit. And the radical spirit searches ceaselessly for the single explanation of the corrupt present and the single road to the glorious future. Berdyaev, who had watched the performance of the orthodox Marxists from a box seat, framed this living triangle in words largely borrowed from the Hungarian Marxist, Georg Lukacs:

> The essence of revolution is *totality,* entireness, in relation to every act of life. The revolutionary is one who in every act he performs relates it to the community as a whole, and subordinates it to the central and complete idea. For the revolutionary there are no *separate* spheres; he tolerates no division of life into parts, nor will he admit any autonomy of thought in relation to action or autonomy of action in relation to thought. The revolutionary has an integrated world-view in which theory and practice organically coalesce. Entirety in everything—that is the basic principle of the revolutionary attitude to life.[5]

And that, we know to our despair, is the basic principle of Marxist radicalism.

We have come perilously close along an indirect route to concluding that the decisive confrontation of orthodox Marxism and the American tradition is one of totalitarianism and liberal democracy. Since we would not want to reach any such conclusion by the back gate, we must approach this difficult question directly. We certainly cannot answer it by arguing that Marx himself was a totalitarian, for totalitarianism, it is agreed, is very much an institutional and ideological phenomenon of the twentieth century, the age of advanced technology and mass man. The question we must face is to what extent Marx was a major source of totalitarianism, more precisely, to what extent he may reasonably be held accountable—in the intellectual sense, I hasten to point out—for the acknowledged totalitarian features and institutions of the Soviet Union and of all other countries that invoke his memory as "the founder of scientific socialism." Let us first take note of the most important of these features and institutions, then see how many of them can be traced to Marx.

The essential, interrelated characteristics of a genuinely totalitarian system would appear to be: [6]

1) the obliteration of all restraints on political power: direct restraints like constitutional and legal prescriptions, indirect restraints like free associations * and inherited patterns of morality, "natural" restraints like the family;

2) the penetration of every nook and corner of the exposed and defenseless society by the restless, protean, dynamic power of the state, that is, the "politicalization" of every form of social and even personal activity;

3) the ubiquitous control and direction of the individual, whose allegiance to the state must be demonstrated actively and continuously;

4) the manipulation of men and power in pursuit of an ideology so revolutionary, millennial, and total that it takes on the form of a secular religion,† and of a militant nationalism.[9]

On only the first of these counts can totalitarianism be compared at all meaningfully to the autocracies and despotisms of the past. They were content with the obliteration of all visible restraints on their power, and they rarely felt the urge or need to exercise more than a fraction of the power they had. They annoyed most men and groups only when these were actively hostile and subversive; wielded power to exploit and to keep order rather than to remake

* In the undevious words of William Z. Foster, "Under the dictatorship all the capitalist parties—Republican, Democratic, Progressive, Socialist, etc.—will be liquidated, the Communist Party functioning alone as the Party of the toiling masses. Likewise, will be dissolved chambers of commerce, employers' associations, rotary clubs, American Legion, Y.M.C.A., Masons, Odd Fellows, Elks, Knights of Columbus, etc." [7] And as Bertram D. Wolfe has pointed out from wide experience, "Mr. Foster really meant that 'et cetera.' "

† Bertram Wolfe finds five determining characteristics in a specifically totalitarian ideology: "1) it is monistic; 2) it is all-inclusive; 3) it is exclusive—it is *allein selig machend;* 4) it is psychologically exhaustive, in that it demands total passion and total engagement; 5) it contains an imminent eschatology." [8]

society; and held a view of life that was narrow, traditional, and aimed largely at security at home and adventure abroad.

The essential institutions of totalitarianism, the instruments through which its unique purposes are formulated and pursued if not always realized, are:

1) the all-encompassing state, a gigantic bureaucracy that busies itself with every aspect of society from the maintenance of order to the care and feeding of lady discus-throwers;

2) the monolithic party, which identifies itself with the people and the state, acting for the former and directing the latter;

3) within the party a small ruling group of praetorian-priests who provide the dynamism in the pattern of total power and guard the purity of the ideology against revision and deviation (and who feel a persistent urge to give their dictatorship over to a dictator);

4) a series of controls through which the media of communication are monopolized by the state and party, and are harnessed to the dictates of the ideology;

5) a parallel series of controls and organizations through which the intellectual and cultural life of the people is similarly monopolized and politicalized; *

* In every area of artistic and literary endeavor, *partiinost* ("I ask myself—what does the party want?") and *narodnost* ("I ask myself—what do the people want?") work hand in hand to produce the stale fruits of "Socialist realism." "A Soviet encyclopedia," an official statement runs, "cannot be a mere collection of information presented in an impartial, neutral and politically indifferent manner. It should present all aspects of human activity and knowledge from the standpoint of a militant Marxist-Leninist world outlook." "Soviet art," another official statement echoes, "is suffused with optimism, cheerfulness, belief in the bright future of the people, in the victory of Communism. It is an art with an affirmative view of life, like all of Soviet ideology." "Soviet psychologists," a voice cuts in from a border area, must "resolutely apply the principle of Bolshevist partisanship and militancy" and place their science "in the service of the party."

I could go on endlessly giving evidence of the domination of "Zhdanovism"—a label which memorializes the reign of Stalin's lieutenant for culture, Andrei A. Zhdanov—over Soviet intellectual life, but I think it will be enough to quote from Zhdanov himself.

To the writers: "Create works of high attainment, of high ideological

6) an elaborate system of organized terror, a new kind of force that serves the needs of a new kind of state by purging the body social of its dissident humors;

7) the trappings of democracy, through which the wielders of total power seek to create the mass base so essential in the age of mass man;

8) and, as the most shocking result of the processes I have mentioned, the "atomization" of society, that is, the creation of a system devoid of buffers between the individual and the state, a society of rootless individuals and nothing more.

This is at best a sketchy rendering of the outlines of totalitarianism. It avoids the question whether there must be a dictator; it begs the question whether militant nationalism must infuse the ideology; it does not touch upon certain other essentials of totalitarianism (the worship of technology, the quest for autarchy, the glorification of the military, the need for scapegoats) that are only extreme versions of features common to all advanced states

---

and artistic content. Help actively to remold the people's consciousness in the spirit of socialism. Be in the front ranks of those who are fighting for a classless socialist society. . . . We are in no way obliged to provide a place in our literature for tastes and tempers that have nothing in common with the ethics and qualities of Soviet people."

To the philosophers: "Our philosophical work does not show either a militant or a Bolshevik tempo." The Soviet Union needs "an organized detachment of militant philosophers, perfectly equipped with Marxist theory . . . a detachment ceaselessly advancing our science, arming the toilers of our socialist society with the consciousness of the correctness of our path, and with confidence, scientifically grounded, in the ultimate victory of our cause."

And to Shostakovich and his erring friends: Remember "Glinka's wonderful words about the ties between the people and the artist: 'Music is created by the people and we artists only arrange it.' . . . Let us not forget that the U.S.S.R. is now the guardian of universal musical culture, just as in all other respects it is the mainstay of human civilization and culture against bourgeois decadence. . . . Therefore, not only the musical, but also the political, ear of Soviet composers must be very keen."

The Soviet Union, it seems plain, has made a mockery of Kautsky's promise of "communism in material production, anarchism in the intellectual." Production in the intellectual area is even more centrally directed and regimented than in the material.[10]

in a troubled world. But it does, I think, call attention to the essentials of the new state, which have been given their most intense application in the Soviet Union.

Now, then, how far and how directly can each of the features and institutions of totalitarianism be traced to Marx? To a large extent, this whole book is an answer to that question, and the reader may look back to the discussions of religion in Chapter II, of perfectibilism in Chapter III, of the family in Chapter V, of the state in Chapter VI, of the quest for certainty in Chapter VII, and may answer it conclusively for himself. Let me confine myself here to a rough estimate of Marx's intellectual contribution to the flowering of various aspects of Communist totalitarianism.

To the obliteration of restraints: a large contribution. His solution to the nagging problem of power was simply to ignore it. He derided the whole pattern of constitutional and moral limits, extended unlimited authority for an indefinite period to the dictatorship of the proletariat, and assumed that the men who prosecuted it would need no oversight other than that provided by history. The contempt for constitutionalism that pervades the Communist mind is a direct legacy from Marx.

To the politicalization of life: not so large, but large enough. No man of the nineteenth century could have imagined the massive scale on which power would be used in the twentieth century to reconstitute and then maintain society on revolutionary principles, but Marx did his share to encourage the leaders of Communism in their monumental audacity. In pulverizing the barriers to political power, in sneering at the instruments of "mere formal freedom," in stripping the family of its private character, Marx opened the way to the dynamic, all-pervading collectivism of Soviet totalitarianism, a system in which, as Djilas can testify, power is both the "end" and the "essence." [11]

To the engulfing of the individual: a large contribution indeed, as we have already learned. Again we must remind ourselves that Marx was a man of the nineteenth century, a time in which the whole duty of the individual to even the most brutal despotism left him with thoughts and purposes and interests of his own. While Marx expected men to be punished for singing the wrong tune, he was still a long way from asserting that they should be punished for not singing the right one—loudly, tunefully, and every day of their lives.* Yet he took away so much maneuverability from the free individual that we may certainly hold him accountable, as accountable as any dead man can be held, for the collapse of individualism under Soviet totalitarianism.[13] He was the nineteenth-century thinker, let it not be forgotten, who did most to destroy the age-old concept of private man: of man the average plodder or sweet eccentric or pig-headed fool who wants to live some part of his life for and by himself. Marx did not see why he should want or need to, and neither do the totalitarians.

To the sway of ideology: equally large. I doubt that we need retrace our steps through Chapters II and VII. It should be enough to recall that Marx took off avidly on the quest for certainty, that he found his certainty in the magic formula of dialectical materialism, and that in finding it he claimed to have found absolute truth. In doing all this he provided a major part of the "mystique" of Soviet Communism, those "mystically derived, relatively abstract goals and imperatives" which Alex Inkeles considers the "most distinctive and basic determinant . . . of totalitarian society," standing above and taking "precedence over considerations of human welfare, of personal and group interest, comfort, and gratification, and of stable and calculable patterns of social relations." [14]

The evidence against Marx seems overwhelming, and I hardly think it necessary to run through every instrument of totalitarianism to establish him as the intellectual father (or would it be the

---

* As Stalin put it in his famous speech on the draft constitution of 1936, "It may be said that silence is not criticism. But that is not true. The method of keeping silence, as a special method of ignoring things, is also a form of criticism." "What we build," Zhdanov echoed, "cannot be built with passive people." [12]

grandfather?) of the Soviet system. Let me conclude with a few words on what Americans would consider the most startling instruments: the party, the terror, and the trappings of mass democracy. To what extent was he a source of each of these strands in the web of totalitarianism?

We have already established Marx's broad if not primary responsibility for the Communist party. He willed its existence and gave it its great mission in the *Manifesto* and the *Address to the Communist League*. He placed in its keeping both the interpretation of the iron laws of history and the definition of morality, instructed it how to exploit the progressive urges of other men and groups, and commanded it to seize and manipulate the instruments of political power. As I pointed out in Chapter VI, he intended the party to be "democratic," that is, a party with a mass membership and responsible leadership; but he must have known that the success of any proletarian revolution would depend on the unhindered freedom of action of a hard core of men who had "the advantage of clearly understanding the line of march." He could hardly have expected them to submit daily accounts to the mass of proletarians. Let us say that the party was Lenin's creation, but let us add that he had a selection of highly useful materials at close hand in Marx's writings, and that Marx certainly did not forbid him the "leap" he took in *What is to be Done?* What is more, he had the example of the master, for Marx behaved like a premature Leninist in his boorish, scheming activities in the First International. Bakunin might say that we have been much too kind to Marx.

We cannot find him guilty of inspiring the terror, which is a Russian institution of ancient lineage. Marx was a revolutionary who was ready to kill if necessary, not a tyrant who needed blood to live; and he was much too sure of the triumph of the proletariat to think of the details of suppressing the bourgeoisie. Yet if not guilty, he is also not innocent. He was, we have learned, a fierce hater, an implacable fighter, a man unafraid of the uses or consequences of violence. Like every true Marxist he merged his conviction of certainty and his urge to revolution into a fanaticism that made it impossible for him to live and work except with men who agreed with him unreservedly. If he did not purge old friends and associates in fact, he certainly did in fancy. Is it too much to say that his treatment of Bakunin and Lassalle was a symbolic rehearsal of Stalin's treatment of Bukharin and Zinoviev? [15] The fact that he himself would never have survived the first purge does nothing to mitigate his peculiar responsibility for the "permanent purge."

Totalitarianism goes far beyond any other despotism in history in the enthusiasm of its search for popular support. The Soviet Union, as we know from the newsreels, has made a fine art of manipulating the techniques of mass participation. It insists that it is "a democracy of a higher type," the "most democratic state in the world"; [16] and it dramatizes this claim in the great parades in Red Square, the "spontaneous" demonstrations before Western embassies, the labored discussions in trade unions and soviets, and the public trials and confessions—above all in the grand spectacle of the near-unanimous elections that choose deputies to the Supreme Soviet.[17] More than that, it pays Western democracy the high tribute of imitating most of the processes of parliamentary government. But the world knows, and surely many Communists must know, too, that there is a wide gap between a monolithic state that uses the people primarily to give weight to the decisions of an irresponsible elite and a loose-jointed state that uses the people or ignores their demands at its immediate peril, between parliamentary institutions that "serve as focal points from which the influence of leaders is radiated out through the populace" and parliamentary institutions that do the actual business of decision-making through discussion and compromise.[18]

I do not wish to rehearse the differences between the Soviet and Western types of democracy, nor to raise again those self-evident facts which make a mockery of the Communist boast.[19]

Our central argument throughout this book has been with the subtleties of Marx, not with the vulgarities of Stalin or Khrushchev; and I am concerned at this point only to prove the simple assertion that the fraudulent, illiberal, unlimited "democracy" of the Communist states has a deep root in the Jacobin "democracy" of Marx. To do that I must turn back to a question I asked before: Was Marx a democrat?—to which the short answer is No. He was not a democrat in spirit, for he was dogmatic, angry, and contemptuous of other men and ideas; nor in principle, for it was he who forged the "solid block of steel"; nor in practice, for he had no use for compromise and concession and behaved like a man "whose deepest internal existence" was "all a wounding and being wounded, a crushing and being crushed." [20] There may have been, as H. B. Mayo decently insists, "a genuinely liberal and humanitarian strain in Marx's protest against the injustices of his age," [21] but he was much too unjust himself to be ranked with democrats like Jefferson and Lincoln or Mill and Bentham. The true democrat knows full well that injustice can work no permanent cure for injustice.

If Marx was a democrat at all, it was in the sense I described in Chapter Six: as a true son of the Jacobins, a man of the plebiscite and mass meeting, of the unchecked majority and the helpless minority, of the pursuit of the One Great Interest. If to hate poverty, praise economic abundance, despise all generals and gentlemen, ridicule the follies of businessmen, and wish an abstraction called "the people" well makes a man a democrat, then Marx deserves the label. But to be a genuine democrat calls for more than that. One must believe in the ultimate rightness of the people's judgments, and favor techniques through which these judgments may be made, felt, changed, and felt again. This is a belief Marx never had; lacking the belief, he had no thoughts about the techniques. One can look in vain in every hole and corner of his work to find a kind word for those ideas and institutions which alone make a political system "democratic" in any meaningful sense of the word: the recognition that the state is not all of society, the existence of genuine limits upon the power of the state, the free conflict of interests within a broad sphere of agreement, the ability of the voters to choose and dismiss the government, the undertaking, in Mayo's words, "not to suppress or persecute opponents but to leave them with their political and civil liberties intact." [22] Marx cared for none of these things because, in his view, they were essentially meaningless. He had his eye on three societies, and in none of them did he find any place for what we know as constitutional democracy. Let me cite his attitude toward the spirit and techniques of compromise as a convincing example: in bourgeois society, compromise is fraudulent because the interests of the major groups are impossible to reconcile; in socialist society, it is subversive because the role of the state is to suppress all other interests except those of the proletariat, certainly not to accommodate them; in communist society, it will be irrelevant because there will be nothing to compromise. So much for the prudent virtue that most political theorists have found to be the chief instrument of the democratic way of life.

If we are honest, then, we can make no other judgments than, first, that the Soviet theory of democracy rests squarely upon the concept of a "scientific" leadership that knows what is good for the people much better than do the people, who cannot in any case be trusted to govern themselves; and second, that Marx is a direct ancestor of this Leninist theory of leadership and of its corollary that legitimacy is sought by grounding authority on the supposed wishes of "the great mass of the proletariat." If Marx would permit us to use his precious key to history and nature, we might even say that his theory of "democracy" carried within it the seeds of its own negation. I doubt that he would care much for the synthesis, the "new state" of the Soviet Union, but he would have trouble trying to prove he had no part in it. He, too, believed in government not *by* but only *for* the people, and for the people in a sense that makes it unnecessary and even impolitic to consult them about their wishes. His prescription for society was undemocratic in its parts and undemocratic in the whole; and the Marxists of the Soviet Union are, to this extent, his devoted heirs.

I hope I have made myself clear in this matter of Marx's share of the intellectual blame for Soviet totalitarianism. I am not saying that he was a totalitarian, for the breed did not exist until the 1920's. I am not pinning the whole or even the primary responsibility for the Soviet system on him, for the Russian revolutionaries might well have found the inspiration for totalitarianism in their own tradition, and their heirs might well behave much the way they do even if they were not dogmatic Marxists. Bolshevism has several prime sources in addition to Marxism. I am certainly not tagging Marx as the chief intellectual source of twentieth-century totalitarianism, for the Nazis demonstrated conclusively that there were other intellectual accessories before the fact.[23] Yet the fact is there—the Soviet Union—and the Marxism of Marx helped considerably to shape it. Lenin made effective use of Marx because the master had laid, not entirely unwittingly, a straight path to the next stage of history, and Stalin made the same use of Lenin.

It may be that I have been unfair to Marx, who was a more admirable man and sensitive humanitarian than were many of the men he tilted at. But even if we concede a major point to men like Sidney Hook, who insists doggedly that Marx's "belief in freedom, equality, and individual personality distinguished [him] radically from all totalitarians who invoke his name," [24] we are left with the truth that he counseled harshly undemocratic means to reach his sweetly democratic ends. This "democrat" opened wide the door to naked power, then put that power in the hands of a "scientific" elite; and we can only say in the words of the Grand Inquisitor, "Thou didst thyself lay the foundations for the destruction of thy kingdom, and no man is more to blame for it." "This is the curse on salvationist creeds," a modern wise man adds, "to be born out of the noblest impulses of man, and to degenerate

into weapons of tyranny." [25] Should we be surprised that the supreme creed of earthly salvation has been transformed into the
dogma of the most savage of all tyrannies? And can we not properly add to the three great confrontations we have already found
at least four more: absolutism versus constitutionalism, statism
versus social pluralism, elitism versus populism—and thus totalitarianism versus democracy? From an admittedly subjective
American point of view, Marxism appears to be deeply and in-
curably infected with totalitarianism. [26]

I have argued that Marx was an important intellectual source
of Soviet totalitarianism. Does it then follow that the Communists
themselves are Marxists, men whose long-range policies and every-
day conduct are molded significantly by a sincere devotion to his
and Engels' writings? I confess to having made such an assumption throughout this book, and now I must try to substantiate it. [27]
There is not much doubt about the devotion or its sincerity.
Communists in the Soviet Union and all over the world assume
without question that the ideas by which they live and prosper
are a direct legacy from "the founders of scientific socialism."
When the Twentieth Party Congress in 1956 exhorted its Central
Committee to guard "the purity of the Marxist-Leninist theory as
the apple of its eye," it was expressing a feeling that permeates
the minds of even the toughest activists in the hierarchies that
govern the Soviet Union. Marxism-Leninism, an ideology in which
the first component is still just as important as the second, is very
much the apple of the party's eye. The men of power in the Soviet
Union and its allies, like the men who are itching for power in
Italy and France and Indonesia, have none of the doubts that
plague some of the men who seek to understand them. They
think of themselves as Marxists, and that is a fact which their
revisionist critics would do well to recognize. [28]
Evidence of this sincere devotion abounds in all parts of the
Soviet system. The principles of Marxism-Leninism are taught and

taught again at every level of education: to all children in the schools,[29] to all students in the universities, to all officers and men in the armed forces, to all recruits for the party cadres. More than that, they infect and inform the whole curriculum of formal education to an extent that makes even the most rigid of our church-directed schools seem by contrast quite derelict in doctrinal duty. The law of the Soviet Union, we are informed by one expert, is *"clothed* in Marxism." Despite all the concessions that have been made to the realities of social existence (for example, in the development of the laws of inheritance), the basic features of the legal system "may be traced to its Marxist heritage." [30] The party's attitude toward both science and religion is a tribute to the continuing influence of dialectical materialism. The state's approach to the whole business of diplomacy is evidence of the continuing appeal of Marx's prediction of our doom.[31] Khrushchev puts the stamp on the finality of his rise to power by allowing *Pravda* to hail him as a "creative theoretician of Marxism-Leninism," and he in turn hails the "theory of Marx" as the guiding star of all his actions. "In questions of ideology," he promised the Supreme Soviet on October 31, 1959, "we shall continue to stand as a rock on the basis of Marxism-Leninism."

There is, to be sure, another side to the story of the role of Marxist ideology in the Soviet Union and indeed among Communists everywhere. The dictates of Marxist piety never stand in the way of the advances or retreats that are forced upon Khrushchev by the relentless problems of running a great state, nor do Soviet scientists, whether native-born or imported from the West, pay any higher tribute than lip service (and often perhaps not even that) to dialectical materialism as they juggle the brilliant equations that send their luniks into orbit. Communist leaders are wonderfully adept at selecting those passages in Marx or Engels (or, for that matter, in Lenin) that appear to bless their improvisations, and one who reads at random in the Soviet press gets the impression that the sacred label "Marxist" is affixed indiscriminately to any idea or institution that serves a useful purpose in the system. Certainly the "creative Marxism" of the heirs of Stalin often seems a good deal more creative than Marxist. And, needless to say, the Soviet Union is full of men, even men high in the party, who are either indifferent to considerations of ideology or strongly (if not openly) contemptuous. Even Khrushchev, the "creative theoretician," has expressed an impatience with those of his colleagues who spend too much time thinking and too little producing. The age of the bureaucrat is following hard upon the age of the theoretician, and the fires of this secular religion are burning lower. The Russians, we are told, are behaving more like Russians and less like Marxists with every year that passes.

Yet they are still, on any count, devout Marxists, and no trifling part of their policy and conduct may be traced directly to their intellectual heritage. I certainly cannot settle the argument, in which dozens of wise men have been immersed for years, over what makes the leaders of the Soviet Union behave the way they do. I am impressed by those experts who insist that it is chiefly because they are Russians or Slavs or totalitarians or technologists or bureaucrats or neurotics or men in a unique geopolitical situation.[32] Yet I am also impressed by those who remind us that these men are conscious Marxists whose hopes, fears, obsessions, slogans, categories, and standards are largely Marxist in origin and cast. Even those Communists who know they are manipulating a theology cynically in order to maintain their power are, like our own cynics, prisoners of the ideological tools they use. Those who believe and those who only profess are committed irrevocably to the pursuit of Marxist purposes in the Marxist spirit. And enough do believe zealously in the "truth" of the official ideology to give a general tone of piety to the business of trying to govern men on Marxist principles. How can we explain the deep sense of mission that sustains the Communist leaders if not in terms of quasi-religious fervor? Where else but from Marxism could they get the confidence, zeal, and energy that drive them relentlessly to foment revolution in fifty or more countries around the world? Whether Marxism is a religion or an ideology, a live theory or a dead dogma, a code to be honored or a myth to be manipulated, a major support of morale or a cover-up for the ubiquitous hunger for power—and I think it could be shown to be *all* these things —it is a force of immense consequence in the Communist world. We will ignore the sincerity of the Communist devotion to Marx at our peril; for from a belief in the validity of his promises, not from self-interest or a taste for power or an inner urge to aggression, stems the overpowering sense of mission which will trouble our sleep for years to come. "The divisions of the Red Army," Raymond Aron writes, "would arouse less anxiety if they did not seem to be in the service of an idea." [33] So, too, would the technicians and diplomats and propagandists of "peaceful coexistence."

Whether the Communists are as faithful as they are sincere is an argument not quite so easily settled. "Who of all the professed Marxists are most faithful to Marx?" is a question I am tempted to answer with another question: "Who of all the professed Christians are most faithful to Christ?" In the house of Marxism, too, there are many mansions. Yet the logic of Marx's dogmatic teachings and the course of events over the seventy-five years since his death have combined to build up the house of "hard" Marxism until, in our view, it towers over all the others, whether of Bernstein, Plekhanov, Luxemburg, Kautsky, Jaurès, Blum, Laski, Cole, or Hook. My discussion of Marxism and totalitarianism was, in effect, a statement of my own reasons for believing that the hard Marxists are the authentic Marxists of the middle of the twentieth century. It is possible that I am giving way too easily to the historical fact that Marxism failed in Germany and succeeded in Russia. I am certainly ready to concede that other children besides Bolshevism lay in the womb of Marxism. Yet they were born dead or died young, and Bolshevism prospered because, among other things, it was the one child willing to pursue the inner logic of Marxism—the revolutionary passion for totality— all the way to power. The Marxism of Khrushchev is, to be sure, a kind of Marxism that the master himself would have some trouble recognizing, and after the shock of recognition might well come the huff of disavowal. Yet Marx is, whether he would admit it or not, the paternal grandfather, and it might help to clinch my argument if we were to course swiftly along the line of succession from Marx to Lenin to Stalin to the epigoni.* In particular, I seek short answers to the questions: what did Lenin do to Marx, what did Stalin do to Lenin, what do Khrushchev and his colleagues appear to be doing to all three of them?

Lenin took it upon himself to project Marx's imaginative teachings into the real world in which men of vision make and consolidate proletarian revolutions on socialist principles.[34] This was not an easy task for a faithful Marxist theoretician, principally because a proletarian revolution in backward Russia was not exactly on the agenda of history for 1917.[35] Marx had written that "no social order ever disappears before all the productive forces for which there is room in it have been developed," [36] and most Marxists in the early years of this century assumed without question that a socialist revolution in Russia was several generations away. The dream that flickered in the minds of a few brave Russians— that the proletarian revolution might come first and the upbuilding of an industrial economy second—was considered to be so un-Marxist as to constitute a major heresy. After some backing and filling, Lenin finally swung around to a career of making an orthodox reality of this heretical dream.[37] As a devoted Marxist who felt the eyes of Marxists everywhere burning hopefully but critically upon him, he devoted almost as much energy to explaining his course of action as to pursuing it. His most important

* I am considering Stalin as one of Lenin's generation.

theoretical task was to win Marx's posthumous approval of the revolution of 1917, and he proved himself equal to the "leap" that had to be made.

Three facts helped Lenin to make it with something to spare. First, Marx himself had not always been rigidly dogmatic about his great dogma of historical materialism.* If he had never quite imagined a complete inversion of the historical process in a retarded country like Russia, he had certainly granted a primacy to politics over economics in periods of revolution. Lenin seized upon this exception boldly and expanded it into a working principle. Second, he peered steadily through the curtain of Menshevik scholasticism and kept his eye on the real Marx. While his more timid opponents took refuge in Marx's theory of history, Lenin stayed close to the whole spirit and purpose of Marx's existence and labors. Marx's spirit was revolutionary, his purpose was revolution; the Lenin of 1917, who honored the revolutionary rather than the historian, could argue convincingly that he was the most dutiful child of all. Engels had known and proclaimed that Marx was "before all else a revolutionary," and Lenin proved it with a flourish. He was, as W. H. Chamberlin has written, "the incarnate doctrine of militant Marxism, the revolutionary Word become flesh." [39] Finally, he was most successful in accomplishing his theoretical task because he had a successful revolution about which to theorize. The Marxists all over the world who protested in the name of the iron laws of history were trampled under foot in the onward rush of history itself. While they talked about

---

* Both Marx and Engels toyed with the notion that Russia, that weird country, might move along a different road to socialism from the one staked out by history for France, Germany, and England. Marx is on record as refusing to give a dogmatic Marxist answer to certain young Russians who wanted to know if their country would have to pass through all the stages of capitalist exploitation before they could hope for revolution. Engels gave the same group encouragement when he wrote in 1885 that the important thing for Russia was "that the revolution should break out"—any revolution, it would seem—and that "when 1789 has once been launched, 1793 will not be long in following." [38]

a revolution, Lenin made one; and Marx, I am certain, would have made the same one, too. Those who insist on miscasting Marx in the role of a reluctant Menshevik, who imagine that he would have let the main chance drift by in 1917, are only poorly acquainted, I fear, with that combative man.

Lenin's particular contributions to Marxist theory, as we noted in Chapter VI, were made largely in the area of political strategy and tactics, an area in which Marx had been vague enough to permit any sufficiently determined and clever Marxist to have his own way. Although each of Lenin's four advances, especially his glorification of power, put a strain on the Marxist heritage, each could be squared with the master's scattered but forceful comments about the Communist party and the dictatorship of the proletariat. Beyond this, Lenin's chief additions were the theory of imperialism, of which more later, and the coining of most of those sharp-edged phrases with which Communists the world over slash their enemies—and friends—so gleefully.[40]

In all his thoughts and actions Lenin remained a devoted Marxist.[41] His head was full of the dialectic, materialism, and the class struggle. One may search his writings in vain for a single expression of exasperation or ridicule or even mild doubt over Marx's fundamental teachings. His astounding opportunism in action was matched only by his astounding piety in doctrine. In the end, he resolved once and for all the tension in Marx's own teachings between democracy and autocracy, and thus opened the door to the result toward which Marx had always pointed: totality. He seized upon those tendencies in Marx's ambiguous teachings that put final reliance for the success of communism not in the grindstone of history but in the sword of the dictatorship of the proletariat. Once he had taken up the sword himself, he had no choice but to use it, and in using it he cut away one by one every humanitarian strand in Marx's web. Marxists who are less than orthodox will continue to revile him and call him wicked. Students of Marx who think that historical materialism of the most deterministic kind is the essence of Marxism will continue to flay him and call him heretical. But Lenin could surely say (although I doubt that he would want to) that as Paul carried Jesus to the Gentiles, so he carried Marx to the Russians. He transformed a theory designed for workers in advanced countries into a theory designed for intellectuals in backward countries—an astounding but not entirely illogical achievement that has meant untold trouble for us in the West.

What Stalin did in the realm of Marxist theory was to take the logic of Lenin's additions and corrections two or three steps further toward totality.[42] With the coarsest of threads and crudest of wheels —"socialism in one country"—he spun that web of dogma, magic, and opportunism which continues to comfort Communists and inspire them to great deeds.* Stalin's most important theoretical blow was struck in *Marxism and Linguistics* (1950), in which he the Leninist came right out and said of his collectivization of agriculture what Lenin the Marxist could never quite bring himself to say about 1917-1920: that a state acting on Marxist principles was capable of telescoping the stages of history and of bringing off a "revolution from above." In his *Economic Problems of Socialism* (1952), he tried to call a halt to the celebrations of the power of the Soviet state in which several overenthusiastic academicians had engaged after reading *Marxism and Linguistics,* but he had put his stamp of approval indelibly on the extreme Bolshevik version of Marxism. Although Stalin denied that the state could "abolish" old laws and "create" new "laws of economic development" (insisting in a classical Marxist vein that such laws change only with changes in economic "conditions"), he gave the

* I think it irrelevant to our purposes to devote attention to Stalin's battle with Trotsky and to his consequent theorizing about the strategy and tactics of Bolshevism in an imperialist world. The doctrine of "socialism in one country" was, to be sure, an important prerequisite of the concept of the "revolution from above," but Stalin could have gone on his theoretical way to the "new kind of state" even without it. As to the question of revolution, what difference does it make to us who holds the gun at any given time? It is always pointed at our heads and always likely to go off.

whole game away to his enthusiastic colleagues in "creative Marxism" by conceding that the "new state" could change the conditions and thus, for all practical purposes, the laws themselves.[43] This concept of the new state, it should be added, found its natural extension under the pressures of World War II in the Stalin-blessed revival of the most intense sort of Russian nationalism.[44]

The heirs of Stalin continue to carry water on both shoulders.[45] They, too, are devout Marxists who load their speeches with quotations from *Capital* and *Anti-Dühring;* they, too, are determined Leninists who deal with their domestic and diplomatic problems in the spirit, only slightly mellowed by time and success, of *What is to be Done?* And they do all this with few signs of intellectual strain, with little apparent awareness of the contradictions that exist between the classical and Bolshevized versions of Marxism. Indeed, one is tempted to conclude that the Marxism of Khrushchev faces with equal ease and confidence—dare we say "dialectically"? —in two quite different directions. When the Communists look at us, the bourgeois capitalists of the recalcitrant West, they do it through the lens of classical Marxism. When they turn to look at themselves, they do it through the lens of dynamic Leninism.[46] This book has been sprinkled with examples of the two-facedness, or two-headedness, of Marxism-Leninism. Let me put them all together in a paired listing of the Marxist laws that appear to govern us and the Marxist laws that appear to govern them. In each instance, the law that applies to us is in italics, the law that applies to them in regular type:

Men are prisoners of history, instruments of a cosmic purpose toward which mankind moves with irresistible force.

Men are makers of history, active agents of a cosmic purpose who can direct the course of events within wide limits.

A society cannot skip any of the stages of history.

A society can telescope stages and hack out shortcuts by determined, revolutionary effort.

The progress of society is explosively dialectical; it is powered by the harsh struggle of hostile classes.

The progress of society is smoothly dialectical; it is driven steadily along by the friendly tension of "self-criticism."

Men cannot make a revolution until economic and social conditions are ripe.

Men can make a revolution when the fruit is still green (even, apparently, before it has begun to grow).

The state is the sign of a society "cleft into irreconcilable antagonisms."

The state is the sign of a society in which the class struggle has ended; it is a new kind of state born out of harmony and common purpose.

Economics is supreme over politics.
Politics is supreme over economics.

The political and cultural activities of men are economically determined.

The economic and cultural activities of men are politically determined.

The state is not equal to the task of social improvement.
The state is capable of altering the whole pattern of society.

The law is a weapon of the ruling class.
The law is an instrument of all-encompassing justice.

Morality is a subjective ideology that serves the purposes of exploitation.

Morality is an objective reflection of eternal principles of human decency.

Classes are by definition antagonistic.

Classes, or rather "strata," are by definition co-operative and "friendly to each other."

Ideas are products of a particular socio-economic situation, and have no real power to influence the course of events.

Ideas are products of great minds who understood the laws of nature and history, and have power to move history, make revolutions, and purge mankind.

Political leaders and intellectuals cannot rise above their class origins to serve all men.

Political leaders and intellectuals can rise above their class origins to serve all men—in fact, two of them did, and that is how the whole affair began.

I could carry this exercise in Marxist-Leninist schizophrenia a good deal further—for example, into the realm of morals and manners, in which our nationalism is "reactionary chauvinism" and theirs is "progressive patriotism," our profit motive is the profit motive and theirs is "Stakhanovism" or "socialist emulation," [47] our laws of inheritance are a form of "parasitism" and theirs are a support of "the welfare both of individual citizens and of socialist society as a whole," [48] our honesty and industry are "rationalizations of self-interest" and theirs are "forces building socialism," our criminals and crimes are "fruits" of capitalism and theirs are "remnants." It should be enough by way of summing up to reduce the contrast between the Marxism that applies to us and the Marxism that applies to them to one of *determinism* and *voluntarism.* [49] Marx could never resolve the tension in his own mind between the assumption that the course of history is directed by a few blind laws and the hope that it might be directed by a few farsighted men, or between the related assumption that the consciousness of all men is determined by their social existence and the knowledge that the consciousness of a few—at least of Marx and Engels—is the result of an act of will. The Marxists of the Soviet Union have resolved this dualism neatly by being tougher than Marx, and having it both ways. Upon us the laws of materialism lay the same old iron hand, and those in our camp who attribute a major role in human behavior or social change to the will of man are "subjectivists, idealists, and voluntarists." Upon them these laws lay a helping hand, and those in their camp who warn against running ahead of history are branded as "half-baked textualists and Talmudists." Voluntarism is a sin called "voluntarism" when we celebrate the importance of men, and a virtue called "socialist vision" when they do. Iron laws command our future, iron men command theirs.

The development of this two-headed Marxism has followed a natural if tortuous course from the beginning. Marx himself was self-contradictory or at least equivocal on several of his major points, and it is not surprising that men who wanted to be pious Marxists and effective Communists at the same time should have resolved his theoretical ambiguities in this particular manner. It has been no easy intellectual task to apply the teachings of Marxism in a society that never knew capitalism very well and has not known it at all for more than thirty years. The Communists have matched their successes in practice with successes in theory only because they, far more skillfully than other men, have been able to look in two directions at the same time. They are permitted and even encouraged to perform this notable feat by two circumstances: first, as Manicheans who await the triumph of their system and annihilation of ours, they have room in their minds for two major systems of belief—a theory of social engineering (the new Marxism) and a theory of social disaster (the old Marxism); and second, as Marxists who have kept their eyes on the revolutionary Marx, they can argue that they have been faithful before all other men who claim the mantle of the master. They have been able to hold these two theories together in that sacred bundle called Marxism-Leninism because they have never questioned the predispositions and purposes that have formed the hard, unchanging core of Communism, at all times and in all countries, since the day when Marx first pronounced our doom:

1) the sentence of death that is passed on capitalism and liberal democracy;

2) the hopes that are placed in socialism and the dictatorship of the proletariat;

3) the quest for certainty that begins with "hatred of all the Gods" and ends in totality;

4) the urge to blast out a new course of history with the dynamite of revolution.

To these beliefs each of the two Marxisms is steadfastly true; through these beliefs their antagonisms are resolved into a dialectically harmonious whole. What mattered most to Marx still matters most to the Bolsheviks—not this or that point of doctrine, nor even the doctrine in its entirety, but the purpose of the doctrine: the violent destruction of capitalism and the eager building of socialism. "The point," let us remember, was not to "interpret" the world but to "change" it.

I will not yield to temptation and say that a higher synthesis of Marxism and Leninism is even now forming, principally because the second never was the antithesis of the first. Lenin, I insist, was an uncritical Marxist who resolved what Sidney Hook calls "the ambiguous legacy" of Marx in favor of dynamism and dogmatism. I would myself go one step beyond Mr. Hook by restating my own conviction that the ambiguity could hardly have been resolved in any other way by men—any men, and not just Russians —who remembered that Marx was "before all else a revolutionary." Marxism did not, to be sure, have to be quite so thoroughly "Russified" as it was in the hands of Lenin and his heirs. No one in his right mind can ignore the obvious fact that the Russians behave the way they do because they are Russians as well as Marxists.

The fact is equally obvious, however, that Marxism came to Russia and flowered as Bolshevism because one whole side of that country's mind and spirit already displayed many of the same characteristics and tendencies: materialism,[50] extremism, messianism, monism, dogmatism, collectivism, maximalism,* and revolutionary radicalism. Russia, I think, brought out the worst in Marx; Marx, I am certain, brought out the worst in Russia. Be that as it may, I find it hard not to believe that any group of men who were bent on making a full Marxist revolution—in Germany, France, Italy, Sweden, Spain, even in England and America—would have arrived in time at essentially Bolshevik methods and Bolshevik principles. That is why it has been doubly important for us to take at least this much of a look at the Soviet Union: because it is the leading country that swears pious allegiance to Marx, and because any modern country that swore such allegiance—even the United States—would surely come in time to Communist totalitarianism, if not necessarily to Stalinist brutality.

Perhaps I should end this discussion by repeating what I said in Chapter I: the present political and intellectual leaders of the U.S.S.R., China, and the satellites, as well as those men in the West who proclaim themselves Communists, are closer to Marx in principle and purpose than most Christians are to Christ. The Russians are Marxists;[53] and this book is both a study of two abstractions called Marxism and the American tradition and an introduction to the study of two realities called the Soviet Union and the United States.

Men who turn their backs on Marxism as theory or ideology are still faced with the perplexing figure of Marx himself. We may turn away from him, too, I suppose, if we take the position that

---

* In Michael Karpovich's definition,[51] "an impatient desire to strive for the immediate realization of the ideal in its entirety, a contempt for gradualism, for the intermediate stages of progress and partial achievements"; or, as H. J. Muller puts it, the "yearning for the universal solution," the "passion for the clean sweep," the "scorn of compromise."[52]

his person and teachings have been swallowed up so completely by the Communists that he is no longer a man to whom we dare or care to listen. On the other hand, we may try to separate the thinker from the revolutionary, the gadfly from the godhead, the critic of capitalism from the plotter for communism, the man of the nineteenth century from the myth of the twentieth, and so go to school with him neither more timidly nor less inquisitively than we do, say, with Machiavelli or Nietzsche or Sorel or Clausewitz or even the Marquis de Sade. This is what I now propose to do. The transition from all that has gone before may prove too abrupt for some of my readers, but I am bound to say that it would be neither sporting nor sensible to ignore the Marx whom social democrats admire and social scientists respect—in both instances somewhat grudgingly.

This fine question of a man's responsibility (especially if he is an intellectual) for events that come long after his death is, in any case, sufficiently arguable so that men who hate Communism may certainly study the father of Communism dispassionately as a man of his own time and climate. Studied in this spirit and situation, Marx looms up as one of the truly great figures in the development of Western thought. To scan the intellectual history of the past three centuries, the centuries that produced us, without pausing for a long look at Marx would be like staging *Julius Caesar* without Caesar, or at least without Caesar's Ghost; for he is, as Eduard Heimann writes, "the authentic product, and in more than one respect the logical culmination of Western intellectual and industrial development." [54] As he drew on Bacon, Hobbes, Locke, Petty, Holbach, Hegel, Ricardo, Adam Smith, Guizot, Saint-Simon, and Quesnay, not to mention Aristotle, Democritus, Heraclitus, and Lucretius, so has he been drawn on—consciously or unconsciously, directly or indirectly, willingly or reluctantly—by almost all thinkers who have flourished since his death. "A return to pre-Marxian social science is inconceivable," Karl Popper writes. "All modern writers are indebted to Marx, even if they do not know it. This is especially true of those who disagree with his doctrines, as I do." [55] Some men parrot Marx, others expand upon him, most of us debate with him; but all of us know that he is standing there like a giant, and we cannot look away lest we brand ourselves cowards or fools.

As we look, we may also learn. We must take him with a lump of sugar,* as we take all sour men; we must treat his certainties as possibilities, as we treat those of all dogmatists; we must argue with him boldly, as we do (or should do) with all men who are used to having their own way; and we must seek persistently to separate his wheat from his chaff, as we expect intelligent people to do for us. Certainly the chaff is plentiful. His descriptions were caricatures; his predictions have fallen flat; his prescriptions are an invitation to be drowned in blood. Only his prophecies strike a responsive chord in our bourgeois minds (after all, who wouldn't like to see the state wither away?), and they are visions of a world that will never be. Yet we cannot go to him, in any mood or for any purpose, without increasing our understanding of the human predicament. If we treat him respectfully, which also means gingerly, we can learn a number of things that we are better off knowing. We can learn them elsewhere, to be sure—from far-sighted men who came before him and from able synthesizers who have come after—but no one teaches any of them with such piquancy or all of them together with such authority as does Marx himself. And what are the most important of these lessons for the men who think for the West? What are the Marxist insights we can make use of in moderation without surrendering any of the values of American democracy? I would suggest these:

Economic forces exert a powerful influence on all aspects of human behavior and social organization.

---

* "The Marxist doctrine," Arthur Koestler writes from withering experience, "is a drug, like arsenic or strychnine, which in small doses have a stimulating, in larger ones a paralyzing effect on the creative system." [56]

The course of history is directed to a significant degree by the way men organize themselves to produce, distribute, and consume the means of existence.

The writing of history must pay respectful attention to economic forces: to patterns of ownership, technology, finance, transportation, the distribution of wealth, the supply of raw materials, and all other institutions and arrangements and aspirations of *homo faber* and *homo economicus*.*

Men cannot be studied as abstractions apart from their social environment, for they are in large part the products of the society in which they were born and raised.

Men's ideas can no more properly be studied as isolated, self-generating phenomena, for they, too—even those that embrace some portion of eternal truth—are molded by the circumstances under which they flourish and the uses to which they are put.

Most ideas, in fact, are to a noticeable extent "ideologies," theories "whose social function—whatever the intentions and illusions of their authors and propagators—is to protect the privileges or justify the pretensions of some class or group in society." [59]

Classes constitute one of the most significant, persistent, influential phenomena of society, and both historians and sociologists must take them fully into account. Few men can be understood fully except in the context of their class origin or allegiance; few events fail to lend themselves to an interpretation in terms of the rise and fall and interaction of social classes.

Society is not so much a pattern as a process in which change follows upon change to all eternity.

* Herbert Butterfield puts it neatly when he says that the Marxist view teaches the historian to "hug the soil and be near to the earth," that it is a useful "hint as to the right end of the stick to pick up." [57] Marx's influence has worked both ways in this area. "Since his time," Lord Lindsay points out, "and largely as the result of his influence, historians have paid increasing attention to the working of the economic factor in history, but economists have also paid increasing attention to the working of the historical factor in economics." [58]

In all apparent unities there are elements of contradiction and discord: in all evil there is good, in all good evil; in all truth there is error, in all error truth; in all peace there are elements of conflict, in all conflict urges toward peace.

To these we might add a few reminders about the facts of life in our society:

The forms of democracy are not yet democracy itself.
Freedom on paper is not yet freedom in fact.
One of the great strides toward freedom was the eight-hour day.
Psychological security is not easily found in an industrial system.
Women are happier, or at least freer to pursue happiness, out of the kitchen.
Beware the man who invoke's God's blessing upon his power or profits.
Capitalism has its ups and downs.
The lowest "downs" generally follow the dizziest "ups," and capitalism must always be especially on guard against overproduction.
Property is power.*

It may be said that no one of these lessons came first from Marx's pen, but he is the man who forced most of them down the throats of the learned world. It may be said that they are all obvious features of our intellectual landscape, but he is the searchlight that first picked them out. And it will be said, by all who read these pages, that they are truisms which surely do not bear repeating. Yet things cannot be classed as truisms until they are first recognized as truths, and Marx did far more than any other thinker of the past century to teach us this fresh point of view that tries to

---

* "And," Sidney Hook writes, "that property which gives power over land, instruments of production, and the things that human beings need to live, is power over the human beings who must live by use of them. The more absolute the power over such things, the more absolute the power over people." [60]

see through the veil of ideology to the solid substance of fact. He helped change the intellectual approach of the entire West; he promoted a fresh understanding of the weaknesses and fallacies of our own way of life; he raised the questions that we are now bound to answer. That he should have learned many of his own lessons so poorly does nothing to reduce his stature as teacher. "All I know," Marx said not entirely in jest toward the end of his life, "is that I am not a Marxist." [61] All we know, I am tempted to say (trusting naively that I will not be quoted out of context), is that we are all Marxists now. While I am about it, I might express my warm agreement with Sidney Hook's observation that "Marxism is one of the best standpoints from which to criticize Communism." Marx's own strictures on ideology, class, and contradiction are weapons that we ought to be using much more skillfully in our war of words with the U.S.S.R.

This is by no means all we can learn from Marx, for he is also a man who teaches us how *not* to think and expound and behave. His intellectual trespasses, most of which I noted in Chapter I, were grievous, and we would do well to keep them in mind as we go about our own inquiries and expositions. A giant may sin and get away with it, but we lesser men may not. Remembering him, let us resolve to define terms, face realities, gather facts, anticipate questions, and respect mysteries. Remembering him, let us beware of the black-and-white picture, the simple explanation, the comforting dogma, the arrogant response to criticism, and above all the conviction of certainty about things that can never be certain. Let us not convert a slice of truth into the whole truth, make *an* explanation of events *the* explanation, mistake the assumption we want to prove for the fact we can prove. And as we seek to profit from his example in the realm of ideas, let us look at the realm of action with eyes that have been sharpened by the sight of both his achievements and his errors. Do we know what makes a man's life truly human, and how to make it so? Do we know what prevents a society from being "politicalized," and how to prevent it? Do we understand the force of what Keynes called "the moral problem of our age," the love of money? [62] Do we see the tight connection between means and ends, and understand how the first cannot be dirty without the second getting dirty, too? Are we prepared to face the consequences for individualism of the profound collectivizing influence of our advanced technology? Are we prepared to control economic forces lest they control us? These are just a few of the hard questions Marx forces us to ask ourselves in Western society. We can thank him for exerting pressure, and thank him, too, for showing us how not to answer them.

We could, I am sure, learn all these lessons from other teachers, but who of them would be at once so dazzling, overpowering, and irritating—which at least one teacher in ten ought certainly to be? Perhaps it is time, even for those who admire him, to do what Sidney Hook suggests and renounce Marxism "as a special school of thought or doctrine," [63] for all his "valid contributions" are now part of the contemporary approach to the study of man and society.* But I hope we will never give up studying Marx. May the old Marxism stay buried and the new wither on the vine, but may Americans never be afraid to learn from the Old Nick himself.

The new Marxism, to our consternation, is blooming on the vine all over the world. Communism makes a strong appeal in many of those countries of Asia and Africa which the surge toward industrialism has left behind, and it makes it first of all to disaffected intellectuals. Some of this appeal arises out of circumstances of history about which, alas, the men of the West can do virtually nothing. We come as white men who advertise our racism sadly or gladly; the Communists come as colored men, or as white

---

* My own feeling is that it is especially those who admire Marx who must renounce Marxism as a creed. One can be a socialist and a democrat but not a Marxist and a democrat, for reasons I have tried to make clear in this book. If I were a socialist, which I am not, I would seek out Proudhon for inspiration and Bernstein for instructions. [64]

men who are prepared to love any man, white or yellow or black or brown, so long as he is "progressive." We seem to be on the long road going down; they are on a dizzy path going up. We have been in Asia and Africa for centuries, and our foibles and pretensions are a matter of firsthand knowledge; they are just appearing for the first time, and they have our example how not to act. The remembered sins of Western imperialism are blown up out of all proportion and recited as a kind of morale-boosting incantation; the unimagined brutalities of Eastern imperialism are hidden by a veil of ignorance and indifference. Many of our ideas are inapplicable in retarded countries; most of theirs were forged in the furnace of a retarded country that wanted desperately to catch up with history. It is hard to deny that, for the moment at least, history is on the side of the Marxists in the great struggle for the ideological-political future of Asia and Africa.

The success of that retarded country, the Soviet Union (and the anticipated success of Communist China), is a second reason for the appeal of Communism to Asia and Africa, a second major handicap against the West. Under the knout of Bolshevism the Soviet Union has caught up with the present and, in at least some areas, has lunged into the future. The Communists have stormed their way to industrialization, with the result that the Leninist version of Marxism has become the leading mystique of rapid industrialization of backward areas. Men who can avert their eyes from the human wreckage that has littered the way to Soviet industrialism are inspired by this example to have a go themselves at a proletarian revolution without a proletariat. Marxism worked once before as the instrument of a Europeanized minority in a nonindustrialized country, and now that it has been thoroughly Leninized it should work every time—thus do many intellectuals like to think. Hating capitalism because it appears to be the spur of Western imperialism, they are excited by the knowledge that socialism (or what they insist upon defining as "socialism") was the answer to Russian aspirations and therefore can be the answer to theirs.[65] No small part of the credit for their bitterly anticapitalist temper must be assigned to Lenin's doctrine of imperialism, a shaky, simple-minded, and yet enormously comforting theory which he took over bodily from an English Liberal, J. A. Hobson, and an Austrian Marxist, Rudolf Hilferding. It identifies Western imperialism with "finance capitalism," and lays the burden of all the woes of the colonial world exclusively on the doorstep of this "highest" and presumably last "stage of capitalism." [66] The damage this fraudulent doctrine continues to do our cause is almost incalculable.

Finally, the appeal of Communism draws heavily on the Marxist legacy, which somehow rings truer in many Asian and African ears than does the legacy of Jefferson and Lincoln. They are angry, and they rouse to Marx's call for revolution. They are disinherited, and they remember that he spoke for the poor and exploited. They are victims of discrimination, and they find themselves on a "universal mailing list." [67] They have seen a vision, and they are told that he saw it first.[68] He writes to them in aphorisms they think they understand. Indeed, the intellectual trespasses that unsettle us make him all the more attractive to men who have no time or use for measured discourse. And he gives them the sense of total dedication they need to endure the present and the sense of total power they need to storm the future. "It was," a young Malayan said after joining the party, "as if I had climbed on the back of a tiger. . . . I had the power of the tiger; I moved as he moved." [69] Marx, let us remember, hated the West, and other men who hate it, surely with more reason, follow him eagerly in his assault upon our ideas and institutions.

What we can and must do to match the appeal of Communism to the thinkers and leaders of the uncommitted world I find hard to say. It would help if we could convince young men like the Malayan that those who ride tigers usually end up inside, but it is not going to be easy to get them to listen to the spokesmen of a country in which dislike or fear or mistrust of men with dark skins is a way of life for at least one-fourth of the people.

But that is the kind of exhortation in which I am resolved not to indulge by way of conclusion. This book was an adventure in ideas, and any moral I feel compelled to draw should be confined to that realm. I will draw several and then have done. These, in my opinion, are the lessons that Americans must get by heart as they sharpen their minds for intellectual combat with Communism.

First, we must not be tempted or bullied by the fierce pressure of events into aping the habits of thought we scorn in the hard Marxists. Let us not set forth on any delusive quest for certainty, nor comfort ourselves with the conviction that we have found it, lest we, too, equate dissent with heresy. Let us not treat all ideas as if they had social significance, lest we, too, strangle ourselves with the cord of "politicalization." Let us eschew ideology, despise dogmatism, and discipline ourselves against extremism, lest we indulge in what Czeslaw Milosz calls "Ketman"—the acrobatic protestation of unswerving faith in the official truth.[70] Above all, let us take note of their monumental presumptuousness,[71] and make our own advances in the world of knowledge step by step, hypothesis by hypothesis, test by test, fact by fact. If it is a "disease of the soul to be in love with impossible things," it is a disease of the mind to believe that all things are possible. We must be daring, but we must first be humble.

Second, we must face the Communists in the arena of ideas with our own forces marshaled on the broadest possible front. They have framed the struggle of their world and ours as one between "socialism" and "capitalism," and we have let them get away with it much too long. The issue between us is not that simple. In the first place, their "socialism" is a harsh form of state capitalism and our "capitalism" is a mixed economy that has been civilized by social controls. Far more important than that veiled truth, however, is the fact that it is not alone our economy that divides us from them, but our free, pluralistic, accommodating patterns of government, social relations, culture, science, education, and religion. It is high time that we sought to undo the damage we have let Khrushchev do with his flat insistence (while we flounder about in our own clichés) that "peaceful co-existence" is an accommodation between socialism and capitalism. We will never put our cause persuasively to the uncommitted world until we make clear how much more encompassing the conflict really is. Our struggle with the Communists is one of society against society and mind against mind; our chief strength lies in a tradition that insists, in defiance of our own urges toward dogmatism and obscurantism, that both be kept open.

So, too, must the future that we carry in our imaginations. Let us not succumb, like the Marxists, to the temptation to look for "tendencies working with iron necessity towards inevitable results," [72] lest it be their version of the closed future that we grimly make our own. There are no such tendencies, and there need be no such results, not if we see the world as it really is. To do this, we must rise serenely above the Manicheanism that fogs the Marxist view of reality. We must not resolve all the torments of our century into a two-sided struggle between the forces of pure light and the forces of total darkness, lest we ourselves end up in a state of frenzied obsession with the enemy. We must not make as intense a religion of anti-Marxism as they have of Marxism, lest we suffer the fate of those who identify the absence of evil with the presence of good.

Above all, we must not slide hopelessly into an apocalyptic view of the struggle between their system and ours, lest we slam the door forever on all hopes of an evolution in Communism that would make it possible for East and West to live together in a reasonably peaceful world. [73] No one in his right mind would predict such an evolution confidently, but hope may still reign where prediction abdicates. It may well be that the commitment of the Communist leaders to the Marxist ideology will never let them rest until Marx's promise of our violent destruction has been fulfilled. If this be true, peaceful co-existence is simply a breathing spell before the last bloody attack, which the Communists hope to launch from within our system. Yet it may also be that the Communists are now so confident of ultimate victory that they can wait patiently for us to stumble and vote our way into Communism. If this be true, peaceful co-existence is a global game which the Soviet Union expects to win by default. And it may even be that the Communists will, over the years of tension, move slowly into an attitude that looks upon our system as a kind of useful enemy to have around, and we will be allowed to continue indefinitely as an example of everything a social order should not be. If this be true, peaceful co-existence is a game that might go on for many hundreds of years, especially if both we and the Communists can claim to be far ahead on points.* The changes that have taken place in Marxism already should be enough to persuade us that other changes are sure to come, changes perhaps so profound in nature that the "hard, unchanging core" I described on page 267 will be transformed out of all recognition. What would be left over would be Marxism only in name, but that, after all, has been the fate of most of the great isms that have held sway in the world. The apocalyptic promise of Marxism, like that of Islam, may endure for centuries—unfulfilled and unrepudiated.

All this, of course, is speculation about a distant and enigmatic future. For the present it should be comfort enough to remember that in this book I have been contrasting two faiths, and that like all faiths they claim a great deal more allegiance than they will ever get. If we were perfect, if our grasp on reality matched the reach of our tradition, we could look forward confidently to a free, peaceful, prosperous world. If they were perfect, if they never

* There is something to be said for the argument that the Communists, as they become more successful, bureaucratic, and "conservative" at home, might become less subversive, ideological, and revolutionary abroad. There is also something to be said for the obvious counterargument.

really doubted Marx's promise that they would inherit the earth, we could look forward grimly to abject surrender or inevitable war. But we, unfortunately, are imperfect democrats and they, fortunately, imperfect Marxists. In the first of those two facts lies the challenge, in the second the hope of a brighter future for America and for the world.

APPENDIX · NOTES · INDEX

APPENDIX: A CHRONOLOGY (PRINCIPALLY LITERARY) OF MARXISM

1818 Marx born in Trier, son of a well-to-do Jewish lawyer

1820 Engels born in Barmen, son of a wealthy textile manufacturer

1835-1836 Marx at University in Bonn

1836-1841 Marx at University in Berlin, where he joins the Young Hegelians

1837 Engels begins a career in the family business

1841 Engels does military service

Marx awarded degree of Doctor of Philosophy by University of Jena; his dissertation deals with differences between Democritean and Epicurean natural philosophy (first published in 1902)

1842 Engels goes to Manchester to work in the firm of Ermen and Engels

1842-1843 Marx contributes to (and later edits) *Rheinische Zeitung* in Cologne

1843-1845 Marx in Paris

1844 Marx and Engels meet

Marx issues *Deutsch-Französiche Jahrbücher* (with a contribution from Engels) with A. Ruge, and writes the economic-philosophical manuscripts (not published in full until 1932)

1844-1850	Engels active in revolutionary politics in France, Belgium, and Germany

1845-1848 Marx in Brussels

1845 Marx and Engels, *The Holy Family*

Marx, *Theses on Feuerbach* (not published until 1888)

Engels, *The Condition of the Working Class in England in 1844*

1846 Marx and Engels, *The German Ideology* (not published in full until 1932)

1847 Marx joins the Communist League

Marx, *The Poverty of Philosophy*

1848 Marx and Engels, *The Communist Manifesto* (in German; first English edition, 1850; first Russian edition, 1882)

1848-1849 Marx returns to Germany, edits *Neue Rheinische Zeitung*, stands trial, is expelled from Germany and then from Paris

1849 Marx settles in London

Marx, *Wage-Labor and Capital*, published in *Neue Rheinische Zeitung* (first published as a book in 1885)

1850 Engels returns to Manchester

Engels, *The Peasant War in Germany*, published in *Neue Rheinische Zeitung* (first published as a book in 1870)

Marx and Engels, *Address to the Communist League*, a circular

Marx, *The Class Struggles in France*, published in *Neue Rheinische Zeitung* (first published as a book in 1895)

1851-1861 Marx serves as correspondent for *New York Tribune*

1851-1852 Engels, *Germany: Revolution and Counter-Revolution*, articles in *New York Tribune* under Marx's name (first published as a book in 1896)

1852 Marx, *The Eighteenth Brumaire of Louis Bonaparte*, published in Weydemeyer's *Die Revolution* (first published as a book in 1869)

1859 Marx, *A Contribution to the Critique of Political Economy*

1864 Founding of International Workingmen's Association (First International); Marx draws up *Inaugural Address and Provisional Rules*

1866	First congress of First International (in Geneva)
1867	Marx, *Capital,* Volume I
1868	Bakunin joins First International
1870	V. I. Ulyanov (Lenin) born in Simbirsk (now Ulyanovsk), son of a minor public official
	Engels, retired from business, moves to London for good; period of closest collaboration with Marx begins
1871	The Paris Commune
	Marx, *The Civil War in France*
1872	Bakunin expelled from First International; it moves to New York
	Engels, *The Housing Question,* published in *Volkstaat* (first published as a book in 1887)
1874	First International dissolved in Philadelphia
1875	Marx, *Critique of the Gotha Programme* (not published until 1891)
1877-1878	Engels (with the aid of Marx), *Anti-Dühring,* published in *Vorwärts,* and then (1878) as a book
1879	J. V. Djugashvili (Stalin) born in Gori, son of a peasant artisan
	Lev D. Bronstein (Trotsky) born in Yanovka, son of an illiterate Jewish kulak
1880	Engels, *Socialism: Utopian and Scientific*
1882	Engels, *Dialectics and Nature* (not published until 1927)
1883	Marx dies in London
1884	Engels (with the aid of Marx's notes), *The Origin of the Family, Private Property and the State*
1885	Marx (thanks to Engels), *Capital,* Volume II
1886	Engels, *Ludwig Feuerbach and the Outcome of Classical German Philosophy,* first published as articles in *Die Neue Zeit,* then (1888) as a book
1887	Lenin's brother hanged for his part in an unsuccessful conspiracy against the life of the Czar; Lenin begins his turn away from liberalism

1889	Second International founded in Paris
1892	Kautsky, *The Class Struggle* (*The Erfurt Program*)
1893	Lenin abandons study of law for career of revolutionary socialism
1894	Marx (thanks to Engels), *Capital,* Volume III
1895	Engels dies in London
1896	Labriola, *Essays on the Materialistic Conception of History* Trotsky joins revolutionary movement
1897-1900	Lenin in Siberia
1897	Plekhanov, *The Materialist Conception of History*
1898	Plekhanov, *The Role of the Individual in History* Founding of Russian Social Democratic party on Marxist principles
1899	Bernstein, *Die Voraussetzungen des Sozialismus und die Aufgaben der Sozialdemokratie* (translated and published as *Evolutionary Socialism*), the great tract of revisionist Marxism Kautsky, *Bernstein und das sozialdemokratische Programm,* an orthodox (for 1899) reply to Bernstein
1900-1905	Lenin in exile in Europe
1901	Stalin joins Social Democratic party
1902	Lenin, *What is to be Done?*
1903	Lenin effects split of Russian Social Democratic party into Bolsheviks and Mensheviks, at meeting in London
1904	Lenin, *One Step Forward, Two Steps Back*
1905	Revolution in Russia Lenin, *Two Tactics of Social Democracy*
1905-1907	Lenin in Russia
1905-1910	Marx (thanks to Kautsky), *Theories of Surplus Value*
1906	Kautsky, *Ethics and the Materialist Conception of History*

1907-1917 Lenin in exile in Europe

1909 Lenin, *Materialism and Empirio-Criticism*

1911 Stalin founds *Pravda*

1914 Lenin, *The Teachings of Karl Marx*

1917

February Overthrow of Czarist government
April Lenin returns to Russia
August Lenin takes refuge in Finland
November The Bolshevik revolution

1917 Lenin, *Imperialism: The Highest Stage of Capitalism*

1918 Lenin, *The State and Revolution* (written in August-September 1917)
Kautsky, *The Dictatorship of the Proletariat*
Lenin, *The Proletarian Revolution and the Renegade Kautsky*

1919 Establishment of Third International (Comintern)
Bukharin and Preobrazhensky, *The ABC of Communism*

1920 Lenin, *"Left-Wing" Communism: An Infantile Disorder*
Trotsky, *Terror and Communism* (retitled *The Defence of Terrorism* and *Dictatorship versus Democracy* in English versions)

1921-1928 U.S.S.R. pursues New Economic Policy (NEP), a temporary return to a limited capitalist system

1922 Stalin chosen General Secretary of party
First Constitution of U.S.S.R.

1924 Lenin dies in Moscow; triumvirate of Kamenev, Stalin, and Zinoviev assumes leadership
Stalin, *Foundations of Leninism*

1926 Stalin, *Problems of Leninism*

1927 Stalin takes over sole leadership; Trotsky expelled from party and exiled to Alma-Ata

1928 Abandonment of NET and adoption of first Five-Year Plan; the "revolution from above" begins in earnest

1929	Trotsky exiled from U.S.S.R.
1932-1933	Trotsky, *History of the Russian Revolution*
1934	Adoption of second Five-Year Plan Stalin's "purges" begin
1936	Stalin, *On the Draft Constitution of the U.S.S.R.* A. Y. Vyshinsky, *The Law of the Soviet State* Adoption of new Constitution of U.S.S.R.
1936-1938	Treason trials in Moscow
1938	Stalin, *Dialectical and Historical Materialism* Third Five-Year Plan
1939	Stalin's report to the Eighteenth Party Congress
1940	Trotsky murdered in Mexico
1941	Hitler invades U.S.S.R.
1945	Stalin, *The Great Patriotic War of the Soviet Union*
1946	Fourth Five-Year Plan
1950	Stalin, *Marxism and Linguistics*
1952	Stalin, *Economic Problems of Socialism*
1953	Stalin dies in Moscow
1956	Twentieth Party Congress; Khrushchev's speech against Stalin and "cult of personality"
1957-1958	Khrushchev emerges as undisputed leader of party and U.S.S.R.
1958	Twenty-first Party Congress

NOTES

CHAPTER ONE · MARX AND AMERICA

1. David A. Shannon, *The Socialist Party of America* (New York, 1955), pp. 258-268, and the works cited at 309.
2. Karl Marx and Friedrich Engels, *Selected Correspondence, 1846-1895* (New York, 1942), pp. 501-502.
3. Quoted in Sidney Hook, *Marx and the Marxists* (Princeton, 1955), p. 64; Marx and Engels, *Selected Correspondence*, pp. 452-455. On this point, see Shannon, *Socialist Party*, pp. 258-262; Daniel Bell, "The Background and Development of Marxian Socialism in the United States," in D. D. Egbert and Stow Persons, eds., *Socialism and American Life* (Princeton, 1952), Vol. I, chap. 6, esp. pp. 217-222; Robert J. Alexander, "Splinter Groups in American Radical Politics," *Social Research*, Vol. XX (1953), p. 282.
4. Hook, *Marx and the Marxists*, p. 63.
5. Theodore Draper, *The Roots of American Communism* (New York, 1957), pp. 189-191.
6. *The Opium of the Intellectuals* (Garden City, 1957), p. 106.
7. Not so civil that I cannot delight in E. H. Carr's sharp attack on the "pseudo-Marxists" in his *Karl Marx: A Study in Fanaticism* (London, 1935), pp. v-vi. For an account of the struggle over the corpse of Marx, see Sidney Hook, *Towards the Understanding of Karl Marx* (New York, 1933), chaps. 3-7. The chief differences of the orthodox Marxists and the revisionists are summarized in S. H. M. Chang, *The Marxian Theory of the State* (Philadelphia, 1931), pp. 14-23.
8. John Plamenatz, *German Marxism and Russian Communism* (London, 1954), p. 251, a brilliant commentary on Marxism and its problems. Among the other studies I have found enlightening guides (and only a fool would refuse to accept guides to Marxism) are: M. M. Bober, *Karl Marx's Interpretation of History* (Cambridge, 1948); Jean-Yves

Calvez, *La pensée de Karl Marx* (Paris, 1956); G. D. H. Cole, *The Meaning of Marxism* (London, 1950); A. L. Harris, "The Social Philosophy of Karl Marx," *Ethics,* Vol. LVIII (1948), No. 3, Pt. ii; Hook, *Marx and the Marxists,* only the latest and clearest of a number of his studies cited in these notes; Werner Sombart, *Der proletarische Sozialismus* (Jena, 1924), Vol. I (*Die Lehre*), still a magisterial presentation after all these years; Maximilien Rubel, *Karl Marx: Essai de biographie intellectuelle* (Paris, 1957), an especially useful introduction to the chronology of Marx's intellectual development; André Piettre, *Marx et Marxisme* (Paris, 1957), which analyzes Marxism under the three headings of philosophy, economics, and theory of revolution; R. N. Carew Hunt, *The Theory and Practice of Communism* (London, 1951), and *Marxism Past and Present* (New York, 1954); J. L. Gray, "Karl Marx and Social Philosophy," in F. J. C. Hearnshaw, ed., *The Social and Political Ideas of Some Representative Thinkers of the Victorian Age* (London, 1933), pp. 116-149; H. J. Laski, *Communism* (London, 1927); H. B. Mayo, *Democracy and Marxism* (New York, 1955), revised and reissued as *Introduction to Marxist Theory* (New York, 1960); A. G. Meyer, *Marxism: The Unity of Theory and Practice* (Cambridge, 1954); and, each in its own way a bright light on Marxism, G. H. Sabine, *A History of Political Theory* (New York, 1950), chaps. 33-34; K. R. Popper, *The Open Society and its Enemies* (Princeton, 1950), chaps. 13-22; and Edmund Wilson, *To the Finland Station* (New York, 1940, 1953). Guides to special topics will be cited throughout these notes.

9. A useful introduction to the orthodox canon, especially since it is an "inside job," is Maurice Cornforth, ed., *Readers' Guide to the Marxist Classics* (London, 1952). A useful introduction to the secondary literature is R. N. Carew Hunt, *Books on Communism* (London, 1959).

10. Of the major biographies of Marx the most substantial is Franz Mehring, *Karl Marx* (London, 1936); of the minor, the most perceptive is Isaiah Berlin, *Karl Marx* (London, 1948). Others well worth seeing are E. H. Carr, *Karl Marx: A Study in Fanaticism* (London, 1935); Karl Korsch, *Karl Marx* (New York, 1938); B. I. Nicolaevsky and Otto Maenchen-Helfen, *Karl Marx: Man and Fighter* (Philadelphia, 1936); Otto Rühle, *Karl Marx* (New York, 1929); Leopold Schwarzchild, *The Red Prussian* (New York, 1947), as biased against Marx as several of the others are for him; Karl Vorländer, *Karl Marx* (Leipzig, 1929). Still others are listed in Egbert and Persons, eds., *Socialism and American Life,* Vol. II, p. 37, and Mayo, *Democracy and Marxism,* pp. 339-340. For comprehensive bibliographies of his and Engels' own works, see M. Rubel, *Bibliographie des oeuvres de Karl Marx* (Paris, 1956), and H.-C. Desroches, *Signification du Marxisme* (Paris, 1949), pp. 251-377.

11. *Ludwig Feuerbach and the Outcome of German Classical Philosophy* (New York, 1941), pp. 42-43 n. Marx's leading biographer, Mehring, agrees that Engels was too modest (*Karl Marx,* pp. 95, 107, 231-237). Gustav Mayer, *Friedrich Engels* (London, 1936), is the only biography worth noting. Engels deserves a major biography.

12. Howard Selsam, ed., *Handbook of Philosophy* (New York, 1949), p. 37.
13. Joseph Stalin, *Leninism* (New York, n.d.), Vol. I, p. 14.
14. Plamenatz, *German Marxism*, pp. 8, 281-305, and "Deviations from Marxism," *Political Quarterly*, Vol. XXI (1950), p. 40. For the lives of Lenin, Stalin, and Trotsky, see the works cited in Egbert and Persons, eds., *Socialism and American Life*, Vol. II, pp. 77-79, and Mayo, *Democracy and Marxism*, pp. 340-341. I must acknowledge my own large debt to Bertram D. Wolfe, *Three Who Made a Revolution* (New York, 1948); Isaac Deutscher, *Stalin* (New York, 1949), *The Prophet Armed: Trotsky, 1879-1921* (New York, 1953), and *The Prophet Unarmed: Trotsky, 1921-1929* (New York, 1959), all of these books to be used with care; Boris Souvarine, *Stalin* (New York, 1939). See also Max Nomad, *Apostles of Revolution* (Boston, 1939); E. H. Carr, *The Bolshevik Revolution*, 3 vols. (New York, 1951-1953), which should be read with Bertram D. Wolfe's review in *Problems of Communism*, Vol. IV, No. 2 (1955), p. 43; Carr, *The Interregnum, 1923-1924* (New York, 1954), and *Socialism in One Country*, 2 vols. (London, 1958); Arthur Rosenberg, *A History of Bolshevism* (London, 1934); W. H. Chamberlin, *The Russian Revolution*, 2 vols. (New York, 1954); G. D. H. Cole, *A History of Socialist Thought* (New York, 1953-58), Vol. IV, Pt. I, chaps. 1-3, 6, 9.
15. Benjamin Schwartz, *Chinese Communism and the Rise of Mao* (Cambridge, 1952), a first-class study; Robert C. North, *Moscow and Chinese Communists* (Stanford, 1953). Karl A. Wittfogel, "The Influence of Leninism-Stalinism on China," *Annals of the American Academy of Political and Social Science*, Vol. CCLXXVII (1951), p. 23, and Benjamin Schwartz, "On the 'Originality' of Mao Tse-tung," *Foreign Affairs*, Vol. XXXIV (1955), p. 67, are the best short studies of Mao's heritage (Leninist-Stalinist) and contributions (not many). Benjamin Schwartz, "New Trends in Maoism?," *Problems of Communism*, Vol. VI, No. 4 (1957), p. 1, brings the story up to date. The best edition of Mao's own writings in English is *Selected Works*, 4 vols. (New York, 1954-56).
16. See Lenin's tribute to Plekhanov's work—"the best of its kind"—in G. Plekhanov, *Essays in Historical Materialism* (New York, 1941), p. 5.
17. See especially Daniel De Leon, *Speeches and Editorials*, 2 vols. (New York, n.d.), published by the New York Labor News Co., and L. B. Boudin, *The Theoretical System of Karl Marx* (Chicago, 1907). For a useful bibliography of American Marxism, see Egbert and Persons, eds., *Socialism and American Life* (Princeton, 1952), Vol. II, Pt. III, esp. pp. 185-191. The works of most of these men may be traced through my index. The early works of Sidney Hook and Max Eastman form a special but important category of American Marxism.
18. For Foster's dreams, see his *Toward Soviet America* (New York, 1932), chap. 5. His *History of the Communist Party of the United States* (New York, 1952), is an astounding view of American history.
19. For basic bibliographies of books about the American tradition, see my *Conservatism in America* (New York, 1955), pp. 315-316; Stow Per-

sons, *American Minds* (New York, 1958), pp. 452-457; Alan P. Grimes, *American Political Thought* (New York, 1955), pp. 459-489; Merle Curti, *The Growth of American Thought* (New York, 1943), pp. 755-816.

20. Daniel Boorstin, *The Genius of American Politics* (Chicago, 1953).
21. *Reason and Revolution* (New York, 1954).
22. *Human Nature: The Marxian View* (New York, 1945), pp. 193 ff.
23. *Reason, Social Myths and Democracy* (New York, 1940), pp. 184 ff. I am inclined to agree with Jacques Barzun that if there must be seven sorts of dialectic, perhaps it would be better to do without any. *Darwin, Marx, Wagner* (2nd ed.; New York, 1958), p. 166 n.
24. As a sample, see Hunt, *Theory and Practice of Communism*, pp. 67-70, 172 ff.; Plamenatz, *German Marxism*, pp. 227 ff., 276-277, 283 ff.; Sabine, *History of Political Theory*, pp. 826 ff.; Mayo, *Democracy and Marxism*, pp. 117 ff.; Chang, *Marxian Theory of the State*, pp. 63 ff.; A. G. Meyer, *Leninism* (Cambridge, 1957), pp. 139 ff.
25. Paul M. Sweezy, ed., *Karl Marx and the Close of his System . . . and Böhm-Bawerk's Criticism of Marx* (New York, 1949).
26. Thorstein Veblen, *The Place of Science in Modern Civilization* (New York, 1919), p. 437 n.
27. *Systèmes Socialistes* (Paris, 1926), Vol. II, p. 342. For an attempt to prove a monumental inconsistency in *Capital*, that between the Hegelian and Darwinian points of view, see Jean Hyppolite, "De la structure du 'Capital' et de quelques présuppositions philosophiques de l'oeuvre de Marx," *Bulletin de la Société française de Philosophie*, Oct.-Dec. 1948, pp. 172-173. For a keen defense of Marx against charges of inconsistency, see A. D. Lindsay, *Karl Marx's Capital* (London, 1925), pp. 9-11.
28. Mayo, *Democracy and Marxism*, pp. 44-45.
29. Plamenatz, *German Marxism*, pp. 35-39, 55-73.
30. *Historical Materialism and the Economics of Karl Marx* (New York, 1914), p. 50.
31. *Historical Materialism*, p. 49.
32. *Communism and Man* (New York, 1940), pp. 139-140.
33. Alexander Gray, *The Socialist Tradition* (London, 1946), p. 316.
34. Franz Borkenau, "Marx's Prophecy in the Light of History," *Commentary*, Vol. VII (1949), p. 430.
35. H. M. Morais, "Marx and Engels on America," *Science and Society*, Vol. XII (1948), p. 3, which claims too much but is a useful guide. Karl Marx and Friedrich Engels, *Letters to Americans* (New York, 1953) contains Engels' revealing preface to the American edition (1887) of his *Condition of the Working Class in England*.
36. Karl Marx and Friedrich Engels, *The Civil War in the United States* (New York, 1937), pp. 279-283; *Letters to Americans*, pp. 65-66; Raya Dunayevskaya, *Marxism and Freedom* (New York, 1958), pp. 81 ff.
37. B. J. Stern, *Lewis Henry Morgan* (Chicago, 1931), esp. pp. 175-188. See Engels' tribute to Morgan in *The Origin of the Family, Private Property and the State* (New York, 1942), pp. 5-6, 15-16, and indeed throughout the book.

38. Gray, *Socialist Tradition*, p. 330.
39. Emile Burns, ed., *A Handbook of Marxism* (New York, 1935), p. 205.
40. *Letters to Americans*, pp. 157-158; *Socialism: Utopian and Scientific* (New York, 1935), pp. 24-25; *Letters to Americans*, p. 287; *Selected Correspondence*, pp. 453, 496-497, 501-502.
41. On De Leon, see Egbert and Persons, eds., *Socialism and American Life*, Vol. II, pp. 140-145. See also Boudin, *Theoretical System of Karl Marx*, an orthodox defense of Marx against the revisionists. Two quite different books by Earl Browder may be read with profit: *What is Communism?* (New York, 1936), for its simple orthodoxy; *Marx and America* (New York, 1958), for its strange mixture of skepticism and belief, of frustration and triumph. Browder's best writings are, unfortunately, fugitive pieces.
42. Algie M. Simons, *Social Forces in American History* (New York, 1920); Morris Hillquit, *Socialism in Theory and Practice* (New York, 1909); John Spargo, *Socialism* (New York, 1909), and *Marxian Socialism and Religion* (New York, 1915); William English Walling, *The Larger Aspects of Socialism* (New York, 1913); Hook, *Towards the Understanding of Karl Marx*. I have been especially instructed by W. A. Glaser, "Algie Martin Simons and Marxism in America," *Mississippi Valley Historical Review*, Vol. XLI (1954), p. 419.
43. Bernard C. Borning, "The Political Philosophy of Young Charles A. Beard," *American Political Science Review*, Vol. XLIII (1949), p. 1177; Morton G. White, *Social Thought in America* (New York, 1952), pp. 119 ff.; Persons, *American Minds*, pp. 328-330, a good review of Marxist influence on American thought. Beard and Lenin had identical debts to J. A. Hobson's *Imperialism* (London, 1902).
44. C. W. Kegley and R. W. Bretall, eds., *Reinhold Niebuhr: His Religious, Social, and Political Thought* (New York, 1956), pp. 8, 65, 71 ff., 137 ff., 158 ff., 301 ff., 436.
45. *The Education of Henry Adams* (New York, 1918), p. 225. See the Marxist treatment of the Adams brothers in Richard Greenleaf, "History, Marxism and Henry Adams," *Science and Society*, Vol. XV (1951), p. 193, and W. A. Williams, "On the Restoration of Brooks Adams," *Science and Society*, Vol. XX (1956), p. 247.
46. Thornton Anderson, *Brooks Adams: Constructive Conservative* (Ithaca, 1951), pp. 67-69.

CHAPTER TWO · THE MARXIST IDEA

1. For discussions of the two major senses in which Marxists use this word, see G. H. Sabine, *Marxism* (Ithaca, 1958), pp. 16-25; H. B. Acton, *Illusion of the Epoch* (Boston, 1957), pp. 116-133, 172-179; J. and M. Miller, "A New Stage in the Study of Marxism," *Soviet Studies*, Vol. VII (1956), p. 280; and Acton's remarks in *Soviet Studies*, Vol. VII (1956), p. 411; S. W. Moore, *The Critique of Capitalist Democracy* (New York, 1957), chap. 4. By far the best

study of this aspect of Marx's thought is Hans Barth, *Wahrheit und Ideologie* (Zurich, 1954), pp. 73-190, esp. 146-164. An interesting Marxist discussion of ideology as an aspect of idealism is Auguste Cornu, *Essai de critique marxiste* (Paris, 1951), pp. 11-32.

2. *The Uses of the Past* (New York, 1954), p. 73; Berlin, *Marx*, p. 267.
3. For typically ritualistic proclamations of this monumental truism, see T. A. Jackson, *Dialectics: The Logic of Marxism and its Critics* (London, 1936), p. 626; John Macmurray, *The Philosophy of Communism* (London, 1933), pp. 36 ff. So far as I can tell, this concept is simply a fuzzy way of saying that Marxists are free to be both dogmatists and pragmatists at the same time—which they (and all of us) are.
4. *Dialectical and Historical Materialism* (New York, 1940), p. 24; Lenin, *What is to be Done?* (New York, 1929), pp. 28-29, 99, 101.
5. *Dialectical and Historical Materialism*, p. 5. For a painfully orthodox presentation of dialectical materialism, see Maurice Cornforth, *Materialism and the Dialectical Method* (New York, 1953). By far the most authoritative study of dialectical materialism is Gustav A. Wetter, *Dialectical Materialism* (New York, 1958), a notable book.
6. Macmurray, *Philosophy of Communism*, pp. 31-33.
7. V. Adoratsky, *Dialectical Materialism* (New York, 1934), p. 37; Henri Lefebvre, *Le matérialisme dialectique* (Paris, 1940), pp. 84 ff.
8. Sidney Hook, *From Hegel to Marx* (New York, 1950), esp. chap. 1; Marcuse, *Reason and Revolution;* Lindsay, *Karl Marx's Capital*, chap. 1; Popper, *Open Society*, pp. 661-662, an immensely useful summary of "views which Marxism takes over from Hegelianism"; Karl Löwith, *Von Hegel bis Nietzsche* (Zurich, 1941), pp. 124-139; Ludwig Landgrebe, "Hegel und Marx," in *Marxismusstudien* (Tübingen, 1954), p. 39; Jean Hyppolite, *Etudes sur Marx et Hegel* (Paris, 1955), esp. pp. 107 ff.; Erich Thier, *Das Menschenbild des jungen Marx* (Göttingen, 1957), chap. 1; Konrad Bekker, *Marx' philosophische Entwicklung, sein Verhältnis zu Hegel* (Zurich, 1940), esp. pp. 6-36; Heinrich Popitz, *Der entfremdete Mensch* (Basle, 1953), Pts. I-II, and the bibliography at pp. 171-172; Auguste Cornu, *Karl Marx et la pensée moderne* (Paris, 1948), a Marxist appraisal of Marx's debt to Hegel and place in the stream of modern ideas. For good, brief reviews of some of Marx's other sources, see Barzun, *Darwin, Marx, Wagner*, pp. 142 ff., 177; Berlin, *Marx*, pp. 14 ff., 89, 142-143, and chaps. 3-4 generally; Gray, *Socialist Tradition*, pp. 300-301. For the English background, see Elie Halévy, *The Growth of Philosophic Radicalism* (Boston, 1955). Wilson, *Finland Station*, is without doubt the most exciting exposition of Marx's intellectual heritage. G. D. H. Cole, *Socialist Thought*, Vol. I, is also important. Julien Benda, *Trois idoles romantiques* (Paris, 1948), pp. 147 ff., insists that dialectical materialism is an expression of Romanticism.
9. *Capital* (Chicago, 1906-1909), Vol. I, p. 25; *Selected Correspondence*, p. 234. Engels, *Ludwig Feuerbach and the Outcome of Classical German Philosophy*, is invaluable for its account of the transformation of the Hegelian dialectic to the Marxist.

10. See his *Anti-Dühring* (Moscow, 1954), esp. chaps. 12-13, in which Marx had a hand; *Feuerbach*, pp. 12, 43 ff.; *Dialectics of Nature* (New York, 1940), esp. chap. 2; *Socialism: Utopian and Scientific*, pp. 45-59. The last book was a separately published part of *Anti-Dühring*.
11. See the review of those laws and assumptions which Lenin found embodied in the dialectic in H. Levy *et al., Aspects of Dialectical Materialism* (London, 1934), pp. 14-16, or T. A. Jackson, *Dialectics*, pp. 635-636. Lenin's *Materialism and Empirio-Criticism* (New York, 1927), was his major attempt to defend dialectical materialism, apply its principles to science, and sink the Marxist "idealists" like Bazarov and Lunacharsky without a trace. See Wolfe, *Three Who Made a Revolution*, chap. 29.
12. Macmurray, *Philosophy of Communism*, p. 14.
13. Bober, *Marx's Interpretation of History*, chap. 2; Hunt, *Theory and Practice of Communism*, pp. 17-28, and *Marxism Past and Present*, chap. 2; Mayo, *Democracy and Marxism*, chap. 3; Wilson, *Finland Station*, chap. 11; Max Eastman, *Marxism: Is it Science?* (New York, 1940), pp. 134-145; Bekker, *Marx' philosophische Entwicklung*, pp. 100-130; Georges Izard, *L'homme est révolutionnaire* (Paris, 1945), chap. 5. See especially Marcuse, *Reason and Revolution;* Hook, *Reason, Social Myths and Democracy*, chaps. 9, 11. No study of the dialectic could be more enlightening than Calvez, *La pensée de Karl Marx*, Pt. III.
14. *Dialectics of Nature*, p. 13; *Socialism: Utopian and Scientific*, p. 49; *Feuerbach*, pp. 12, 44; Marx, *Poverty of Philosophy* (Chicago, 1910), pp. 116, 119; Adoratsky, *Dialectical Materialism*, p. 33.
15. *Dialectical and Historical Materialism*, p. 8.
16. Marx, *Selected Works* (New York, n.d.), Vol. I, pp. 355-357, an edition in which, of course, important writings of Engels are also to be found. I have used the translation in the first American edition (1904) as printed in Burns, ed., *Handbook of Marxism*, pp. 371-373, and I have taken the liberty of channeling Marx's flood of thoughts into paragraphs. For a lengthy critical analysis of this passage, see Karl Federn, *The Materialist Conception of History* (London, 1939).
17. *Feuerbach*, p. 31.
18. B. D. Wolfe, *Khrushchev and Stalin's Ghost* (New York, 1957), pp. 218, 220; Boris Meissner, *The Communist Party of the Soviet Union* (New York, 1956), pp. 223-245. The "new texts" of which I speak are the still untranslated *Political Dictionary* of 1958 (*Politicheskii Slovar*), the party history of 1959 (*Istoriia Kommunisticheskoi Partii Sovetskogo Soivza*), and a collection of essays issued in 1959 (*Voprosy Stroitelstva Kommunizma v SSSR*). I am grateful to Jan Triska and Frederick Hargadon for helping me to translate and understand key passages in the new party history—of which, to tell the truth, there are precious few of an ideological character. On the faithfulness of Khrushchev to Stalin on this and most other points of Marxist ideology, see Leopold Labedz, "Ideology: The Fourth Stage," *Problems of Communism*, Vol. VIII, No. 6 (1959), p. 1. On the new history, see *Current Digest of the Soviet Press*, August 12, 1959, and Leopold

Labedz, "Khrushchev's New Party History," *New Leader*, October 12, 1959.

19. *Dialectical and Historical Materialism*, pp. 15-19. It is interesting to note that all of Stalin's many quotations in support of his exposition are from Engels and Lenin. On Stalin as philosopher, see Wetter, *Dialectical Materialism*, chap. 10; Nathan Leites, "Stalin as an Intellectual," *World Politics*, Vol. VI (1953), p. 45. William Edgerton, translator, *A Soviet History of Philosophy* (Washington, 1950), is a useful introduction to the interests and issues of Soviet philosophy. Percy E. Corbett, "Postwar Soviet Ideology," *Annals of the American Academy of Political and Social Science*, Vol. CCLXIII (1949), p. 45, is a sharp account of the sterility of current Soviet Marxism.

20. Selsam, ed., *Handbook of Philosophy*, p. 53.

21. *Selected Works*, Vol. I, p. 225. Italics mine.

22. *German Ideology* (New York, 1947), pp. 14-15. Italics mine.

23. *Dialectical and Historical Materialism*, p. 29.

24. For a review of the struggle between "mechanistic" and dialectical materialism in Soviet philosophy, see John Somerville, *Soviet Philosophy* (New York, 1946), chap. 7; Wetter, *Dialectical Materialism*, chap. 7. For the current orthodox "line" on this subject, see Cornforth, *Materialism and the Dialectical Method*, chaps. 3-5. Engels said his piece in *Feuerbach*, pp. 26 ff.

25. For insights into Feuerbach's more immediate influence, see Acton, *Illusion of the Epoch*, pp. 116 ff.; Hook, *From Hegel to Marx*, chaps. 7-8. Marx and Engels considered England—in the persons of Bacon, Hobbes, Locke, Hartley, and Priestley—the foundation of modern materialism. See the passage from Marx's *Holy Family* in Engels, *Socialism: Utopian and Scientific*, pp. 10-12.

26. See Engels' testimony in *Socialism: Utopian and Scientific*, p. 6.

27. Egbert and Persons, eds., *Socialism and American Life*, Vol. II, pp. 192-197.

28. Bukharin, *Historical Materialism* (New York, 1925), p. xiv.

29. J. B. S. Haldane, in the preface to Engels, *Dialectics of Nature*, p. xv.

30. For an example of the agonies of an intelligent man who seeks to defend the Marxist dialectic, see G. D. H. Cole, *What Marx Really Meant* (London, 1934), chap. 9. And for the rigid application of dialectical materialism to nature, see J. D. Bernal in H. Levy *et al.*, *Aspects of Dialectical Materialism*, pp. 89-122, 147-154. J. B. S. Haldane, *The Marxist Philosophy and the Sciences* (New York, 1939), pp. 28-29, deserves full credit for applying the dialectic to skidding cars, at least to his own and to London buses.

31. On this point, see Gerhart Niemeyer, *An Inquiry into Soviet Mentality* (New York, 1956), pp. 33-35.

32. Wilson, *Finland Station*, pp. 190-191.

33. Mao Tse-tung, *Selected Works*, Vol. I, p. 202. I cannot deny that the italics are mine.

34. *Selected Correspondence*, pp. 475-477.

35. *The Origin of Russian Communism* (London, 1955), pp. 98-100.

36. For examples of Marx's and Engels' contempt for the bourgeois habit of transforming an ideology into "eternal laws of nature and of reason," see *Selected Works*, Vol. I, pp. 223, 226; S. W. Moore, *Critique of Capitalist Democracy*, p. 35 n.; *Anti-Dühring*, Pt. I, chap. 9. Yet they, too, could never conquer the habit of talking about "natural" "forms" or "behavior" or even "laws," presumably because they, too, like the rest of us, were natural-law thinkers at bottom. See, for example, *Capital*, Vol. I, pp. 14, 393, 533, 709-710; *Anti-Dühring*, p. 195.

37. Z. Barbu, "Marxist Philosophy and European Thought," *Philosophical Quarterly*, Vol. III (1953), p. 150, is excellent on Marxism's strange fondness for all the philosophical positions it derides—metaphysics, dogmatism, subjectivism, and idealism.

38. *Socialism: Utopian and Scientific*, p. 7. For the natural-law essence of Marx's own thinking, see Hans Kelsen, *The Communist Theory of Law* (New York, 1955), pp. 20-23, 39-40.

39. For a classic example, see the quotation from the Soviet theoretician L. Rudos in Sidney Hook, ed., *The Meaning of Marx* (New York, 1934), pp. 78-79. When Stalin was asked where and when Lenin expounded dialectical materialism, he answered, "Where and when did he not expound it?" Levy *et al.*, *Aspects of Dialectical Materialism*, p. 122.

40. M. Cornforth, *Dialectical Materialism: An Introductory Course* (London, 1952), Vol. I, p. 126.

41. Stalin, *History of the Communist Party of the Soviet Union* (New York, 1939), p. 355. I. M. Bochenski, *Der Sowjetrussische dialektische Materialismus* (Berne, 1950), is a highly informative short account of what Lenin and his followers have made of Marx's dialectical materialism. See G. L. Kline, "A Philosophical Critique of Soviet Marxism," *Review of Metaphysics*, Vol. IX (1955), p. 90, an account of B. Petrov, *Filosofskaya nishcheta marksizma* (Frankfurt, 1952), a devastating assault on dialectical materialism in the Soviet Union. See also Gustav Wetter, "Dialectical Materialism and Natural Science," *Soviet Survey*, January-March 1958, p. 51; Brian Simon, ed., *Psychology in the Soviet Union* (Stanford, 1957), pp. 3-9.

42. Some of the best and most sensible writing about Marxism has been done on this subject. See Acton, *Illusion of the Epoch*, pp. 133 ff.; Berlin, *Marx*, chap. 6; Bober, *Marx's Interpretation of History*, esp. Pt. V; J. M. Cameron, *Scrutiny of Marxism* (London, 1948), chaps. 1, 3; Federn, *Materialist Conception of History;* Herbert Butterfield, *History and Human Relations* (London, 1951), pp. 66-100; Gray, *Socialist Tradition*, pp. 301 ff.; Hook, *Towards the Understanding of Marx*, chaps. 11-13; Hunt, *Theory and Practice of Communism*, pp. 35-51; Mayo, *Democracy and Marxism*, chaps. 2, 5; Popper, *Open Society*, esp. chap. 15; Plamenatz, *German Marxism*, chap. 2; E. R. A. Seligman, *The Economic Interpretation of History* (New York, 1907), chaps. 2-5; Venable, *Human Nature*, esp. chap. 11; Wilson, *Finland Station*, a work of art. Special studies of value are Leonard Krieger, "Marx and Engels as Historians," *Journal of the History of Ideas*,

Vol. XIV (1953), p. 381; H. Trevor-Roper, "Marxism and the Study of History," *Problems of Communism,* Vol. V, No. 5 (1956), p. 36.
43. Bertrand Russell, *Bolshevism: Practice and Theory* (New York, 1920), p. 124; Plamenatz, *German Marxism,* pp. 12-13.
44. John Plamenatz, "The Communist Ideology," *Political Quarterly,* Vol. XXII (1951), p. 16.
45. *Selected Works,* Vol. I, p. 402; Marx to Annenkov, *Selected Correspondence,* pp. 5-18.
46. *Socialism: Utopian and Scientific,* 54. Chapter 3 of this book is a remarkable twenty-page compression of the theory of historical materialism employed in *Capital,* Vol. I. Engels, *The Peasant War in Germany* (New York, 1926), is an interesting example of applied historical materialism. A standard exposition of the "hard" Marxist philosophy of history is Maurice Cornforth, *Historical Materialism* (New York, 1954).
47. Engels, *Socialism: Utopian and Scientific,* p. 49.
48. Sombart, *Der proletarische Sozialismus,* Vol. I, chap. 24, is excellent on the Communist myths of Paradise Lost and Paradise Regained.
49. Engels occasionally looked far into the future to foresee the end of all life on earth. Venable, *Human Nature,* p. 14 n.; Engels, *Dialectics of Nature,* p. 20.
50. Georgi Dimitrov, *Selected Speeches and Articles* (London, 1951), p. 36.
51. Burns, *Handbook,* pp. 354-355.
52. *Selected Correspondence,* pp. 472-484, 516-519. Plekhanov, *The Materialist Conception of History* (New York, 1940), and Antonio Labriola, *Essays on the Materialistic Conception of History* (Chicago, 1908), are classics of historical materialism. Alexander Dallin, "Recent Soviet Historiography," *Problems of Communism,* Vol. V, No. 6 (1956), p. 24, is a useful review of current attempts to write Marxist-Leninist history.
53. Samuel Beer, ed., *The Communist Manifesto* (New York, 1953), p. xxi.
54. *Historical Materialism,* p. 44. See Nathan Leites, *A Study of Bolshevism* (Glencoe, Ill., 1953), pp. 67-73.
55. *Selected Works,* Vol. I, p. 16; Engels, *Feuerbach,* pp. 48-49.
56. *Selected Works,* Vol. I, pp. 204-206; *Anti-Dühring,* p. 41.
57. Soviet theoretician G. F. Aleksandrov, quoted in Hunt, *Marxism,* p. 84.
58. *State and Revolution* (New York, 1932), pp. 15-20, 34; Stalin, *Leninism,* Vol. I, pp. 30-41, 47-48.
59. *The Poverty of Philosophy,* pp. 190-191, quoting George Sand.
60. For an analysis of the role of the hero in Marxist history, see Sidney Hook, *The Hero in History* (Boston, 1955), chaps. 5, 10. See also the exchange over the inevitability of socialism between Hook, *Towards the Understanding of Karl Marx,* pp. 110-114, and Max Eastman, *The Last Stand of Dialectical Materialism* (New York, 1934).
61. Engels, *Feuerbach,* pp. 48-49.
62. H. J. Blackham, *The Human Tradition* (Boston, 1953), p. 103.

63. Sir John Maynard, *Russia in Flux* (New York, 1948), pp. 122-123.
64. *Selected Correspondence*, p. 517; *Selected Works*, Vol. II, p. 315.
65. No text in the canon is more revealing of the harshness of this dilemma for the honest Marxist than Plekhanov, *The Role of the Individual in History* (New York, 1940), esp. pp. 43-48, 55-60. For an analysis of the history-making importance Lenin ascribed to the man of Communist ideas, see Max Eastman, *Marx and Lenin: The Science of Revolution* (New York, 1927), pp. 144, 150-152, 167-168. And for the attempt of an American Marxist to evaluate the roles of "acquiescence" and "activity" in Marx's thought—and to have it both ways —see Theodore Brameld, *A Philosophic Approach to Communism* (Chicago, 1933).
66. *Socialism: Utopian and Scientific*, p. 68.
67. Max Eastman called it an "escalator" in his *Marxism: Is it Science?* (New York, 1940), p. 15. Others have conceived of it as a locomotive.
68. Bukharin, *Historical Materialism*, p. 51.
69. Cameron, *Scrutiny of Marxism*, p. 71.
70. For a discussion of Marxist and democratic theories of history, and for a guide to the best sources, see Egbert and Persons, eds., *Socialism and American Life*, Vol. I, pp. 409-425 (by David F. Bowers), and Vol. II, pp. 197-205.
71. *Selected Works*, Vol. I, p. 357.
72. See generally Isaiah Berlin, *Historical Inevitability* (London, 1954). For a Marxist reply to both Berlin and Popper, see Lewis, *Marxism and the Open Mind*, chap. 2.
73. A. A. Ekirch, *The Idea of Progress in America, 1815-1860* (New York, 1944).
74. Cameron, *Scrutiny of Marxism*, p. 31.
75. "Why I am not a Communist," in Hook, ed., *The Meaning of Marx*, pp. 54-55.
76. Margaret T. Hodgen, "Karl Marx and the Social Scientists," *Scientific Monthly*, Vol. LXXII (1951), p. 252; Federn, *Materialist Conception of History*, pp. 233-235. For a devastating attack on Marxist history, which makes much of "the complete absence of any great Marxist historians," see Trevor-Roper, "Marxism and the Study of History," pp. 40-41. A more friendly view is Rudolf Schlesinger, "Recent Soviet Historiography," *Soviet Studies*, Vol. I (1949-1950), p. 293; Vol. II (1950-1951), pp. 3, 138, 265.
77. For a sharp criticism of Marx's historical method, see Julien Benda, *La trahison des clercs* (Paris, 1927), p. 239.
78. See Cornforth, *Materialism and the Dialectical Method*, chap. 11, and Andrei Zhdanov, *Essays on Literature, Philosophy, and Music* (New York, 1950), pp. 71-72, for standard expositions. See Alex Inkeles, *Public Opinion in Soviet Russia* (Cambridge, 1950), chap. 14, for the practical manifestations of this concept.
79. Franz Borkenau, "Marx's Prophecy in the Light of History," *Commentary*, Vol. VII (1949), p. 430; V. G. Simkhovitch, *Marxism versus Socialism* (New York, 1913); Sidney Hook, "What is Living and

What is Dead in Marxism," *Southern Review,* Vol. VI (1940), p. 293.

80. Popper, *Open Society,* esp. chaps. 1, 13, 15; Aron, *The Opium of the Intellectuals,* chap. 5.
81. Bertram D. Wolfe, "The Prophet and his Prophecies," *Problems of Communism,* Vol. VII, No. 6 (1958), p. 24.
82. *Anti-Dühring,* p. 438; *Capital,* Vol. I, pp. 91, 83.
83. *Gesamtausgabe,* Vol. I, p. 607. (See note 11, chap. 3.)
84. *Religion* (New York, 1933), p. 42. For an especially interesting discussion of Marxism as atheism, see Desroches, *Signification du Marxisme,* pp. 165-180. Engels' remarks on the fad of spiritualism in *Dialectics of Nature,* pp. 297 ff., make amusing and revealing reading —with which it is hard to disagree.
85. Selsam, ed., *Handbook of Philosophy,* p. 105.
86. *Gesamtausgabe,* Vol. I, p. 607.
87. *Gesamtausgabe,* Vol. I, p. 607.
88. *Religion,* p. 7.
89. *Religion,* p. 14.
90. Lenin, *Collected Works* (New York, 1930), Vol. XVIII, p. 296.
91. *Gesamtausgabe,* Vol. VI, p. 278. Not all Marxists after Marx have been able to dispose of Christianity quite this easily. See Lewis' musings on "Communism the Heir to the Christian Tradition," *Marxism and the Open Mind,* chap. 10.
92. *Gesamtausgabe,* Vol. I, p. 608; *Capital,* Vol. I, pp. 91-92.
93. *Anti-Dühring,* pp. 439-440. On the hard times of religion in the Soviet Union, see N. S. Timasheff, *Religion in Soviet Russia, 1917-1942* (New York, 1942), which has an excellent bibliography at p. ix; Timasheff, "Religion in Russia, 1941-1950," in W. Gurian, ed., *The Soviet Union* (Notre Dame, 1951), pp. 153-194; John S. Curtiss, *The Russian Church and the Soviet State, 1917-1950* (Boston, 1953); Bauer et al., *How the Soviet System Works* (Cambridge, 1956), pp. 61-64.
94. *Religion,* p. 10.
95. N. Bukharin and E. Preobrazhensky, *The ABC of Communism* (London, 1922), pp. 229, 247 ff.
96. *Gesamtausgabe,* Vol. I, p. 608.
97. For excellent critiques of Marx's methods in this field, see Edward Rogers, *A Christian Commentary on Marxism* (New York, 1952), esp. pp. 139-144; Mayo, *Democracy and Marxism,* chap. 7; Bober, *Marx's Interpretation of History,* pp. 353-358. A recent confrontation of interest is Martin C. D'Arcy, *Communism and Christianity* (New York, 1957), esp. chaps. 6-8, and the select bibliography at pp. 241-242. See also Berdyaev, *Origin of Russian Communism,* chap. 7; Walter Dircks, "Le Marxisme dans une vision chrétienne," *Esprit,* May-June 1948, pp. 783-798; Charles W. Lowry, *Communism and Christ* (New York, 1952); Fulton J. Sheen, *Communism and the Conscience of the West* (New York, 1948); John C. Bennett, *Christianity and Communism* (London, 1949).
98. *Young Bolshevik,* No. 5-6 (1946), p. 58, quoted in W. Gurian, *Bolshevism* (Notre Dame, 1953), p. 149; Lenin, *Religion,* p. 5.

99. *Handbook of Philosophy,* p. 10; Cornforth, *Materialism and the Dialectical Method,* p. 122.
100. *Selected Works,* Vol. I, p. 473; Burns, *Handbook,* p. 228.

CHAPTER THREE · MARXIST MAN

1. Venable, *Human Nature: The Marxian View,* a most useful treatise by a most reasonable Marxist; Bober, *Marx's Interpretation of History,* chap. 4; Sheed, *Communism and Man,* Pt. I, chap. 7, and Pt. II, chap. 1.
2. For Marx's preference for "sociologism" over "psychologism," see Popper, *Open Society,* chaps. 13-14, 23. For the Marxist rejection of Freud, which was not easy, see the useful bibliography in Egbert and Persons, eds., *Socialism and American Life,* Vol. II, pp. 359-360, and for the most recent rejection of his "reactionary idealistic teaching," see "Freud and Pavlov," *Soviet Survey,* July-September 1959.
3. *Dialectics of Nature,* p. 13.
4. *The Poverty of Philosophy,* p. 160.
5. Erich Thier, "Etappen der Marxinterpretation," in *Marxismusstudien* (Tübingen, 1954), pp. 1-38, has given considerable thought to the misunderstood connection between the "young Marx" and the "old Marx."
6. *Gesamtausgabe,* Vol. III, pp. 125, 156; *Capital,* Vol. I, pp. 197-206, where labor is described as the "everlasting nature-imposed condition of human existence"; Engels, *Dialectics of Nature,* pp. 279 ff.
7. Paul Tillich, *Der Mensch im Christentum und im Marxismus* (Stuttgart, 1953), p. 6.
8. *Literature and Revolution* (New York, 1925), p. 255.
9. *German Ideology,* p. 7. Italics mine.
10. Third "Thesis on Feuerbach," *Selected Works,* Vol. I, p. 472.
11. These writings are to be found in German in the *Historisch-kritische Gesamtausgabe,* edited by D. Riazanov and V. Adoratsky (Berlin, 1927-1932), Vol. III, Pt. I, pp. 29-172. An English translation of parts of them is now available in Dunayevskaya, *Marxism and Freedom,* pp. 288 ff. See generally Karl Löwith, "Man's Self-Alienation in the Early Writings of Marx," *Social Research,* Vol. XXI (1954), p. 204; Marcuse, *Reason and Revolution,* pp. 258-295, an expansion of a pioneering study in this area; H. P. Adams, *Karl Marx in his Earlier Writings* (London, 1940), a useful guide; Robert C. Tucker, "Marxism—Is It Religion?," *Ethics,* Vol. LXVIII (1958), pp. 125, 127-130; Mehring, *Marx,* pp. 544-547; Popitz, *Der entfremdete Mensch,* Pt. III; Acton, *Illusion of the Epoch,* pp. 223 ff.; S. W. Moore, *Critique of Capitalist Democracy,* pp. 124-134; Erich Voegelin, "The Formation of the Marxian Revolutionary Idea," *Review of Politics,* Vol. XII (1950), pp. 275, 286 ff. For a Marxist version of the earliest years, see Auguste Cornu, *Karl Marx et Friedrich Engels* (Paris, 1955), Vol. I, esp. chap. 3, or *The Origins of Marxian Thought* (Springfield, Ill., 1957), chaps. 3-5.
12. To tell the truth, French Catholic philosophy has done much better.

I am especially indebted to Calvez, *La pensée de Karl Marx*, Pt. I, for my own imperfect grasp of this concept.

13. For the importance of this concept in *Capital*, and indeed for Marx's whole economic theory, see Pierre Bigo, *Marxisme et humanisme* (Paris, 1953), pp. 27-34; Hyppolite, *Etudes sur Marx et Hegel*, pp. 142-168; Henri Bartoli, *La doctrine économique et sociale de Karl Marx* (Paris, 1950), pp. 83 ff. Popitz, *Der entfremdete Mensch*, pp. 109, 165-170, suggests that alienation is the philosophical basis of dialectical materialism. For fresh thoughts on this whole matter, see Daniel Bell, "The 'Rediscovery' of Alienation," *Journal of Philosophy*, Vol. LVI (1959), p. 933.

14. David Braybrooke, "Diagnosis and Remedy in Marx's Doctrine of Alienation," *Social Research*, Vol. XXV (1958), pp. 325, 326.

15. Bartoli, *La doctrine de Karl Marx*, p. 19.

16. Venable, *Human Nature*, chap. 9.

17. *Capital*, Vol. I, p. 399, and chap. 14 generally.

18. *Capital*, p. 396; *German Ideology*, pp. 20-22, 43 ff.; *Poverty of Philosophy*, pp. 138-157.

19. Marx, *Poverty of Philosophy*, p. 153.

20. Kenneth Burke, *Attitudes Toward History* (New York, 1937), Vol. I, p. 53.

21. S. W. Moore, *Critique*, p. 125.

22. *Capital*, Vol. I, p. 708.

23. Hyppolite, *Etudes sur Marx et Hegel*, p. 151.

24. *Gesamtausgabe*, Vol. III, p. 114.

25. *German Ideology*, p. 22. As Gray, *Socialist Tradition*, pp. 328-329, points out, "the cattle themselves might have some objection to being reared in this casual manner."

26. *Anti-Dühring*, p. 278.

27. R. A. Bauer, *The New Man in Soviet Psychology* (Cambridge, 1952); Joseph Wortis, *Soviet Psychiatry* (Baltimore, 1950); Brian Simon, ed., *Psychology in the Soviet Union* (Stanford, 1957). All these studies emphasize Pavlov's importance to Soviet purposes in the broad field of manipulative psychology.

28. "Morals of Soviet Man," *Trud*, May 24, 1947, quoted in W. Gurian, *Bolshevism* (Notre Dame, 1953), pp. 140-141. See S. Kovalyov, *Ideological Conflicts in Soviet Russia* (Washington, 1948), a translation of an important article in *Bolshevik*.

29. Wilson, *Finland Station*, p. 449.

30. Robert C. Tucker, "Stalin and the Uses of Psychology," *World Politics*, Vol. VIII (1956), p. 455; Julian Huxley, "Why Lysenko is Important," *New Republic*, December 5, 1949, and *Heredity, East and West* (New York, 1949), pp. 1-34; E. N. Megay, "Lysenkoism and the Stateless Society," *Journal of Politics*, Vol. XV (1953), p. 211; Bertram D. Wolfe, *Six Keys to the Soviet System* (Boston, 1956), pp. 69-87; H. H. Plough, "Bourgeois Genetics and Party-Line Darwinism," *American Scholar*, Vol. XVIII (1949), p. 291; H. J. Muller, "The Destruction of Science in the U.S.S.R.," *Saturday Review of Literature*, Dec. 4, 11, 1948. For a careful account of Lysenko's experiments see P. S. Hudson and R. H.

Richens, *The New Genetics in the Soviet Union* (Cambridge, Eng., 1946). No secondary account can quite give the flavor of Lysenko's own *The Science of Biology Today* (New York, 1948).

31. Quoted in Bauer, *Soviet Psychology,* p. 81.
32. Sixth "Thesis on Feuerbach," *Selected Works,* Vol. I, p. 473.
33. *German Ideology,* p. 69.
34. On this point, see M. Watnick, "Georg Lukacs," *Soviet Survey,* January-March 1958, pp. 60, 65, and works there cited.
35. *Dictatorship versus Democracy* (New York, 1922), p. 63.
36. *Critique of the Gotha Programme* in *Selected Works,* Vol. II, p. 566.
37. *Capital,* Vol. I, p. 330.
38. *Anti-Dühring,* pp. 147-148.
39. A. L. Harris, "Utopian Elements in Marx's Thought," *Ethics,* Vol. LX (1949), pp. 79, 87-89.
40. *Capital,* Vol. I, p. 195. See Engels' strictures on this "freedom" in his *Condition of the Working Class in England* (New York, 1887), pp. 51-52.
41. *Gesamtausgabe,* Vol. I, p. 595.
42. *Gesamtausgabe,* Vol. I, p. 599.
43. R. A. Bauer *et al., How the Soviet System Works* (Cambridge, 1956), pp. 100-101.
44. *Anti-Dühring,* p. 158.
45. Venable, *Human Nature,* p. 191.
46. *Capital,* Vol. III, pp. 954-955. On this point, see Popper, *Open Society,* p. 295; Lindsay, *Marx's Capital,* pp. 36-37.
47. Engels, *Socialism: Utopian and Scientific,* p. 73. A latter-day Marxist view of liberty may be found in Rudolf Schlesinger, *Marx: His Time and Ours* (London, 1950), pp. 402 ff.
48. Even, I fear, with so reasonable a Marxist as John Lewis. See his contribution to the UNESCO symposium on human rights in his *Marxism and the Open Mind* (London, 1957), pp. 53-76, and also 77-93. And note Stalin's insistence, in his famous interview with Roy Howard in 1937, that "we have not built this society in order to cramp individual freedom." A. Vyshinsky, *The Law of the Soviet State* (New York, 1954), p. 539. For an excellent critique of Marxist ideas about freedom, see H. B. Parkes, *Marxism: An Autopsy* (New York, 1939), chap. 4.
49. I know of no book that gives a more completely orthodox statement of the Marxist concept of liberty than Roger Garaudy, *La liberté* (Paris, 1955), esp. Pts. II, IV. Christopher Caudwell, *Studies in a Dying Culture* (London, 1938), chap. 8, is an eloquent Marxist statement of the irreconcilability of the two liberties, one a "bourgeois illusion," the other the "social consciousness of necessity."
50. Note Vyshinsky's comment, so much at odds with our way of thinking, that "any contrasting of civil rights with the state is alien to socialist public law." *Law of the Soviet State,* pp. 562-563.
51. Lewis, *Marxism and the Open Mind,* p. 58.
52. For a useful bibliography on this subject, see Egbert and Persons, eds., *Socialism and American Life,* Vol. II, pp. 340-342. Sombart, *Der proletarische Sozialismus,* Vol. I, chap. 9, is an excellent introduction.

53. *Critique of the Gotha Programme* in *Selected Works*, Vol. II, p. 567.
54. *Anti-Dühring*, p. 148.
55. *Selected Works*, Vol. I, p. 237.
56. John Strachey, *The Theory and Practice of Socialism* (New York, 1936), p. 117. Barrington Moore, Jr., *Soviet Politics—The Dilemma of Power* (Cambridge, 1956), pp. 405 ff., puts the necessary connection between industrialism and a "system of organized social inequality" with particular conviction. So, in his own way, does Milovan Djilas, *The New Class* (New York, 1958), esp. pp. 37 ff. Engels beat them both to the draw by pointing out in *Anti-Dühring*, p. 193, that "each new advance of civilization is at the same time a new advance of inequality."
57. Marguerite Fisher, *Communist Doctrine and the Free World* (Syracuse, 1952), p. 216. See R. N. Carew Hunt, *A Guide to Communist Jargon* (London, 1957), pp. 69-73; B. Moore, *Soviet Politics*, pp. 182-188, 236-246, 404.
58. *Law of the Soviet State*, p. 209. For the sad story of Lenin's doctrine of "maximum income," see Carr, *Bolshevik Revolution*, Vol. II, pp. 112-115. See his orthodox comments on equality in *State and Revolution* (New York, 1932), pp. 76-82.
59. *Selected Works*, Vol. II, pp. 560-568; Lenin, *State and Revolution*, pp. 75-85.
60. Stalin, *Leninism*, Vol. II, pp. 373-377.
61. *Anti-Dühring*, pp. 148-149. The italics are Engels'.
62. *Critique of the Gotha Programme* in *Selected Works*, Vol. II, p. 566. The italics are mine.

CHAPTER FOUR · MARXIST SOCIETY: THE CLASSES

1. A classic statement is in Engels, *Feuerbach*, pp. 50-52.
2. I am aware, of course, of Marx's differences with Darwin, some of which are summed up in Venable, *Human Nature*, chap. 6; Bober, *Marx's Interpretation of History*, pp. 35-39; Eastman, *Marx and Lenin*, Pt. I, chap. 6. For the early American Marxist use of Darwin, see Richard Hofstadter, *Social Darwinism in American Thought* (Philadelphia, 1945), pp. 95-97. Marx, it is said, had wanted to dedicate the first volume of *Capital* to Darwin, but the latter, ever modest, declined this signal honor. See Engels' admiring comments in *Socialism: Utopian and Scientific*, pp. 48, 61; *Feuerbach*, pp. 46, 67; *Dialectics of Nature*, pp. 19, 234-236, 279 ff.; *Anti-Dühring*, pp. 36-37, 97-107, 471.
3. *Origin of the Family*, p. 161. It is the persistence of this sort of thinking that has led Herbert Read, *Existentialism, Marxism and Anarchism* (London, 1949), p. 17, to accuse Marxists of clinging to "an antiquated darwinism."
4. From "A Great Beginning" (1919), *Selected Works* (1950-1951), Vol. II, Pt. II, p. 224. For a useful summary of Marx's views, see R. Bendix and S. M. Lipset, eds., *Class, Status and Power* (Glencoe, Ill., 1953),

pp. 26-35. See also Hunt, *Marxism,* chap. 6; Mayo, *Democracy and Marxism,* chap. 3; Plamenatz, *German Marxism,* chap. 5; Bober, *Marx's Interpretation of History,* chap. 5.

5. Venable, *Human Nature,* p. 113.
6. *Selected Works,* Vol. II, p. 415. See generally Georg Lukacs, *Geschichte und Klassenbewusstsein* (Berlin, 1923), pp. 57 ff.
7. *Selected Works,* Vol. II, p. 415.
8. *Poverty of Philosophy,* p. 189.
9. *Capital,* Vol. III, pp. 1031-1032; *Peasant War,* pp. 15-21.
10. R. Aron, "Social Structure and the Ruling Class," *British Journal of Sociology,* Vol. I (1950), pp. 1, esp. 3-5. Bukharin, *Historical Materialism,* pp. 282-285, makes a bravely orthodox attempt to deal with the obvious plurality of social classes.
11. *Selected Works,* Vol. I, p. 205.
12. *Selected Works,* Vol. I, p. 210.
13. *Selected Works,* Vol. I, pp. 207-208. On the continuing difficulties of defining this word so as to show respect for those good friends of the U.S.S.R., the "progressive bourgeoisie," see Hunt, *Guide to Communist Jargon,* pp. 3-7.
14. Engels, in a footnote to the English edition of 1888 of the *Communist Manifesto* in *Selected Works,* Vol. I, p. 204 n.
15. *Selected Works,* Vol. I, p. 216.
16. Soviet Academician G. F. Aleksandrov, in a broadcast quoted in Hunt, *Marxism,* p. 84.
17. Marx, *Poverty of Philosophy,* p. 189.
18. No modern critic has been more lucid on this particular Marxist myth than Aron, *The Opium of the Intellectuals,* chap. 3.
19. *Gesamtausgabe,* Vol. I, pp. 619-620. See especially Sheed, *Communism and Man,* pp. 102-106; Sombart, *Der proletarische Sozialismus,* Vol. II (*Die Bewegung*), chaps. 1-2, 4.
20. See generally David Mitrany, *Marx against the Peasant* (Chapel Hill, 1951), a most useful work. Mao's famous tract of 1927 casting the peasantry in the role of the proletariat is in his *Selected Works,* Vol. I, pp. 21-59. See Schwartz, *Chinese Communism,* pp. 73-78, 117-126, 178-179, 189 ff.
21. *Peasant War,* p. 18; *Selected Works,* Vol. II, p. 211.
22. *Theories of Surplus Value* (New York, 1952), pp. 148-197, esp. 161-162, 175-177, 194-197.
23. On the rise of a similar class in Communist society, see Ernst Halperin, "The Metamorphosis of the New Class," *Problems of Communism,* Vol. VIII, No. 4 (1959), p. 17.
24. N. Bukharin and E. Preobrazhensky, *The ABC of Communism* (London, 1922), pp. 168-169.
25. Marx, *Selected Works,* Vol. I, p. 222. For a provocative, broadly Marxist study of the plight of the American "petty bourgeoisie" in the 1930's, see Lewis Corey, *The Crisis of the Middle Class* (New York, 1935).
26. *Selected Correspondence,* p. 376. Bartoli, *La doctrine de Karl Marx,* pp. 306-349, and Sombart, *Der proletarische Sozialismus,* Vol. I, chaps. 26-28, are excellent reviews of the Marxist theory of the class struggle.

27. *Capital*, Vol. I, p. 21; Lenin, *State and Revolution*, pp. 70, 75.
28. *Socialism: Utopian and Scientific*, pp. 68-69; *Anti-Dühring*, pp. 407, 411.
29. Popper, *Open Society*, pp. 275-279, 663-664; Lenin, *State and Revolution*, p. 82.
30. *The Yogi and the Commissar* (London, 1945), p. 126.
31. *Anti-Dühring*, pp. 405 ff.; *German Ideology*, pp. 43 ff. Stalin's major (and lame) attempt to deal with this problem is in his *Economic Problems of Socialism in the U.S.S.R.* (New York, 1952), pp. 22-26.
32. *Leninism*, Vol. I, p. 387. On this subject, see A. L. Harris, "Utopian Elements in Marx's Thought," *Ethics*, Vol. LX (1950), p. 79.
33. Carr, *Marx*, p. 81.
34. Quoted in Sheed, *Communism and Man*, p. 195 n.
35. On the difficulties inherent in this concept, see Gray, *Socialist Tradition*, pp. 499-504. Sabine, *Marxism*, chap. 3, is a powerful indictment from the democratic point of view.
36. Russell, *Freedom versus Organisation* (New York, 1934), p. 218; Gonnard, *Histoire des doctrines économiques* (5th ed.; Paris, 1947), pp. 324-325; Stalin, *Marxism and Linguistics* (New York, 1951), pp. 19-20.
37. Sabine, *Marxism*, p. 34.
38. Harry K. Wells, *Pragmatism: Philosophy of Imperialism* (New York, 1954), p. 190.
39. A. M. Scott, *The Anatomy of Communism* (New York, 1951), pp. 27-31, 80-82.
40. "On the Draft Constitution" (1936), in Stalin, *Selected Writings* (New York, 1942), pp. 382-384; Vyshinsky, *Law of the Soviet State*, pp. 123, 135-140. See generally Julian Towster, *Political Power in the U.S.S.R.* (New York, 1948), pp. 313-336; Alex Inkeles, "Social Stratification and Mobility in the Soviet Union," in Bendix and Lipset, eds., *Class, Status and Power*, pp. 609-622; B. Moore, *Soviet Politics*, chaps. 8, 14; Bauer *et al.*, *How the Soviet System Works*, chaps. 17-20; W. W. Kulski, "Classes in the Classless State," *Problems of Communism*, Vol. IV, No. 1 (1955), p. 20; and the articles on "The Classless Society" by Robert A. Feldmesser and Seweryn Bialer in *Problems of Communism*, Vol. IX, No. 2 (1960), p. 31. The special problem of the peasants is well handled in Barrington Moore, Jr., *Terror and Progress: U.S.S.R.* (Cambridge, 1954), chap. 3. Hugh Seton-Watson, "The Soviet Ruling Class," *Problems of Communism*, Vol. V, No. 3 (1956), p. 10, is a most instructive piece.
41. S. F. Bloom, *The World of Nations: A Study of the National Implications in the Work of Karl Marx* (New York, 1941), not a very reliable book but the only one on the subject; Michel Collinet, *La tragédie du Marxisme* (Paris, 1948), Pt. III. For Engels' early grasp of what Disraeli was to call the "two nations" of England, see his *Condition of the Working Class*, p. 83. Bertram D. Wolfe, "Nationalism and Internationalism in Marx and Engels," *American Slavic and East European Review*, Vol. XVII (1958), p. 403, presents convincing evidence of Marx's sense of nationality and his strong concern for Germany's interests.
42. *Selected Works*, Vol. I, p. 225.

43. Wolfe, *Three Who Made a Revolution,* chap. 33; Meyer, *Leninism,* chaps. 7, 10; A. D. Low, *Lenin on the Question of Nationality* (New York, 1958).
44. Hugh Seton-Watson, "1917-1957: An Historical Perspective," *Problems of Communism,* Vol. VI, No. 6 (1957), pp. 1, 4.
45. Howard Selsam, *Socialism and Ethics* (New York, 1943), pp. 175-187, is example enough of the double talk of the hard Marxist trying to appeal to hard nationalists.
46. Frederick C. Barghoorn, *Soviet Russian Nationalism* (New York, 1956); Towster, *Political Power in the U.S.S.R.,* chaps. 4-5.
47. Wolfe, *Three Who Made a Revolution,* p. 588.
48. Popper, *Open Society,* p. 316; Marcuse, *Reason and Revolution,* pp. 283-295; Dunayevskaya, *Marxism and Freedom,* pp. 60, 64-65, 295. See generally John D. Lewis, "The Individual and the Group in Marxist Theory," *Ethics,* Vol. XLVII (1936), p. 45. H. M. Kallen, "Communism as a Secret Individualism," *Social Research,* Vol. XVII (1950), p. 293, argues that the will-to-believe of the devout Marxist is an expression of profound individualism. Communism is a religion; hence it is a "secret individualism."
49. *Capital,* Vol. I, p. 15.
50. Belfort Bax, *The Ethics of Socialism* (London, 1890), pp. 19 ff., quoted in Selsam, *Socialism and Ethics,* pp. 140-141.
51. Quoted in Hook, *Marx and the Marxists,* p. 32.
52. Vyshinsky, *Law of the Soviet State,* p. 644. See Julian Towster, "Vyshinsky's Concept of Collectivity," in E. J. Simmons, ed., *Continuity and Change in Russian and Soviet Thought* (Cambridge, 1955), pp. 237-254.
53. For a useful review of the Chinese "leap," see H. F. Schurmann, "The Communes: A One-Year Balance Sheet," *Problems of Communism,* Vol. VIII, No. 5 (1959), p. 7. For the place of the individual in the Communist cadre, see Philip Selznick, *The Organizational Weapon* (New York, 1952), pp. 25-29. See the testimony of André Gide, *Return from the U.S.S.R.* (New York, 1937), p. 25, as well as Bauer *et al., How the Soviet System Works,* Pt. III.
54. Bauer, *New Man in Soviet Psychology,* p. 142.
55. Lewis, "Individual and Group," *Ethics,* Vol. XLVII (1936), p. 54.
56. From his famous interview of 1934 with H. G. Wells, printed by the *New Statesman and Nation* as *Stalin-Wells Talk* (London, 1934), p. 7; Vyshinsky, *Law of the Soviet State,* pp. 55, 197, 539-540, 562-563. An American echo is Harry F. Ward, *The Soviet Spirit* (New York, 1944), chap. 16.
57. Selsam, *Socialism and Ethics,* pp. 129-132, 145.

CHAPTER FIVE · MARXIST SOCIETY: THE INSTITUTIONS

1. *Fundamental Problems of Marxism* (London, n.d.), p. 72; Bukharin, *Historical Materialism,* chap. 6. A useful introduction to this problem is Walter Theimer, *Der Marxismus* (Berne, 1950), chap. 5.

2. *Laissez-Faire and Communism* (New York, 1926), p. 99. Perhaps the most judicious brief assessment of Marx as economist is Joseph Schumpeter, *Capitalism, Socialism, and Democracy* (3rd ed.; New York, 1950), chap. 3. See also Joan Robinson, *An Essay on Marxian Economics* (London, 1942), who, in comparing Marx with the orthodox economists of his time, judges that his "intellectual tools" were "far cruder," but his "sense of reality far stronger." For a stoutly orthodox Marxist view, see Maurice Dobb, *Marx as Economist* (New York, 1945); for a far friendlier view than my own, see Ben B. Seligman, "Marxian Economics Revisited," *Dissent*, Vol. V (1958), p. 342; and for an interpretation of Marx as a "magnificent dynamic," see W. J. Baumol, *Economic Dynamics* (New York, 1951), pp. 20-35. Paul M. Sweezy, *The Theory of Capitalist Development* (New York, 1942), is by all odds the most serious and successful attempt to present the fundamentals of Marxist economics to an American audience.

3. Carr, *Karl Marx*, p. 277.

4. On this crucial point, see especially Sombart, *Der proletarische Sozialismus*, Vol. I, pp. 10-11.

5. L. E. Mins, ed., *Engels on Capital* (New York, 1937), pp. 43-92, gives Engels' own synopsis of Marx's sprawling first volume of *Capital*. Ernest Untermann, the translator of *Capital*, did the same job for an American audience in *Marxian Economics* (Chicago, 1907).

6. *Capital*, Vol. I, p. 709. Bukharin, *ABC of Communism*, chaps 2-3, is a compendium of violent strictures on capitalism.

7. Foster, *Toward Soviet America*, p. 319.

8. *Capital*, Vol. I, p. 834.

9. *Gesamtausgabe*, Vol. III, p. 82.

10. *Capital*, Vol. I, p. 836. For a concise review of the Marxist distinction among accumulation, concentration, and centralization of capital, see Popper, *Open Society*, p. 687. A glossary of Marx's economic terms is in W. J. Blake, *Elements of Marxian Economic Theory* (New York, 1939), pp. 710-721.

11. Gray, *Socialist Tradition*, pp. 323-324, finds all of five different Marxist interpretations of this law.

12. H. W. B. Joseph, *Karl Marx's Theory of Value* (London, 1923), a thorough whipping of a dead horse that will not stay dead; Bartoli, *La doctrine de Karl Marx*, pp. 127-156; Lindsay, *Karl Marx's Capital*, chaps. 3-4; Gray, *Socialist Tradition*, pp. 308-322; Croce, *Historical Materialism and the Economics of Karl Marx*, chap. 4; Robinson, *Essay on Marxian Economics*, chap. 3; F. R. Salter, *Karl Marx and Modern Socialism* (London, 1921), chap. 5; Schumpeter, *Capitalism, Socialism, and Democracy*, pp. 23-25; Popper, *Open Society*, pp. 358-365, 696-697; Bober, *Marx's Interpretation of History*, pp. 182-199. Marx's theory may be found in clearest form in *Capital*, Vol. I, Pts. III-V, esp. pp. 207-244; *Theories of Surplus Value*, esp. pp. 305 ff.; *Value, Price and Profit* (New York, 1935), esp. pp. 40 ff. Engels' neat summary of this "essential character" of capitalism is in *Socialism: Utopian and Scientific*, p. 52; *Engels on Capital*, pp. 4-7; *Anti-Dühring*, pp. 282-284. The most memorable of all debates on Marx's theory of value was carried

on between Eugen von Böhm-Bawerk and Rudolf Hilferding around the turn of the century. Paul M. Sweezy has put together and edited their writings on this subject (*Karl Marx and the Close of His System,* New York, 1949).

13. *Capital,* Vol. I, pp. 257, 282, 291, 363; Vol. III, p. 106.
14. M. Beer, *The Life and Teachings of Karl Marx* (New York, n.d.), p. 156.
15. *Selected Works,* Vol. I, p. 223; Engels, *Socialism: Utopian and Scientific,* p. 32; *German Ideology,* pp. 39-42; *Selected Correspondence,* pp. 293, 350, 375; *Anti-Dühring,* pp. 132-133.
16. *Theorien über den Mehrwert* (2nd ed.; Stuttgart, 1910), Vol. I, p. 382. See generally the interesting Marxist study by Mikhail Lifshitz, *The Philosophy of Art of Karl Marx* (New York, 1938). Edward A. Shils, "Daydreams and Nightmares," *Sewanee Review,* Vol. LXV (1957), p. 587, argues that most of the savage criticism of contemporary American mass culture emanates from writers who "are, or were, Marxian socialists."
17. *State and Revolution,* p. 79.
18. *Toward Soviet America,* pp. 2, 69. Chapter I of this book is especially interesting as a Communist indictment of American capitalism written in the depths of the Great Depression.
19. *Communism, Fascism, or Democracy?* (New York, 1938), p. 112.
20. *Capital,* Vol. I, pp. 81-96.
21. Bertram D. Wolfe, "Marx—The Man and His Legacy," *American Mercury,* Vol. LXV (1947), pp. 368, 372.
22. For summaries of the Marxist handling of this problem, see Schumpeter, *Capitalism, Socialism, and Democracy,* pp. 49-54; Hunt, *Theory and Practice of Communism,* pp. 161-167; Marguerite Fisher, *Communist Doctrine and the Free World* (Syracuse, 1952), chap. 6. Lenin's *Imperialism* (1916) is based squarely on J. A. Hobson's famous study of the same name (1902) and Rudolf Hilferding's *Finanz-Kapital* (1910). E. M. Winslow, *The Pattern of Imperialism* (New York, 1948), pp. 92-110, is a useful introduction to Hobson's thesis.
23. *Selected Works,* Vol. II, p. 437.
24. *Capital,* Vol. I, pp. 836-837.
25. *Capital,* Vol. I, pp. 466-478, esp. 468, where Marx asks workingmen to "distinguish between machinery and its employment by capital, and to direct their attacks, not against the material instruments of production, but against the mode in which they are used." See Kautsky's thoroughly Marxist hopes for machinery in his *Economic Doctrines of Karl Marx* (London, 1936), pp. 178-179, a major piece of Marxist exposition.
26. *Capital,* Vol. III, pp. 221, 773.
27. *Capital,* Vol. I, p. 52. Engels speaks in *Anti-Dühring,* p. 411, of "one single vast plan" for industry. Karl Kautsky made a brave attempt to describe what would take place "On the Day after the Social Revolution," in *The Social Revolution* (Chicago, 1903), pp. 103 ff.
28. E. H. Carr, *The Soviet Impact on the Western World* (New York, 1954), chap. 2.

29. *Selected Works,* Vol. IX, p. 338. See Vyshinsky, *Law of the Soviet State,* pp. 198 ff., for a valiant attempt to bring Marx's blessings to the Soviet style of state planning.
30. *Selected Works,* Vol. I, pp. 223-225.
31. *The Origin of the Family, Private Property and the State* (New York, 1942), pp. 65-66, the most sacred of all Marxist texts in this whole area of domestic relations. For a sympathetic review of his ideas, see B. J. Stern, "Engels on the Family," *Science and Society,* Vol. XII (1948), p. 42. A hardly less sacred Marxist classic was August Bebel's immensely popular *Women and Socialism* (1879) (New York, 1910).
32. *Toward Soviet America,* p. 306.
33. *Capital,* Vol. I, p. 536.
34. Engels, *Origin of the Family,* p. 67; Karl Kautsky, *The Class Struggle* (Chicago, 1910), pp. 127-129, an orthodox Marxist statement.
35. *Origin of the Family,* p. 67.
36. *Women and Society* (New York, 1938), pp. 11-14; Trotsky, *Literature and Revolution,* p. 253, who speaks of "endless collective creativeness" as the solution to all problems of domestic life.
37. *Letters to Dr. Kugelmann* (New York, 1934), p. 83.
38. William Petersen, "The Evolution of Soviet Family Policy," *Problems of Communism,* Vol. V, No. 5 (1956), p. 29, and the many references there cited; Harold Berman, *Justice in Russia* (Cambridge, 1950), chap. 12; Rudolf Schlesinger, *The Family in the U.S.S.R.* (London, 1949); John N. Hazard, *Law and Social Change in the U.S.S.R.* (London, 1953), chap. 10; Nicholas S. Timasheff, *The Great Retreat* (New York, 1946), chap. 8.
39. *Selected Works,* Vol. I, pp. 224, 228; Vol. II, p. 583; *Anti-Dühring,* pp. 406-410, 440-446; *Capital,* Vol. I, p. 534; Burns, *Handbook of Marxism,* p. 562. Engels, I am happy to say, was a stout advocate of "knowledge of the ancient languages."
40. Bauer, *New Man in Soviet Psychology,* p. 43.
41. George Counts, ed., *I Want to be Like Stalin* (New York, 1947). See also his *The Challenge of Soviet Education* (New York, 1957); Wolfe, *Six Keys to the Soviet System,* pp. 87-98; Maurice J. Shore, *Soviet Education* (New York, 1947), an uncritical yet useful book, especially the notes and bibliography at pp. 267-339; E. Koutaisoff, "Soviet Education and the New Man," *Soviet Studies,* Vol. V (1953), p. 103; George L. Kline, ed., *Soviet Education* (New York, 1957), a collection of essays by former Soviet pedagogues; Nicholas DeWitt, "Upheaval in Education," *Problems of Communism,* Vol. VIII, No. 1 (1959), p. 25, for the recent trend back to the "complete unity of mental and physical labor." For other works in this general field, see Egbert and Persons, eds., *Socialism and American Life,* Vol. II, pp. 383-391.
42. From the Soviet journal *Culture and Life,* quoted in Gurian, *Bolshevism,* pp. 141-142.
43. From the Soviet journal *Pedagogy,* quoted in Counts, *I Want to be Like Stalin,* p. 14.
44. A clear and startling look into the Marxist-Leninist mind in American education is provided by Theodore Brameld, "Karl Marx and the

American Teacher," *Social Frontier,* January 1935; Howard D. Langford, *Education and the Social Conflict* (New York, 1936); Zalmen Slesinger, *Education and the Class Struggle* (New York, 1937), esp. chaps 4, 10.
45. *Condition of the Working Class,* p. 186.
46. *What is to be Done?,* pp. 54 ff., 105 ff. Lenin's *"Left-Wing" Communism, An Infantile Disorder* (New York, 1940), pp. 30-39, makes instructive reading on Bolshevik plans for "free" trade unions.
47. Bauer *et al., How the Soviet System Works,* pp. 65-66, 139; John N. Hazard, *The Soviet System of Government* (Chicago, 1957), pp. 56-60, 191, and *Law and Social Change in the U.S.S.R.,* chap. 7; Isaac Deutscher, *Soviet Trade Unions* (London, 1950); Merle Fainsod, *How Russia is Ruled* (Cambridge, 1953), pp. 88-89, 133-134, 422-423, 432-436; Solomon S. Schwarz, "Soviet Trade Unions Today," *Problems of Communism,* Vol. III, No. 6 (1954), p. 25.
48. *ABC of Communism,* p. 279.
49. For a typically two-faced statement, see Foster, *Toward Soviet America,* pp. 291-296.
50. *Selected Works,* Vol. I, pp. 219-220, 227-228; Vol. II, p. 166; *Anti-Dühring,* pp. 181-186, 223-226, 243-247, 371-374; *German Ideology,* pp. 58 ff., 97 ff.; Marx, *Poverty of Philosophy,* pp. 168-181; *Capital,* Vol. I, pp. 835-837, 848; Dunayevskaya, *Marxism and Freedom,* pp. 290 ff.
51. *Law of the Soviet State,* p. 178. See pp. 193-198 for the official Soviet view on personal property—an eye-opener, especially in its disingenuous defense of the famed bourgeois right of inheritance. See generally Hazard, *Law and Social Change in the U.S.S.R.,* chap. 1.
52. In his *Reason, Social Myths and Democracy,* p. 135, Sidney Hook appears to take a contrary position, asserting that Marx considered "the possession of some property" to be "necessary to the enjoyment of personality."
53. *Critique of the Gotha Programme* in *Selected Works,* Vol. II, p. 556.
54. Some very sharp-eyed reader may note that I have drawn on my *Conservatism in America,* pp. 38-39, for much of this material. I have done my best to render it less "conservative" and more commonly acceptable.
55. *Selected Correspondence,* p. 57. On Marx's understanding of the distinction and relations between state and society, see Collinet, *La tragédie du Marxisme,* pp. 42-54; Hans Kelsen, *Sozialismus und Staat* (Leipzig, 1923), pp. 20-33.

CHAPTER SIX · THE MARXIST STATE

1. *Leninism,* Vol. I, p. 14.
2. Chang, *Marxian Theory of the State;* Bober, *Marx's Interpretation of History,* pp. 128-142; Hunt, *Marxism,* chap. 8; Plamenatz, *German Marxism,* chap. 7; Kelsen, *Communist Theory of Law,* chap. 1, and

Sozialismus und Staat, chaps. 2-3; Max Adler, *Die Staatsauffassung des Marxismus* (Vienna, 1922), an acute Marxist interpretation with which Kelsen joined issue.

3. *Origin of the Family,* p. 158.
4. *Origin of the Family,* p. 155 (italics mine); Lenin, *State and Revolution,* pp. 7 ff.
5. *Origin of the Family,* pp. 156-157.
6. *Selected Works,* Vol. II, pp. 324-325.
7. *Origin of the Family,* p. 157. Italics mine.
8. *Origin of the Family,* p. 156.
9. Engels, *Feuerbach,* pp. 53-54.
10. *Selected Works,* Vol. II, pp. 501-502; *The Civil War in France* (New York, 1940), p. 59.
11. *Capital,* Vol. III, p. 919.
12. *Selected Works,* Vol. I, p. 355.
13. *Feuerbach,* p. 53.
14. S. W. Moore, *Critique of Capitalist Democracy,* is an odd but useful study of the Marxist-Leninist theory of our state. It is especially useful for its exhaustive annotation of primary sources on such matters as the definition of "state" (p. 18 n.), the role of reform in capitalism (p. 51 n.), and the pattern of public authority in the classless and stateless society (pp. 43-44 n.).
15. *Selected Works,* Vol. I, p. 207.
16. *Selected Works,* Vol. II, p. 496.
17. *Origin of the Family,* pp. 157-158; Lenin, *State and Revolution,* p. 14.
18. *Selected Works,* Vol. II, pp. 458-459.
19. Roy Pascal, *Karl Marx: Political Foundations* (London, 1943), pp. 11-12.
20. *Selected Works,* Vol. I, pp. 235-236.
21. For the example of the factory acts, which Marx found to be hastening rather than delaying the death of capitalism, see *Capital,* Vol. I, p. 552.
22. *Selected Correspondence,* pp. 475-477.
23. *Selected Works,* Vol. II, p. 579; Engels, *Origin of the Family,* pp. 66, 157.
24. *Gesamtausgabe,* Vol. VI, pp. 397-398.
25. *Selected Works,* Vol. II, pp. 154-168.
26. Wolfe, *Three Who Made a Revolution,* p. 122. Lenin's *"Left-Wing" Communism, An Infantile Disorder* is a bold embroidery on this text. For the Bolshevik approach to coalitions and "deals," see Nathan Leites, *Operational Code of the Politburo* (New York, 1951), pp. 40-46, 88-90, who points out that "any agreements between the Party and outside groups must be regarded as aiding the future liquidation of these groups."
27. *Selected Works,* Vol. I, p. 190; *Selected Correspondence,* pp. 309-310.
28. *Selected Correspondence,* p. 57; *Selected Works,* Vol. II, pp. 219, 577.
29. *State and Revolution,* pp. 36, 39 ff., 70, 75.
30. *Selected Correspondence,* p. 337.
31. *ABC of Communism,* p. 81.
32. The best studies are Edward S. Mason, *The Paris Commune* (New York, 1930), which pays particular attention to the place of the

Commune in Marxist thought and mythology; Frank Jellinek, *The Paris Commune of 1871* (London, 1937).

33. *Selected Works*, Vol. II, p. 460. Mehring, *Marx*, pp. 447 ff., gives a useful review of the theoretical contradictions into which Marx fell by embracing the Commune so eagerly.

34. For a revisionist Marxist view of the "democratic" nature of the dictatorship in Marx, see Lucien Laurat, *Marxism and Democracy* (London, 1940), pp. 40 ff.

35. *Selected Correspondence*, pp. 307-315, 325-326, 330-331; *Selected Works*, Vol. II, pp. 494-512, 525, in which (*The Civil War in France*) Marx salutes the Commune as "the glorious harbinger of a new society." On the emotional and intellectual importance of the Commune to Marx, see Arthur Rosenberg, *Democracy and Socialism* (New York, 1939), pp. 204-208, and *History of Bolshevism*, p. 18; Rubel, *Karl Marx*, pp. 409-416; Cole, *Socialist Thought*, Vol. II, pp. 148 ff. See also Lenin, *State and Revolution*, pp. 29, 32 ff., 56, 64-65; and *The Paris Commune* (New York, 1934), a collection of his scattered writings on this subject; Trotsky, *Dictatorship versus Democracy*, pp. 69 ff.

36. See Engels' remarks in *Selected Works*, Vol. II, p. 456.

37. *Dictatorship versus Democracy*, p. 84.

38. On this whole subject, see generally J. L. Talmon, *The Origins of Totalitarian Democracy* (London, 1952).

39. *Origin of the Family*, p. 158.

40. *Socialism: Utopian and Scientific*, pp. 68-69. For a collection of Marx's sayings on the subject, see Chang, *Marxian Theory of the State*, pp. 58-59.

41. *Historical Materialism*, p. 71.

42. Popper, *Open Society*, pp. 674-675. For a contrary view, see Hunt, *Theory and Practice of Communism*, pp. 64-65.

43. A crude model for which, so it would seem, was the Iroquois confederacy—"A society which still has no *state*"—as described by Engels, *Origin of the Family*, pp. 84-85.

44. S. F. Bloom, "The 'Withering Away' of the State," *Journal of the History of Ideas*, Vol. VII (1946), p. 113; Kelsen, *Sozialismus und Staat*, pp. 41-49, 90-113.

45. Hans Kelsen, *The Political Theory of Bolshevism* (Berkeley, 1948), is a useful guide to this subject, but no Western text can take the place of Vyshinsky's *Law of the Soviet State*.

46. *State and Revolution*, pp. 71-73. For a recent orthodox Marxist account of bourgeois democracy, see Garaudy, *La liberté*, Pt. III.

47. Vyshinsky, *Law of the Soviet State*, p. 546; Foster, *Toward Soviet America*, p. 133.

48. Even, according to Lenin, in England and the United States. See his correction (by elimination) of Marx's apparent willingness to exempt these two advanced countries, in Marx and Engels, *Selected Correspondence*, p. 310.

49. Vyshinsky, *Law of the Soviet State*, pp. 6, 12, 63.

50. Bukharin, *ABC of Communism*, pp. 40, 172.

51. *Selected Works*, Vol. II, pp. 154-168. See also Engels' remarks in *Selected Works*, Vol. II, p. 28 n. A guide to the writings of Marx and

Engels on which the Communists rely for canonical support of their kind of party is Cornforth, ed., *Readers' Guide to the Marxist Classics*, pp. 44-47.

52. *Selected Works*, Vol. I, pp. 218-219.
53. For a useful introduction to this famous tract, see Wolfe, *Three Who Made a Revolution*, pp. 152-166. Lenin's *One Step Forward, Two Steps Back* (1904) is also important for his development of the theory of the autocratic party, but for our purposes is much too occasional a piece. On Lenin's theory of the state, see Kelsen, *Communist Theory of Law*, chap. 2.
54. *What is to be Done?*, pp. 12, 15, 57, 61, 75, 82, 94 ff., 105, 110 ff., 168.
55. *What is to be Done?*, p. 168.
56. Gurian, *Bolshevism*, p. 130. See Wolfe, *Khrushchev and Stalin's Ghost*, pp. 280-287.
57. W. H. Chamberlin, ed., *Blueprint for World Conquest as Outlined by the Communist International* (Washington, 1946), pp. 73-74.
58. See generally Selznick, *The Organizational Weapon*.
59. *Toward Soviet America*, p. 241.
60. *State and Revolution*, p. 30. For an interesting perspective on the place of this work in Lenin's development, see R. V. Daniels, "The State and Revolution: A Case Study in the Genesis and Transformation of Communist Ideology," *American Slavic and East European Review*, Vol. XII (1953), p. 22. See also *"Left-Wing" Communism*, pp. 9-10, 29.
61. *The Proletarian Revolution*, in Lenin, *Selected Works* (1950-1951), Vol. II, Pt. II, p. 55. This book is the primary source of Lenin's clearest, most uncompromising thoughts on the dictatorship of the proletariat. For his opinion of democracy—both his and ours—see *State and Revolution*, pp. 14, 17-18, 31, 39 ff., 59, 65, 71 ff., 82, 96-97.
62. *State and Revolution*, pp. 15-17, 21, 38-39, 68-74, 79, 83-85.
63. Yet see his painfully orthodox Marxist speech on the state to a group of university students, in Lenin, *Marx-Engels-Marxism* (Moscow, 1951), pp. 490-512.
64. *Dictatorship versus Democracy*, pp. 169-170.
65. *ABC of Communism*, pp. 75, 81. Lenin began to speak in 1918 of an "entire historical epoch"; *Selected Works* (1950-1951), Vol. II, Pt. II, p. 61.
66. *Dictatorship versus Democracy*, p. 170.
67. See Towster, *Political Power in the U.S.S.R.*, pp. 28-37; Meyer, *Leninism*, chaps. 1-2. On the special problem of the soviets, see Hazard, *Soviet System of Government*, pp. 37 ff.; B. Moore, *Soviet Politics*, pp. 37, 41-42, 128-138, 270-273; Towster, *Political Power in the U.S.S.R.*, pp. 176-208.
68. Lenin, *Selected Works* (1937), Vol. VII, p. 123.
69. Selznick, *The Organizational Weapon*, p. 17.
70. Lenin, *Collected Works* (New York, 1932), Vol. XXI, p. 39. See generally Feliks Gross, *The Seizure of Political Power* (New York, 1958), chaps. 7-10.

71. His view of the dictatorship of the proletariat is in *Foundations of Leninism* (1924), printed in *Leninism*, Vol. I, pp. 41-51.
72. H. W. Laidler, ed., *Social-Economic Movements* (New York, 1944), p. 428. Stalin's most important comments on the party and its role are in his *Foundations of Leninism* and *Problems of Leninism* (1926), both in *Leninism*, Vol. I, esp. pp. 87-99, 276-296. For Stalin's standard explanation why there could be only one party in the U.S.S.R., see Vyshinsky, *Law of the Soviet State*, pp. 627-628; and for a direct Soviet reply to the Western assertion of the incompatibility of a one-party system with democracy, see G. F. Aleksandrov, *The Pattern of Soviet Democracy*, translated by Leo Gruliow (Washington, 1948), pp. 21-25.
73. Hazard, *Soviet System of Government*, chap. 2; Towster, *Political Power in the U.S.S.R.*, chaps. 6-8; Fainsod, *How Russia is Ruled*, Pt. II; Djilas, *The New Class*, pp. 70 ff. On the new status of the party, see Merle Fainsod, "The Party in the Post-Stalin Era," *Problems of Communism*, Vol. VIII, No. 1 (1958), p. 7. On the party as the embodiment of history, see Arthur Koestler, *The Invisible Writing* (London, 1954), pp. 25-26, quoting from his novel *Darkness at Noon*. And on the party as the "priesthood of truth," see *Facts on Communism* (Washington, 1959), pp. 85-87, a document prepared for the House Committee on Un-American Activities by Gerhart Niemeyer.
74. See Khrushchev's concession on this point, reported in the New York *Times*, March 19, 1958.
75. Leites, *Study of Bolshevism*, chap. 10.
76. B. Moore, *Soviet Politics*, pp. 61-64; Inkeles, *Public Opinion in Soviet Russia*, pp. 11-21.
77. For Lenin's anticipation of this connection, see the comment quoted in J. Martov, *The State and the Socialist Revolution* (New York, 1938), p. 31 n.; for Trotsky's, see his comment in Wolfe, *Three Who Made a Revolution*, p. 253; for Plekhanov's, see *Problems of Communism*, Vol. V, No. 5 (1956), p. 47.
78. *Leninism*, Vol. I, p. 44.
79. See especially his report to the Eighteenth Party Congress, in Stalin, *Selected Writings*, pp. 468-474.
80. *Leninism*, Vol. I, p. 43
81. A. Y. Vyshinsky, *The Teachings of Lenin and Stalin on Proletarian Revolution and the State* (London, 1948), pp. 115-116. For a revealing expression of Stalin's respect for the uses of political power, see *Stalin-Wells Talk*, pp. 11, 16.
82. *Marxism and Linguistics* (New York, 1951), pp. 27-28. For the background of this issue and its importance for Soviet ideology, see J. Ellis and R. W. Davies, "The Crisis in Soviet Linguistics," *Soviet Studies*, Vol. II (1951), p. 209; M. Miller, "Marx, Stalin and the Theory of Language," *Soviet Studies*, Vol. II (1951), p. 364; J. Kucera, "Soviet Nationality Policy: The Linguistic Controversy," *Problems of Communism*, Vol. III, No. 2 (1954), p. 24. On the success of the "revolution from above," see B. Moore, *Soviet Politics*, chap. 15.

316 Notes

83. *Economic Problems of Socialism in the U.S.S.R.* (New York, 1952). See I. Deutscher, "Dogma and Reality in Stalin's 'Economic Problems,'" *Soviet Studies,* Vol. IV (1953), p. 349; Peter Meyer, "In Defense of Reaction," *Problems of Communism,* Vol. III, No. 1 (1954), p. 14. Stalin first talked of a "revolution from above" in 1939, in the *History of the Communist Party,* p. 305, but not until 1950 did he make this idea crystal clear.

84. For the satellite states a new conceptual category, that of "people's democracy," has been devised. See H. G. Skilling, "'People's Democracy' in Soviet Theory," *Soviet Studies,* Vol. III (1951), pp. 16, 131; Benjamin Schwartz, "China and the Soviet Theory of People's Democracy," *Problems of Communism,* Vol. III, No. 5 (1954), p. 8; Hunt, *Guide to Communist Jargon,* pp. 113-117; Z. K. Brzezinski, *The Soviet Bloc* (Cambridge, 1960). An authoritative statement is given by Dimitrov, *Selected Speeches and Articles,* pp. 233-237.

85. *Selected Works* (1937), Vol. IX, p. 54.

86. For the corresponding shift in the theory of law—from a pattern of exploitation expected to wither away with the state to a venerated system of virtually classless norms—see Towster, *Political Power in the U.S.S.R.,* pp. 15-17; Henri Chambre, *Le Marxisme en Union soviétique* (Paris, 1955), chaps. 1-5; Berman, *Justice in Russia,* pp. 37-50, 201-205; Kelsen, *Communist Theory of Law,* esp. pp. 33-34, 38, 62 ff., 77 ff., 89 ff. (on E. B. Pashukanis), p. 112 ff. (on the rejection of Pashukanis), p. 116 ff. (on Vyshinsky, the theoretician of the new law), p. 193. Rudolf Schlesinger, *Soviet Legal Theory* (London, 1945), is a much too friendly approach to this subject, for the truth seems to rest with Kelsen's judgment: "The deplorable status of Soviet legal theory, degraded to a handmaid of the Soviet government, should be a grim warning to social scientists that true social science is possible only under the condition that it is independent of politics." An interesting recent development—the partial exhuming of Pashukanis, at least in his role as expert in international law—is noted by John N. Hazard, "Pashukanis is no Traitor," *American Journal of International Law,* Vol. LI (1957), p. 385.

87. Lenin, *Selected Works* (1937), Vol. IX, p. 54.

88. *Teachings of Lenin and Stalin,* p. 115. Stalin's rejection of Bukharin's "anarchism" is chronicled in Hazard, *Communist Theory of Law,* pp. 109-110.

89. I am indebted for my understanding of the theory of the new Marxist state to Vernon Aspaturian's perceptive article, "The Contemporary Doctrine of the Soviet State and its Philosophical Foundations," *American Political Science Review,* Vol. XLVIII (1954), p. 1031. See also Towster, *Political Power in the U.S.S.R.,* pp. 10-15. The further development of the new orthodoxy in the post-Stalin era is chronicled in Leopold Labedz, "Ideology: The Fourth Stage," *Problems of Communism,* Vol. VIII, No. 6 (1959), p. 1. It would almost (but not quite) be worth having the whole world go Communist to observe the antics of Marxist theoreticians as they explained why, even then, the state refused to wither away.

90. Again I have drawn, with some editing of a "liberalizing" nature, on my *Conservatism in America*, esp. pp. 31-36, 72-73, 263-266.
91. Vyshinsky, *Law of the Soviet State*, pp. 166, 220, 312 ff. See Towster, *Political Power in the U.S.S.R.*, pp. 52, 61-62, 184-186, for typical Marxist statements on federalism and the separation of powers. On Soviet federalism, see Hazard, *Soviet System of Government*, chap. 6; Richard Pipes, *The Formation of the Soviet Union: Communism and Nationalism, 1917-1922* (Cambridge, 1955). Lenin sealed the theoretical doom of federalism in *State and Revolution*, pp. 46, 60-62.
92. On this concept, see Hunt, *Guide to Communist Jargon*, pp. 53-56; B. Moore, *Soviet Politics*, pp. 64 ff., 81, 139, 232; Towster, *Political Power in the U.S.S.R.*, pp. 186, 207-208; Fainsod, *How Russia is Ruled*, pp. 180-181. This is an essentially party concept now transferred in application to the whole state.
93. Popper, *Open Society*, p. 316.
94. Fisher, *Communist Doctrine*, p. 166.
95. *Capital*, Vol. I, p. 354.
96. *Works* (9th ed.; Boston, 1889), Vol. V, p. 166.
97. R. A. Dahl, "Marxism and Free Parties," *Journal of Politics*, Vol. X (1948), p. 787.
98. Berlin, *Marx*, p. 108; Nomad, *Apostles of Revolution*, p. 199.
99. Quoted in Kelsen, *Sozialismus und Staat*, p. 86. Bakunin's strictures on Marx's political theory have been collected and translated by K. J. Kenafick, *Marxism, Freedom and the State* (London, 1950).

CHAPTER SEVEN · THE MARXIST TEMPER

1. Sabine, *History of Political Theory*, pp. 844 ff.
2. Harry K. Wells, *Pragmatism: Philosophy of Imperialism* (New York, 1954), p. 202, quoting if not citing Stalin, *Dialectical and Historical Materialism*, p. 17.
3. *Marxism*, p. 18.
4. On the place and problems of science in the Soviet Union, see Eugene Rabinowitch, "Survey of Soviet Science," *Problems of Communism*, Vol. VII, No. 2 (1958), p. 1; I. D. London, "Toward a Realistic Appraisal of Soviet Science," *Bulletin of Atomic Physicists*, Vol. XIII (1957), p. 169; Alexander Vucinich, *The Soviet Academy of Sciences* (Stanford, 1956); Eric Ashby, *Scientist in Russia* (New York, 1947), which has an interesting chapter on the influence of dialectical materialism on scientific research; R. Bauer, "The Soviet Attitude toward Science," and H. J. Muller, "Science under Soviet Totalitarianism," both in C. J. Friedrich, ed., *Totalitarianism* (Cambridge, 1954); Ruth C. Christman, ed., *Soviet Science* (Washington, 1952), an extremely sober and useful survey conducted by nine American scientists.
5. Maurice Cornforth, *Dialectical Materialism: An Introductory Course* (London, 1952), Vol. I, p. 126; Wells, *Pragmatism*, p. 197; *History of the Communist Party of the Soviet Union*, pp. 114-115; Stalin, *Dialectical and Historical Materialism*, pp. 19-20.

6. *Selected Works,* Vol. I, p. 16. And in the preface to a German edition of *The Eighteenth Brumaire* in *Selected Works,* Vol. II, pp. 314-315, Engels compared Marx's law of history with "the law of the transformation of energy."

7. *Darwin, Marx, Wagner,* p. 139. Marx's attack on the Utopians is described in Martin Buber, *Paths in Utopia* (London, 1949), chaps. 2-7.

8. Foreword to J. D. Bernal, *Marx and Science* (New York, 1952), p. 4. See the devastating review of this pamphlet by H. G. Wood, "Marx and Science," *Hibbert Journal,* Vol. LIV (1955-1956), p. 226.

9. Quoted in Wood, "Marx and Science," pp. 227-228.

10. Venable, *Human Nature,* p. viii.

11. Barrington Moore, Jr., *Terror and Progress: U.S.S.R.* (Cambridge, 1954), p. 106.

12. *Historical Materialism,* pp. xi-xii. The introduction to this famous and thoroughly Marxist book is a case study of the "scientism" I am trying to describe. For an example of the absurdities in which a Western scientist must indulge in order to proclaim Marx a genuine man of science, see Bernal, *Marx and Science,* any page, and Haldane, *Marxist Philosophy and the Sciences,* esp. pp. 45 ff.

13. *Democracy and Marxism,* p. 218. Mayo's entire chapter 6 is a useful and destructive analysis of "Marxism and Scientific Method."

14. On this point, see especially Jules Monnerot, *Sociologie du Comunisme* (Paris, 1949), most of which has been translated and published as *Sociology and Psychology of Communism* (Boston, 1953); Bartoli, *La doctrine de Karl Marx,* pp. 62-64.

15. Robert C. Tucker, "Marxism—Is It Religion?," *Ethics,* Vol. LXVIII (1958), p. 125; W. Gurian, "Totalitarian Religions," *Review of Politics,* Vol. XIV (1952), p. 3; Mayo, *Democracy and Marxism,* chap. 7; Eduard Heimann, "Atheist Theocracy," *Social Research,* Vol. XX (1953), p. 311, and *Vernunftglaube und Religion in der modernen Gesellschaft* (Tübingen, 1955), chap. 6; A. C. Macintyre, *Marxism: An Interpretation* (London, 1953), esp. pp. 101-102; Howard Fast, *The Naked God* (New York, 1957), pp. 45, 76, and esp. 101-106; Crossman, ed., *The God That Failed.*

16. For the Marxist parallels of Christian dogma, see Calvez, *La pensée de Karl Marx,* pp. 592-602. Raymond Aron, *The Century of Total War* (Boston, 1955), p. 116, is not the only sensible writer to insist that "Marxism is a Christian heresy."

17. Wolfe, *Three Who Made a Revolution,* p. 506.

18. See Popper's critique of Arnold Toynbee's extreme emphasis on Marx's Jewishness in *Open Society,* p. 437; Toynbee, *A Study of History* (London, 1939), Vol. V, pp. 177-180, 581-587.

19. Will Herberg, "From Marxism to Judaism," *Commentary,* Vol. III (1947), p. 26.

20. Quoted in J. Hampden Jackson, *Marx, Proudhon and European Socialism* (New York, n.d.), pp. 63-64.

21. *Marxism and Linguistics,* p. 47.

22. For a crushing characterization of Lenin as a dogmatist, see Berdyaev, *Origin of Russian Communism,* pp. 118-119.

23. See Lenin's use of this statement in Burns, *Handbook of Marxism*, p. 541. T. A. Jackson, *Dialectics* (London, 1936), p. 33, calls Marxism "the completest refutation" of "all dogmatisms . . . the world has hitherto known."
24. Macmurray, *Philosophy of Communism*, p. 61.
25. For a somewhat contrary view, see Popper, *Open Society*, p. 672.
26. *Bolshevism: Practice and Theory*, p. 6.
27. "Marxism and Belief," *Quarterly Review*, Vol. CCXCII (1954), pp. 510, 514.
28. *The Rebel* (New York, 1954), pp. 20-21.
29. Leites, *Operational Code of the Politburo*, pp. 1, 3, 13, 56-57.
30. See especially Sabine, *Marxism*, pp. 36 ff.
31. On this point, see Lenin's remarks quoted in Fisher, *Communist Doctrine*, p. 122; Scott, *Anatomy of Communism*, pp. 49 ff.; Gurian, *Bolshevism*, pp. 122-124.
32. *Soviet Attitudes Toward Authority* (New York, 1951), p. 15.
33. *Communism and Man* (New York, 1940), p. ix.
34. *Origin of Russian Communism*, p. 151; Laski, *Communism*, pp. 51-52.
35. *Anti-Dühring*, p. 132.
36. *Selected Works* (1950-1951), Vol. I, Pt. I, p. 75.
37. Bertrand Russell, *Philosophy and Politics* (London, 1947), pp. 20-23.
38. For a thorough demolition of Marxism's pretensions to the status of science, see Max Eastman, *Marxism: Is it Science?*, Pt. V.
39. William James, *Pragmatism* (New York, 1907), pp. 54-55.
40. Selsam, ed., *Handbook of Philosophy*, pp. 97-98.
41. Venable, *Human Nature*, p. 199; Popper, *Open Society*, pp. 277-278. On the question of Marx's alleged empiricism, see Venable, *Human Nature*, pp. 9-12, 195-198; Scott, *Anatomy of Communism*, pp. 32 ff. I am inclined to rest with the latter's neat answer that Marx and Engels were "empiricists operating within an *a priori* framework." For a learned analysis of Marx's "Theses on Feuerbach" and denial of their pragmatism, see N. Rotenstreich, "Marx's Thesen über Feuerbach," *Archiv für Rechts- und Sozialphilosophie*, Vol. XXXIX (1951), pp. 338, esp. 354-355.
42. See Raymond Bauer's comments in Friedrich, ed., *Totalitarianism*, pp. 141 ff. For Lenin's peremptory rejection of pragmatism, see his *Materialism and Empirio-Criticism* (New York, 1927), p. 355 n.
43. *Pragmatism*, p. 187 ff.
44. In the introduction to Wells's *Pragmatism*, p. 8. His own neat confrontation of pragmatism and Marxism is at pp. 9-10, Wells's at pp. 200-202.
45. *Pragmatism*, pp. 14, 25, 208, 186. On the whole tangled problem of Dewey's intellectual war with Marxism, see his own statements in *Freedom and Culture* (New York, 1939), pp. 74-102, and "Why I am not a Communist," in Hook, ed., *The Meaning of Marx*, pp. 54-56; as well as Sidney Ratner, "The Development of Dewey's Evolutionary Naturalism," *Social Research*, Vol. XII (1953), pp. 127, 139-146, and

Jim Cork, "John Dewey, Karl Marx, and Democratic Socialism," *Antioch Review*, Vol. IX (1949), p. 435.

46. *Freedom and Culture*, pp. 101-102.
47. Quoted in Eastman, *Marxism: Is it Science?*, p. 132.
48. *State and Revolution*, p. 7.
49. *Dictatorship versus Democracy*, p. 63.
50. Carr, *Marx*, p. 75.
51. Mehring, *Marx*, p. 172; Jackson, *Marx, Proudhon and European Socialism*, p. 93.
52. Quoted in Jackson, *Marx, Proudhon and European Socialism*, p. 66. Wilson, *Finland Station*, p. 313, thinks it "a serious misrepresentation of Marx to minimize the sadistic element in his writing." Engels and Lenin both shared this combative habit.
53. *Selected Works*, Vol. I, p. 17; Sombart, *Der proletarische Sozialismus*, Vol. I, pp. 59-73, a remarkable word-portrait. When asked in a parlor game what fault he hated most, Marx replied, in one word, "servility." Piettre, *Marx et Marxisme*, p. 3 n.
54. Eastman, *Marx and Lenin: The Science of Revolution*, p. 262; Blackham, *The Human Tradition*, p. 110.
55. *Marxisme, existentialisme, personnalisme* (Paris, 1950), pp. 16-27.
56. *Freedom and Culture*, p. 92. See the examples collected by Bochenski, *Der sowjetrussische dialektische Materialismus*, pp. 66 ff.
57. *Introduction to Marxism* (London, 1957), p. 74.
58. G. M. Stekloff, *History of the First International* (London, 1928), pp. 240-241.
59. Franz Mehring, ed., *Aus dem literarischen Nachlass von Karl Marx, Friedrich Engels* (Stuttgart, 1902), Vol. III, p. 199.
60. Bober, *Marx's Interpretation of History*, pp. 262-263.
61. *German Ideology*, p. 69.
62. On this point, see the works cited above in note 24 to chap. 1. On the un-Marxist nature of the Bolshevik revolution of 1917, see Sabine, *Marxism*, pp. 4 ff.; Popper, *Open Society*, pp. 300-301.
63. *State and Revolution*, p. 34. For a standard Marxist view of revolution as the motive power of history, see Bukharin, *Historical Materialism*, chap. 7.
64. *Leninism* (New York, 1928), Vol. I, pp. 117-118. For an opinion contrary to the one I have been arguing here, see John Somerville, *The Communist Trials and the American Tradition* (New York, 1956). For an opinion critical, if not completely contrary, see David Spitz, *Democracy and the Challenge of Power* (New York, 1958), pp. 36-39, 186-188.
65. Gurian, *Bolshevism*, p. 12; Stefan Possony, *A Century of Conflict* (Chicago, 1953), pp. xvii-xx. See J. Middleton Murry's opinion, not the most astute for which he is known, that "the only point on which I can imagine the sincere Christian and the sincere Marxist at issue is on the question of violence," in Murry *et al.*, *Marxism* (New York, 1935), pp. 6-7.
66. New York *Times*, August 23, 1958.

67. *Collected Works,* Vol. XXIII, pp. 122-123; Trotsky, *Dictatorship versus Democracy,* pp. 48 ff. For a useful collection of quotations from Lenin's many thoughts on revolution, see M. Fisher, *Communist Doctrine,* chap. 9.

68. *Open Society,* p. 339. Laurat, *Marxism and Democracy,* pp. 32 ff., denies that Marx's mind was wedded to violence.

69. Among the useful surveys of the role of terror in the Soviet Union are Z. K. Brzezinski, *The Permanent Purge* (Cambridge, 1956); Hazard, *Soviet System,* chap. 5; Merle Fainsod, *How Russia is Ruled* (Cambridge, 1953), chap. 13; Moore, *Terror and Progress: U.S.S.R.,* chap. 6; Bauer *et al., How the Soviet System Works,* chap. 7; J. Gliksman, "Social Prophylaxis as a Form of Soviet Terror," in Friedrich, ed., *Totalitarianism,* pp. 60 ff.; W. Leonhard, "Terror in the Soviet System: Trends and Portents," *Problems of Communism,* Vol. VII, No. 6 (1958), p. 1, which argues that, although a "return full circle" to the excesses of the Stalinist terror is quite unlikely, "the terror apparatus will remain" as an integral part of the Soviet system.

70. *Law of the Soviet State,* p. 162.

71. See the works cited in Egbert and Persons, eds., *Socialism and American Life,* Vol. II, p. 326. Lenin, *A Letter to American Workers* (New York, 1934), p. 9, called the Revolution of 1776 one of the "great, really liberating, really revolutionary wars"—a quite un-Marxist judgment, to say the least.

72. *Seedtime of the Republic* (New York, 1953), p. 445. It is only fair to say that Marx, in the *Manifesto,* considered the proletarian movement to be one of the "immense majority in the interests of the immense majority," but he hardly expected this majority to make the revolution —or even to recognize the need for it.

73. Will Herberg, in Egbert and Persons, eds., *Socialism and American Life,* Vol. I, p. 495.

74. Carr, *Marx,* p. 75. Carr traces this belief of Marx to the Romanticism of the 1830's and 1840's. See also the interesting remarks on hate and love in Sheed, *Communism and Man,* pp. 170-171; Gray, *Socialist Tradition,* p. 505.

75. Sheed, *Communism and Man,* p. 170.

76. *Selected Works,* Vol. I, p. 223; *Selected Correspondence,* pp. 293, 350, 375; *Anti-Dühring,* pp. 30-32, 132-133; *Origin of the Family,* p. 162; Roger Garaudy, *Le Communisme et la morale* (Paris, 1947), esp. pp. 11 ff., in which the Marxist view of bourgeois morality as an "appendage of religion" is clearly stated; Venable, *Human Nature,* p. 163. Robert C. Tucker, "The Cunning of Reason in Hegel and Marx," *Review of Politics,* Vol. XVIII (1956), pp. 269, esp. 290 ff., is a remarkable exposition of one of the major reasons for Marx's amorality, and especially for his moral differences with the Utopians.

77. *Anti-Dühring,* pp. 131-132; Cornu, *Essai de critique marxiste,* pp. 58 ff.; *Selected Works,* Vol. I, p. 223; Hunt, *Marxism,* p. 2.

78. *Socialism and Ethics* (New York, 1943), pp. 8-9, 32. See also his "The Ethics of the Communist Manifesto," *Science and Society,* Vol. XII (1948), p. 22; *Philosophy in Revolution* (New York, 1957), chap.

5. For a subtle attempt to come to grips with this problem from a moderate Marxist point of view, see Lewis, *Marxism and the Open Mind*, chap. 5.

79. *Socialism and Ethics*, p. 98.
80. *Anti-Dühring*, p. 133.
81. *Selected Works*, Vol. II, p. 442.
82. *State and Revolution*, p. 74.
83. *Socialism and Ethics*, p. 34.
84. *Selected Works* (1950-1951), Vol. II, Pt. II, pp. 482-487; Bukharin, *ABC of Communism*, p. 82; Leites, *Study of Bolshevism*, chap. 3; Trotsky, *Dictatorship versus Democracy*, p. 63, who makes a flat distinction between the "White Terror and the Red" on the basis of the class nature and historical purpose of each.
85. This bouquet was gathered by George L. Kline, "Recent Soviet Philosophy," *Annals of the American Academy of Political and Social Science*, Vol. CCCIII (1956), pp. 126, 134. For important discussions of this whole problem, see Cameron, *Scrutiny of Marxism*, chap. 2; Acton, *Illusion of the Epoch*, pp. 180 ff.; Hunt, *Theory and Practice of Communism*, chap. 7; Mayo, *Democracy and Marxism*, pp. 226 ff.; M. Polanyi, "The Magic of Marxism," *Bulletin of the Atomic Scientists*, Vol. XII (1956), p. 211; M. Rubel, *Pages choisies pour une éthique socialiste* (Paris, 1948), pp. v ff., the pages of which are cleverly chosen from Marx's own writings.
86. Selsam, *Socialism and Ethics*, p. 96. See especially pp. 69-70 and 92-99 for the "Marxist approach to ethics."
87. See Gabriel Almond, *The Appeals of Communism* (Princeton, 1954), chaps. 1-2, for a useful if somewhat too intellectualized account of the virtues to be displayed by Communist leaders, as well as the orthodox statement in the famed *vade mecum* of "J. Peters," *The Communist Party: A Manual on Organization* (New York, 1935), pp. 112-113. The emphasis on the most heavily bourgeois brand of morality as the current ideal pattern of conduct within the Soviet Union has been remarked by hundreds of observers.
88. *Communist Manifesto: Socialist Landmark* (London, 1948), p. 86. I think we should read "sought" for "wrought."
89. Gurian, *Bolshevism*, p. 15. See Selsam's interesting way of handling this problem in *Socialism and Ethics*, pp. 209 ff.
90. Jack Lindsay, *Marxism and Contemporary Science* (London, 1949), p. 196; Laski, *Communist Manifesto*, p. 87.
91. *Darwin, Marx, Wagner*, p. 177.
92. Quoted in Hook, *Marx and the Marxists*, pp. 88-89.
93. *On Liberty* (Everyman's edition), p. 70.
94. Hunt, *Theory and Practice of Communism*, p. 82, paraphrasing A. L. Rowse.
95. Hook, ed., *Meaning of Marx*, p. 56.
96. Hunt, *Theory and Practice of Communism*, p. 84.
97. Selsam, "Ethics of the Manifesto," p. 31.
98. Leites, *Operational Code*, p. 9.
99. Hunt, *Theory and Practice of Communism*, p. 77.

100. In Egbert and Persons, eds., *Socialism and American Life*, Vol. I, p. 442; *Marx and the Marxists*, p. 88.
101. *The New Class* (New York, 1957), p. 162.
102. John N. Hazard, introduction to *The Law of the Soviet State*, translated by Hugh W. Babb (New York, 1954). A few of the relevant pages are 5-6, 10-38, 336, 344, 501-503, 541-552, 724.
103. *Origin of Russian Communism*, p. 184.
104. William Z. Foster, quoted in D'Arcy, *Communism and Christianity*, pp. 38-39. Note Monnerot's characterization of Communist Russia as the "twentieth-century Islam" in *Sociology of Communism*, pp. 18 ff.
105. Ladislaus Rieger in Richard McKeon, ed., *Democracy in a World of Tensions* (Chicago, 1951), p. 360.
106. Clinton Rossiter, "The American Mission," *American Scholar*, Vol. XX (1950-1951), p. 19; Edward M. Burns, *The American Idea of Mission* (New Brunswick, N. J., 1957), esp. chaps. 1, 4. On the Marxist faith in progress, see Meyer, *Marxism*, chap. 3; Mayo, *Democracy and Marxism*, pp. 31-32. Barghoorn, *Soviet Russian Nationalism*, chap. 8, discusses the relationship of messianism and chauvinism in the Soviet mind.
107. Foster, *Toward Soviet America*, p. 145.
108. Lenin, *What is to be Done?*, p. 80.
109. Marx, *Selected Works*, Vol. I, p. 219. On the "vocation of leadership" in the Communist party, see Sidney and Beatrice Webb, *Soviet Communism: A New Civilization?* (New York, 1936), Vol. I, chap. 5.

CHAPTER EIGHT · AMERICA AND MARX

1. Cameron, *Scrutiny of Marxism*, p. 25.
2. On the intellectual dangers of working within such a system, see Arthur Koestler, *Arrow in the Blue* (New York, 1952), pp. 260-261, and for an intelligent Marxist's warning of the sorrowful consequences of intellectual monism, see Pierre Hervé, *La révolution et les fétiches* (Paris, 1956).
3. The text of Mao's speech is printed in the New York *Times*, June 19, 1957. An interesting commentary is Michael Walzer, "When the Hundred Flowers Withered," *Dissent*, Vol. V (1958), p. 360.
4. H. M. Roelofs, *The Tension of Citizenship* (New York, 1957).
5. *Origin of Russian Communism*, p. 105; Lukacs, *Geschichte und Klassenbewusstsein*, pp. 39-41, a statement no student of Marxism can safely ignore.
6. Brzezinski, *The Permanent Purge*, pp. 1-8, a compelling short analysis of totalitarianism; Sigmund Neumann, *Permanent Revolution* (New York, 1942), a pioneering work in this area; Hannah Arendt, *The Origins of Totalitarianism* (New York, 1951), Pt. III, which emphasizes the roles of terror, propaganda, and ideology; Hans Kohn, *Revolutions and Dictatorships* (Cambridge, 1939), pp. 179-199; C. J. Friedrich and Z. Brzezinski, *Totalitarian Dictatorships and Autocracy* (Cambridge 1956), now the best and most definitive study; Friedrich, ed., *Totali-*

tarianism, especially the contributions of Friedrich, Inkeles, and Gurian; Wolfe, *Six Keys to the Soviet System,* pp. 236-247. A special study of great significance is Karl A. Wittfogel, *Oriental Despotism* (New Haven, 1957). George Orwell, *Nineteen Eighty-Four* (New York, 1949), may yet be judged to have surpassed any of these works in insight into the true nature of totalitarianism.

7. *Toward Soviet America,* p. 275.
8. Friedrich, ed., *Totalitarianism,* p. 134. On the role of ideology in totalitarian systems, see Erich Fromm, *Escape from Freedom* (New York, 1941), esp. pp. 225 ff., 265-268, and Karl Mannheim, *Ideology and Utopia* (New York, 1936), esp. Pts. II, IV. Leites, *Study of Bolshevism,* pp. 19, 25, 29, 399 ff., 429, makes much of the fear of "annihilation" as an explanation of the Bolshevik penchant for totality.
9. Barghoorn, *Soviet Russian Nationalism,* a penetrating study of this fascinating subject; Timasheff, *The Great Retreat,* chap. 7.
10. Hunt, *Guide to Communist Jargon,* p. 98; B. Moore, *Terror and Progress—U.S.S.R.,* p. 111; Wortis, *Soviet Psychiatry,* p. 296; Zhdanov, *Essays on Literature,* pp. 15, 25, 40, 67-68, 83, 95-96; Kautsky, *The Social Revolution,* p. 183. For assessments of the fantastic extent to which culture is harnessed to Communist purposes, and for insights into the sorrowful implications for both the artist and his art, see George S. Counts and Nucia Lodge, *The Country of the Blind* (Boston, 1949); B. Moore, *Terror and Progress—U.S.S.R.,* chaps. 4-5; Wolfe, *Six Keys to the Soviet System,* pp. 41-117; W. Z. Laqueur and G. Lichtheim, eds., *The Soviet Cultural Scene* (London, 1958); Djilas, *The New Class,* pp. 124-146, who thinks that Communism's "tyranny over the mind" will nail it "to a cross of shame in history"; and the series of articles on China in *Soviet Survey,* April-June, 1958. "Socialist Realism," *Soviet Survey,* July-September, 1959, is a brilliant exposition of this subject by a troubled (and anonymous) Insider. Specific case studies are the series of articles by E. J. Simmons and others in "Russia since Stalin," *Annals of the American Academy of Political and Social Science,* Vol. CCCIII (1956), pp. 89-138; Dwight Macdonald, "The Soviet Cinema," *Probems of Communism,* Vol. III, No. 6 (1954), p. 33, and Vol. IV, No. 1 (1955), p. 29; J. Ruehle, "The Soviet Theater," *Problems of Communism,* Vol. VIII, No. 6 (1959), p. 11, and Vol. IX, No. 1 (1960), p. 40; N. A. Gorchakov, *The Theater in Soviet Russia* (New York, 1957), a tragic tale; Jacob Landy, "Soviet Painting and Socialist Realism," *Problems of Communism,* Vol. II, No. 3 (1952), p. 15; Andrey Olkhovsky, *Music under the Soviets* (New York, 1955). Shocking evidence from another field, which one would suppose to be neutral, is given in S. E. Schattman, "Dogma vs. Science in Soviet Statistics," *Problems of Communism,* Vol. V, No. 1 (1956), p. 30. None of these studies can match Czeslaw Milosz, *The Captive Mind* (New York, 1955), for insight into the spiritual slavery of the intellectual under Communism.
11. *The New Class,* p. 169. On Marxism as an important source of the urge toward "politicalization," see Waldemar Gurian, *The Rise and Decline of Marxism* (London, 1938), chap. 10.

12. Wolfe, *Six Keys to the Soviet System*, p. 152; Lewis, *Marxism and the Open Mind*, p. 68. A fascinating revelation of the Soviet distrust of individualism can be found in Khrushchev's observations on the spiritual ineptitude of Jews for collective living, printed in *Le Figaro* of Paris, April 7, 1958. See Irving Howe's comments in *Dissent*, Vol. V (1958), pp. 217-220, and the dispatch in the New York *Times*, April 11, 1958.

13. B. Moore, *Terror and Progress—U.S.S.R.*, pp. 158-161, 203-207, points out that "the process of atomization" may well have gone further in the Soviet Union "than in any previous society in human history."

14. "The Totalitarian Mystique," in Friedrich, ed., *Totalitarianism*, pp. 87 ff.

15. Koestler, *The Invisible Writing*, p. 27.

16. N. S. Timasheff, "The Soviet Concept of Democracy," *Review of Politics*, Vol. XII (1950), p. 506; Hazard, *Soviet System of Government*, esp. chap. 1. See Vyshinsky's claims in *Law of the Soviet State*, pp. 42, 161, 168 ff., as well as Aleksandrov, *Pattern of Soviet Democracy*, esp. pp. 6-18.

17. G. B. Carson, Jr., *Electoral Practices in the U.S.S.R.* (New York, 1955), esp. pp. 93 ff.

18. Hazard, *Soviet System of Government*, p. 12.

19. Mayo, *Democracy and Marxism*, chaps. 8-9; Parkes, *Marxism: An Autopsy*, esp. chaps. 6-7; John K. Turner, *Challenge to Karl Marx* (New York, 1941), chap. 23, a friendly view. A. Landy, *Marxism and the Democratic Tradition* (New York, 1946), p. 204, insists stoutly that Marxism "is the embodiment and expression of the progressive interests and consistently democratic aspirations of the masses of mankind"—as do, of course, all American Communists.

20. Wilson, *Finland Station*, p. 325.

21. *Democracy and Marxism*, p. 110.

22. *Democracy and Marxism*, p. 257.

23. According to Herman Rauschning, *The Voice of Destruction* (New York, 1940), p. 131, Hitler considered the German Communists far better qualified candidates for Nazism than the social democrats. The transit from Communism to Nazism and back again has proved remarkably easy for many Germans.

24. *Marx and the Marxists*, pp. 16-17.

25. Talmon, *Origins of Totalitarian Democracy*, p. 253.

26. No book in the English language could take a more blandly contrary view than John Strachey, *The Theory and Practice of Socialism* (New York, 1936), which was heralded at the time of publication as the "first application of Communist principles to the special conditions of the Anglo-Saxon countries." Mr. Strachey would have left us so many remnants of bourgeois democracy (pp. 108, 122, 147 ff., 150 ff., 207 ff., 223 ff.) that he sounds like a Marxist without real Marxist convictions. An interesting forerunner of Strachey's sweetly reasonable book was H. M. Hyndman, *England for All* (London, 1881).

27. The most penetrating studies of the career of Marxism in the Soviet Union are Wetter, *Dialectical Materialism*, Pt. II, and Bochenski, *Der sowjetrussische dialektische Materialismus*. Herbert Marcuse, *Soviet*

Marxism: A Critical Analysis (New York, 1958), is to be used with care.

28. B. Moore, *Soviet Politics—The Dilemma of Power*, is a careful and insightful study of the role of Marxist-Leninist ideology in the conduct of affairs in the Soviet Union. See also Bauer *et al., How the Soviet System Works*, esp. pp. 29-35, 166-168, 211-212; Selznick, *Organizational Weapon*, pp. 36-42; Chambre, *Le Marxisme en Union soviétique;* Richard Lowenthal, "Ideology and Power Politics," *Dissent*, Vol. V (1958), p. 301.

29. K. Hulicka, "Political Education in Soviet Schools," *Soviet Studies,* Vol. V (1953), p. 138.

30. Berman, *Justice in Russia*, pp. 8, 102-104.

31. B. Moore, *Soviet Politics*, chaps. 16-17; Adam Ulam, "Expansion and Coexistence: Counterpoint in Soviet Foreign Policy," *Problems of Communism*, Vol. VIII, No. 5 (1959), p. 1; Jan Triska, "A Model for Study of Soviet Foreign Policy," *American Political Science Review,* Vol. LII (1958), pp. 64, esp. 69-71, 82. Raymond L. Garthoff, *Soviet Military Doctrine* (Glencoe, Ill., 1953), pp. 37-43, 65-67, is a judicious short analysis of the influence of Marxist-Leninist ideology on the Soviet "principles of war." See also Possony, *Century of Conflict.*

32. Daniel Bell, "Ten Theories in Search of Reality," *World Politics,* Vol. X (1958), p. 327; "Ideology and Power Politics: A Symposium," *Problems of Communism,* Vol. VII, No. 2 (1958), pp. 10-35. Marcuse, *Soviet Marxism*, makes much of massive industrialization as a decisive factor in Soviet ideology, behavior, and morality. A revealing study of one of the least ideological of Soviet elites is David Granick, *The Red Executive* (New York, 1960).

33. *The Century of Total War*, p. 116.

34. Meyer, *Leninism*, who explains Lenin's advances on Marx largely in terms of his fundamental "pessimism" about the historical process; Gray, *Socialist Tradition*, chap. 17; Plamenatz, *German Marxism and Russian Communism*, Pt. II; Henri Lefebvre, *La pensée de Lénine* (Paris, 1957), a presentation that blends orthodoxy with sophistication; Hunt, *Theory and Practice of Communism*, chap. 15; Sabine, *History of Political Theory*, pp. 798 ff., esp. 840-841; Eastman, *Marx and Lenin,* Pt. II, chaps. 4-5, which emphasize Lenin's role as the "scientific engineer of revolution"; M. Salvadori, *The Rise of Modern Communism* (New York, 1952), pp. 9-11.

35. On this point, the "paradox of Marxism," see Sabine, *Marxism*, pp. 4 ff.

36. *Selected Works,* Vol. I, pp. 356-357.

37. He took his first long steps in this direction in his *Two Tactics of Social Democracy in the Democratic Revolution* (1905), and *The Lessons of the Revolution* (1910), both in *Selected Works* (1950-1951), Vol. I, Pt. II, pp. 11, 182. A study of importance for understanding the development of Bolshevism is Leopold Haimson, *The Russian Marxists and the Origins of Bolshevism* (Cambridge, 1955). See also Berdyaev, *Origin of Russian Communism*, chap. 5; Wetter, *Dialectical Materialism*, Pt. I, chaps. 3-4; Maynard, *Russia in Flux*, chap. 7.

38. See the noted exchange (and preparations therefor) between Marx and Vera Zasulich, *Marx-Engels Archiv* (Frankfurt, n.d.), Vol. I, pp. 309-342; Wolfe, *Three Who Made a Revolution*, pp. 110 ff.; Rubel, *Karl Marx*, pp. 424-434; P. W. Blackstock and B. F. Hoselitz, eds., *The Russian Menace to Europe* (Glencoe, Ill., 1952), pp. 218-226, 275-281; Hunt, *Marxism*, pp. 68-72; Wilson, *Finland Station*, pp. 348-349; Marx and Engels, *Selected Correspondence*, pp. 436-438, 508-510, 352-355, and *Selected Works*, Vol. I, p. 192. Berdyaev, *Origin of Russian Communism*, p. 74, insists that Marx and Engels were "mensheviks" in their attitude toward Russia's future!

39. *The Russian Revolution*, Vol. I, p. 140; Lefebvre, *La pensée de Lénine*, p. 13.

40. Hunt, *Guide to Communist Jargon*, p. xi. And see Harry Hodgkinson, *Doubletalk: The Language of Communism* (London, 1955).

41. See his pious expositions of Marx's teachings in *Selected Works* (1950-1951), Vol. I, Pt. I, pp. 75-81; *The Teachings of Karl Marx* (New York, 1930).

42. On Stalin's Marxism, see Plamenatz, *German Marxism and Russian Communism*, pp. 266-280; Waldemar Gurian, "From Lenin to Stalin," *Review of Politics*, Vol. XII (1950), p. 379; Meyer, *Leninism*, pp. 282 ff.; Hook, *Marx and the Marxists*, pp. 107-122, and *Reason, Social Myths and Democracy*, chap. 8; Hunt, *Theory and Practice of Communism*, chaps. 16-18; S. D. Bailey, "The Revision of Marxism," *Quarterly Review*, Vol. CCXCI (1953), p. 177; Chambre, *Le Marxisme en Union soviétique*, chap. 13. Stalin's final explanation of the doctrine of "socialism in one country," which includes an attempt to project it back to Lenin, is in *Marxism and Linguistics*, pp. 42-43. This explanation, as Klaus Mehnert, *Stalin versus Marx* (London, 1952), pp. 109-111, correctly points out, "relativizes" the absolute teachings of Marx and Engels.

43. *Economic Problems of Socialism*, esp. pp. 7-12, 14-15.

44. For a look at some of the fruits, see Mehnert, *Stalin versus Marx*, an absorbing little book; A. Powell, "The Nationalist Trend in Soviet Historiography," *Soviet Studies*, Vol. II (1951), p. 372; and Stalin's own *The Great Patriotic War of the Soviet Union* (New York, 1945).

45. Robert C. Tucker has commented wisely on the fate of Stalin since his death in "The Metamorphosis of the Stalin Myth," *World Politics*, Vol. VII (1954), p. 36, and "The Politics of Soviet De-Stalinization," *World Politics*, Vol. IX (1957), p. 550.

46. For discussions of this dichotomy, the "distinction between Marxism as a scheme of analysis and as a tool of revolution," see Bauer, *New Man in Soviet Psychology*, chap. 2; Berman, *Justice in Russia*, chap. 1; Maynard, *Russia in Flux*, p. 119. For a perceptive review of the major ambiguities in Marxism, see M. M. Drachkovitch, *De Karl Marx à Léon Blum* (Geneva, 1954), chaps. 1-2.

47. Vyshinsky, *Law of the Soviet State*, pp. 206, 570; P. F. Yudin, *The Nature of Soviet Society* (New York, 1951), pp. 15-17.

48. Vyshinsky, *Law of the Soviet State*, p. 198.

49. Hunt, *Guide to Communist Jargon,* pp. 161-165; Aspaturian, "Contemporary Doctrine of the Soviet State," esp. pp. 1035-1041, 1048-1053.
50. Simon, ed., *Psychology in the Soviet Union,* emphasizes the materialist tradition created by Herzen, Chernishevsky, Sechenov, Pavlov, and others.
51. Gurian, ed., *The Soviet Union,* p. 22. Karpovich blames the pre-1917 Leninist underground for Communist extremism, and absolves the Russian character.
52. *The Uses of the Past,* pp. 290-291. Two quite different works that argue the spiritual and intellectual affinity of Marxism and the Russian character (or at least the character of the old intelligentsia) are Berdyaev, *Origin of Russian Communism,* pp. 13-14 (the affinity of Lenin and Peter the Great!), 18, 20-21, 113, 144, 149-151, and Leites, *Study of Bolshevism.* The fact that Berdyaev's approach is mystic and Leites' psychoanalytic serves only to heighten the impact felt by one who reads these two books together. Berdyaev's *The Russian Idea* (New York, 1948) is a hardly less important contribution than his *Origin of Russian Communism,* and his *Dostoevsky* (New York, 1957) is an open window into those parts of the Russian character that evolved into Bolshevism. Sir Bernard Pares, Sir John Maynard, and Edward Crankshaw are three other distinguished members of this school. See generally Simmons, ed., *Continuity and Change in Russian and Soviet Thought,* which has a notable series of articles on Russian messianism.
53. For a contrary view of considerable force, see Daniel Norman, *Marx and Soviet Reality* (London, 1955). And for a useful survey of recent attempts to distinguish Western Marxism (*Marxisme occidental*) from Bolshevik Marxism (*Marxisme défiguré*) see Helmut Dahm, "Ist die sowjet-russische Dialektik latenter Existentialismus?," *Ostprobleme,* Vol. VII (1956), pp. 1485-1500. On the "Russification" of Marxism, see Berdyaev, *Origin of Russian Communism,* pp. 106-107, 149-151.
54. "Marxism and Underdeveloped Countries," *Social Research,* Vol. XIX (1952), p. 322. On the influence of Marx on subsequent intellectual development, see Hook, *Marx and the Marxists,* pp. 35 ff.; Mayo, *Democracy and Marxism,* pp. 55 ff., 232-233; Bober, *Marx's Interpretation of History,* chap. 19; Barzun, *Darwin, Marx, Wagner,* pp. 213 ff., 321 ff.; B. D. Wolfe, "Marx—the Man and his Legacy," *American Mercury,* Vol. LXV (1947), pp. 368, esp. 373-374.
55. *Open Society,* p. 275.
56. *The Invisible Writing,* pp. 28-29.
57. *History and Human Relations,* pp. 81-82.
58. *Karl Marx's Capital,* p. 30.
59. Plamenatz, *German Marxism,* p. 313.
60. In the article cited below, note 63.
61. *Selected Correspondence,* p. 472.
62. *Laissez-Faire and Communism,* p. 134.
63. *Marx and the Marxists,* p. 125. No man has sought more earnestly than Hook to tell us "what is living and what is dead in Marxism." His latest and most reflective effort is "What's Left of Karl Marx?,"

Saturday Review of Literature, June 6, 1959. See also the continuing symposium on "Marxism—Yesterday and Today" in *Problems of Communism,* inaugurated by Bertram D. Wolfe and George Lichtheim in Vol. VII, No. 6 (1958), pp. 24 ff.

64. On the former, see Henri de Lubac, *The Un-Marxian Socialist* (New York, 1948), a superior book; Jackson, *Marx, Proudhon and European Socialism;* George Woodcock, *Pierre-Joseph Proudhon* (London, 1956); and Buber, *Paths in Utopia*—all of which take pains to distinguish him from Marx. On the latter, see Peter Gay, *The Dilemma of Democratic Socialism* (London, 1953), and his own *Evolutionary Socialism* (London, 1909). Karl Vorländer, *Kant und Marx* (Tübingen, 1911), esp. pp. 179-189, gives a good summary of Bernstein's efforts to inject Kantian ethics into Marxist socialism.

65. For wise thoughts on this subject, with which I do not entirely agree, see Alex Inkeles and Oleg Hoeffding, "The Soviet Union: Model for Asia?," *Problems of Communism,* Vol. VIII, No. 6 (1959), pp. 30, 38. On the "myth" of Russian socialism, see Aron, *Century of Total War,* pp. 341 ff., esp. 350-355, and on the Soviet Union as the "opium" of the anticapitalist intellectuals in Europe as well as in Asia, see Aron, *The Opium of the Intellectuals,* and Koestler, *The Yogi and the Commissar,* pp. 129-130.

66. See above, note 22, chap. 5, as well as Raymond Aron, "The Leninist Myth of Imperialism," *Partisan Review,* Vol. XVIII (1951), p. 646, a thorough job of demolition; David G. Smith, "Lenin's 'Imperialism': A Study in the Unity of Theory and Practice," *Journal of Politics,* Vol. XVII (1955), p. 546, a useful summary; Hunt, *Guide to Communist Jargon,* pp. 82-88, and *Theory and Practice of Communism,* pp. 161-167; Meyer, *Leninism,* chap. 11. The faithful American echo of Lenin's voice is recorded in Victor Perlo, *American Imperialism* (New York, 1951).

67. Leo Lowenthal, in Friedrich, ed., *Totalitarianism,* p. 222.

68. Harold Lasswell, *World Politics and Personal Insecurity* (Glencoe, Ill., 1950), pp. 128-137, emphasizes the strategic superiority of Marxist symbolism, especially in its prophecy of the golden future. See also Morris Watnick, "The Appeal of Communism to the Underdeveloped Peoples," in B. F. Hoselitz, ed., *The Progress of Underdeveloped Areas* (Chicago, 1952), pp. 152-172, which makes clear the importance of the discontented intellectuals; Heimann, "Marxism and Underdeveloped Countries"; Adam B. Ulam, "The Historical Role of Marxism and the Soviet System," *World Politics,* Vol. VIII (1955), pp. 20, esp. 29-30.

69. Lucian W. Pye, *Guerrilla Communism in Malaya* (Princeton, 1956), p. 248, a rewarding book. See also Walter Z. Laqueur, *Communism and Nationalism in the Middle East* (London, 1956), esp. pp. 289-299; Gene D. Overstreet and Marshall Windmiller, *Communism in India* (Berkeley, 1959); W. Macmahon Ball, *Nationalism and Communism in East Asia* (Melbourne, 1952), a book that underscores the lack of appeal of liberal ideas for young Asian leaders; John H. Kautsky, "From Marx to Mao," *Soviet Survey,* June-July 1957, pp. 35-40; Mal-

colm Kennedy, *A History of Communism in East Asia* (New York, 1957); Frank N. Trager, ed., *Marxism in Southeast Asia* (Stanford, 1960). The appeal of Communism in another area is examined by R. J. Alexander, *Communism in Latin America* (New Brunswick, N. J., 1957), esp. chap. 1.

70. *The Captive Mind,* chap. 3, in which Milosz expounds on an Islamic custom first described by Gobineau.

71. On this aspect of Communism, see especially Henri de Lubac, "The New Man—the Marxist and the Christian View," *Dublin Review,* Vol. CCXXI (1948), p. 5.

72. *Capital,* Vol. I, p. 13.

73. For some wise thoughts about the future of the Soviet Union (and of its ideology), see B. Moore, *Terror and Progress—U.S.S.R.,* chap. 7, and "The Outlook," *Annals of the American Academy of Political and Social Science,* Vol. CCCIII (1956), pp. 1-10; Bauer *et al., How the Soviet System Works,* chap. 25; Harvey Wheeler, "Problems of Stalinism," *Western Political Quarterly,* Vol. X (1957), p. 634; Raymond Aron and Sidney Hook, "Evolution in Communism," *Problems of Communism,* Vol. VI, No. 6 (1957), pp. 5-18; Arnold Toynbee, "The Question: Can Russia Really Change?," New York *Times Magazine,* July 24, 1955; Walter Lippmann, *The Communist World and Ours* (Boston, 1959); George Kennan, "The Internal Soviet Scene," *The Listener,* November 14, 1957; and the comments of Charles E. Bohlen printed in the New York *Times,* April 18, 1957. An extreme and absurdly hopeful view is expressed in Isaac Deutscher, *Russia in Transition* (New York, 1957). Whatever the future of Communism and Marxism, we may well believe André Gide's words of twenty years ago that "the Soviet Union has not yet finished instructing and astonishing us," in *Return from the U.S.S.R.,* p. 62.

INDEX

Acton, H. B., 293
Adams, Brooks, 25, 293
Adams, Henry, 25, 293
Adams, H. P., 301
Adams, John, 15, 75, 172, 187, 191, 233
Adler, Max, 312
Adoratsky, V., 294
Alderson, Stanley, 203
Aleksandrov, G. F., 46, 298, 305, 315, 325
Alexander, Robert J., 289, 330
Alienation, 54, 57, 68-71, 77-78, 132-133, 148, 302
Almond, Gabriel, 322
American tradition, 5-6, 14-16, 38-42, 239-240, 243
  contrasted with Marxism, 7-9, 19, 38-41, 42, 59-61, 63-64, 74-80, 92, 112-121, 137-140, 141, 144, 145-146, 149-150, 194, 218-220, 226-228, 233-235, 239-244, 255, 277-280
  in economics, 135-141
  in history, 49-52, 114
  in politics, 182-186
  in psychology, 63-64, 74-80, 184
  in religion, 24, 39-40, 58-61, 141
  in social relations, 110-112
  temper of, 205-208, 217-220, 233-235
  classes in, 110-121
  equality in, 91-92
  individualism in, 92, 110, 120-121, 137, 241-242
  liberty in, 85-89
  morality in, 226-228
  property in, 136, 150
Anderson, Thornton, 293
Arendt, Hannah, 323
Aron, Raymond, 8, 99-100, 258, 305, 318, 329, 330
Ashby, Eric, 317
Aspaturian, Vernon, 316

Babb, Hugh W., 323
Bailey, S. B., 327
Bakunin, Mikhail, 13, 191, 211, 250, 251, 317
Ball, W. Macmahon, 329
Barbu, Z., 297
Barghoorn, Frederick C., 307, 323, 324

Barth, Hans, 294
Bartoli, Henri, 69, 302
Barzun, Jacques, 198, 226, 292, 294
Bauer, R. A., 302, 303, 317, 319
Baumol, W. J., 308
Bax, Belfort, 119, 307
Beard, Charles A., 25, 293
Bebel, August, 167, 310
Becker, Carl, 15
Beer, Max, 130, 309
Beer, Samuel, 45, 298
Bekker, Konrad, 294
Bell, Daniel, 326
Benda, Julien, 294, 299
Bendix, Reinhard, 304
Bennett, John C., 300
Berdyaev, Nicolas, 40, 204-205, 230-231, 244, 318, 327, 328
Berlin, Isaiah, 290, 299
Berman, Harold, 256, 310, 316
Bernal, J. D., 14, 296, 318
Bernstein, Eduard, 9, 221, 258, 274 n., 329
Bigo, Pierre, 302
Blackham, H. J., 298
Blackstock, P. W., 327
Blake, W. J., 308
Blanqui, Auguste, 166
Bloom, S. F., 9, 306, 313
Bober, M. M., 213, 289
Bochenski, I. M., 297, 320, 325
Bohlen, Charles F., 330
Böhm-Bawerk, Eugen von, 16, 309
Bolshevism, 11, 17, 73, 79, 172-182, 210, 253, 254, 258-259, 263, 268, 275, 324, 326, 328
  see Communism, Lenin, Soviet Union, Stalin
Boorstin, Daniel, 292
Borkenau, Franz, 292, 299
Borning, Bernard C., 293
Boudin, L. B., 13, 291, 293
Bourgeoisie, 70, 98, 100-101, 127, 158-159, 162, 305
Bowers, David, 299
Brameld, Theodore, 299, 310-311
Braybrooke, David, 302
Browder, Earl, 9, 293
Brzezinski, Z. K., 316, 321, 323

331